NINE
ROADS
TO
RENEWAL

NINE
ROADS
TO
RENEWAL
by WALDEN HOWARD

WORD BOOKS
WACO, TEXAS

First Printing, 1967
Second Printing, 1968
Third Printing, 1969
Fourth Printing, 1970

Printed in U.S.A.

FOREWORD

At last someone has done it. For ten years people have been asking me where they could find examples of churches with steeples and ordinary congregations in which men and women have risked committing themselves to a search for corporate renewal in the Body of Christ.

Since the Babylonian exile, when the temple in Jerusalem was destroyed and the Jewish people became the "people of the book," the great reformations among the People of God have had at their core small groups of deeply committed individuals, people who not only have witnessed to those things which they have seen and heard, but who have captured in writing the significant outlines and forms of renewal as they emerge—thus making new creative possibilities available to whole generations.

As Editor of *Faith at Work*, and now as author of *Nine Roads to Renewal*, Walden Howard stands squarely in the center of this tradition. He has gathered samples of various strands from across America, and has shown us something of the patterns God is weaving in the Church today.

I predict that this book will be widely read and equally useful, since it shows the reader clearly, and from the inside, nine authentic corporate shapes which Christian ministers and laymen are discovering together for their obedience to the living Lord.

—KEITH MILLER

Austin, Texas
July, 1967

CONTENTS

INTRODUCTION

It was a warm April morning. I settled into my seat on the commuter bus to Manhattan. The day before, the latest issue of *Faith at Work* magazine had been safely "put to bed." Now, as the bus rolled along in the stream of New York-bound traffic, I began, in my mind, to put together the next issue. One ingredient was missing: a solid, lead-off story.

For two years, as editor of *Faith at Work*, I had lived in the pressure and drama of gathering and refining stories of personal faith. For half that time I had known Jim Galbraith, a photographer's model who divided his time between New York studios and his home in southern New Jersey. Jim stopped by for the Tuesday noon men's fellowship meeting in our midtown office occasionally, and reported to us the latest news of exciting things that were happening to individuals through his home church in Salem. He kept urging me to come to Salem to "do a story."

That morning as I sat on the bus Jim came to mind—Jim and Salem. *That's the story I need*, I thought to myself. *When I get to the office I'll call Jim first thing*. But I never got the chance.

The phone was ringing as I walked in. "This is Jim Galbraith. The Lord seemed to tell me to call you this morning." And so, by one of those "coincidences" that those who seek to live by God's guidance can come to expect, I was in Salem just four days later meeting Jim's friends, hearing their stories, and compiling the first of what was to become a series of reports on churches and groups of people who are discovering a new way of life.

The road to Salem led next to Houston, and later to Sioux Falls, to Madison, Boston, Bethlehem, Cleveland, and Pittsburgh. My journey resulted in a series of reports that have brought practical help and know-how to thousands of readers of *Faith at Work* magazine. Now, for the first time, nine of these stories are brought together in this book to form one continuous story.

They are one story in the deepest sense. The story involves men and women from different geographical areas and church traditions. They differ theologically, culturally, and temperamentally, but they have discovered a common way of life.

None of these people, nor their churches, is perfect. If you visit any of them, as I hope you will, you will find the human blemishes common to us all. You will also find that changes have occurred since the stories were written. Some have found the going more difficult than they expected and their progress has been disappointing. Others have moved ahead with surprising rapidity.

For most of the people you will meet in this book the story is unfinished, a report "as of now," or at least as of the time of writing. For one or two the last chapter has been written. Donnajean Funk, whose witness is so much a part of the Salem story, died, triumphantly, in January, 1967, enhancing her witness for Christ in death as well as in life. And John Bruere, whose leadership revitalized Calvary Presbyterian Church in Cleveland, died suddenly in September, 1967.

But the witness of this book is not, after all, to individuals, nor even to the churches they attend. It is to a "life-style" which they demonstrate. It is to a life lived together with others in a depth of honesty and commitment that in turn leads both to individual, personal commitment to God through Jesus Christ and to the witness and service in the world.

The masthead of *Faith at Work* magazine attempts to spell out such a life-style. "This magazine expresses Life lived un-

der the Lordship of Jesus Christ," it says; "a life committed
to others in open, honest fellowship; a life of involved concern
for individuals and society; and a life demonstrating that faith
brings changes to people and situations."

To define Christianity in terms of life and experience is
Biblically sound. Jesus called individuals to respond with their
lives to God's call. ("If any man would come after me, let
him deny himself and take up his cross daily and follow me.")
He fashioned those who responded into a community demanding a commitment to one another as binding as their
commitment to God. ("By this all men will know that you
are my disciples, if you have love for one another.") He sent
them out into the world as witnesses and servants. ("Go therefore and make disciples of all nations.")

Many dissatisfied persons in our time have discovered this
three-dimensional life-style experimentally. They have found
it because it works. An analogy can be seen in the conclusions
of a young minister who, in his search for effective principles
of spiritual healing, carefully analyzed numbers of agencies
who seek to rehabilitate narcotics addicts. He reports that, to
his knowledge, only three groups are achieving notable results.
They differ radically in philosophical presuppositions but
operate with the same life-style. One group is Pentecostal,
another vaguely theistic, and the third frankly humanistic. But
this they have in common: they hold up to addicts a new
system of values and tell them they can become changed
people; they bring them into a community of people like
themselves for support and encouragement; and as soon as
they take their first step toward wholeness they are given
responsibility to help others. Who can doubt that, despite
their different understandings of reality, it is the power of
God that they have released because they have discovered
the ways in which God works? If God operates according
to preestablished laws, they who find those laws find access
to God's power.

So it is with "a faith that works" that the groups in this book are concerned. This is not to suggest that they are avoiding the hard theological questions which are pressed on beleaguered Christians in this age of confusion and change. Nor are they avoiding the hard questions about the relevance of traditional structures in the Church. What they are doing— or at least what is reported of them here—is creating authentic situations in which such questions can best be answered: not in ivory-towered seclusion or as uninvolved spectators but from the depth of involvement.

The order in which these stories appear suggests a natural progression in emphasis: from the individual to the group to the world, though every story bears the marks of all three. Each church has its specialty, its strengths as well as its weaknesses, and for purposes of study and evaluation each chapter closes with several pertinent questions that will enable the reader, or study groups, to think through the principles it reveals and their application to each situation.

The "road to renewal" leads first to "Averagetown, U.S.A.," the city of Salem, New Jersey, which in many ways typifies American society. Here the three stages of the life-style unfold in the experience of a Presbyterian church: from individuals who find wholeness in Christ, through the "honeymoon" stage of new-found fellowship in the Christian family, to the first probing efforts at creative witness and ministry in the world.

From Salem the road leads to Houston, Texas, and an Episcopal church where the reporting of Christian experience as it is currently being lived undergirds the preaching, teaching, and evangelism of an alive congregation. From Sioux Falls, South Dakota, a Baptist church reports how the simple technique of laymen's witness can make traveling teams a powerful instrument for transmitting new life. Next, Mennonite young people report a particular form of such traveling teams that best fits their own needs and those of their denomination.

The road leads to Madison, Wisconsin, where a Presbyterian church reports the success of honest encounter between its members and inmates of one of Wisconsin's correctional institutions. A visit to Boston reveals the fact that even pastors who feel imprisoned can find release through small group encounter.

From Boston we go to Bethlehem, Pennsylvania, where a prestigious city church illustrates the strategy of structuring *koinonia* at the center of its life and organization. In Cleveland, Ohio, another Presbyterian church demonstrates the kind of involvement in the changing neighborhoods of an inner city to which depth commitment can lead.

Finally, in Pittsburgh, Pennsylvania, alert Christians from many churches reveal how group fellowship leads not only to individual conversion but to encounter with many social problems. It was in Pittsburgh that Dr. Sam Shoemaker, to whom *Faith at Work* owes much of its impetus, summed up the whole style of life for which this book, and the journey it records, argues. Addressing his friends at the close of the glorious years of ministry that brought into being the Pittsburgh Experiment, he said, "Get changed; get together; get going!"

If we will follow that terse advice, each one of us will find the authentic form new life needs to take in his own church and community.

—WALDEN HOWARD

New York, N. Y.
October, 1967

1

Salt in Salem

Three steps to a new style of life.

Salem, New Jersey, is not on the main road to anywhere. To reach it you leave the New Jersey Turnpike at its southernmost exit, shortly before the highway bridges the Delaware River into Wilmington and funnels its long streams of impatient cars on south to Baltimore and Washington. Off the highway everything is suddenly quiet and you're in the rich, flat farm country where almost three hundred years ago the English Quaker, John Fenwick, bought some land from the Indians and established his colony. Soon after that Salem was built, a town older than Philadelphia and rich in atmosphere and historic interest.

Salem is a good town. Its 10,000 population is typically all-American, with a healthy balance of whites and Negroes, Republicans and Democrats, Protestants, Catholics, and Jews, workers and the "country club set." The town is relatively self-contained with sufficient agriculture and industry to provide employment for its citizens. Here H. J. Heinz bottles much of its catsup, Anchor-Hocking molds glassware, and Mannington Mills produces vinyl floor covering in a community relatively unaffected by the problems of race hatred, political corruption, crime and juvenile delinquency.

Salem, politically, is a "bellwether town." NBC's David Brinkley featured it on an hour-long TV special in 1964 as "Averagetown, U.S.A." because of the fact that in four consecutive national elections it had voted for the presidential winner by the same margin as the nation. But who likes to have his home town called average? The residents of Salem don't. Typical? That's better, and it makes better sense of this story because it implies that what is happening in Salem can happen in your town and in mine.

Standing tall in the center of Salem is the 165-foot spire of the Presbyterian church, built to that height in 1856 to outdo the Episcopalians (as everyone knows), and for over one hundred years a mute testimony both to the spiritual aspirations and the "superiority" of its worshipers. But to outsiders, the church often seemed cold and unfriendly.

Then, some years ago, fresh from theological seminary and full of enthusiasm, Chuck and Nancy Murray came to serve their first charge in the Presbyterian church, and their coming was like a sprinkling of salt. From the first, Chuck refused to be called "Reverend" and encouraged everyone to be on a first-name basis.

Chuck's sermons were warm and conversational and intensely practical. He brought the Word of God right down to cases, illustrating it from his own life and implying, "It will work for you, too." He had surrendered his life to Christ in a breakfast group for young businessmen in California, and his first effort was to reproduce the pattern that had so deeply influenced him. In the pattern of his Lord, he began to seek disciples, calling men and women who wanted to give themselves fully to God to meet for prayer and instruction. But no one responded to his initial invitation.

The breakthrough came when Ken and Ada Campbell went to Washington, D.C., to a Presidential Prayer Breakfast. Inspired by the faith of business and government leaders and by the knowledge that they met weekly for disciplined prayer, Bible study, and personal dialogue, they came back to Salem to assist Chuck in starting a Thursday morning breakfast group for men.

The first women's group, however, was started only after weeks of prayer. Finally the time seemed ripe and Chuck inserted into the Sunday bulletin a simple announcement: "Those who want a closer walk with God will please meet at the manse at such-and-such-a-time." They had prayed for eight women and eight women responded. Committing themselves to a weekly meeting and seeking God's structure, they felt led to divide their meetings into three parts, one each for Bible study, prayer, and personal reporting of what God had done that week in their lives. "If He hadn't done anything that week," one woman recalls, "you were in trouble." Prayer and faith were contemporary and practical.

Soon the group grew in numbers and depth and divided into two groups. Five years later, there were eleven groups, two for men and nine for women. Dozens of other groups have come to life as a result in other churches in surrounding towns and throughout a nine-state area wherever people have been touched by the witness of these contagious young Christians from Salem.

The groups are *ecumenical* (almost every church is represented in them) and *interracial* (when the N.A.A.C.P. tested them and found that Negroes were welcome, a number of them stayed). They bridge all social barriers (a woman may find her maid in her prayer group), and more and more the prayers and witness of these men and women are reaching into every area of life of Salem: its business and politics as well as its homes and churches. Those who are actively engaged in prayer groups number about one per cent of the town's population. "That's not many," you say. But how much salt does it take to season the whole?

Malcolm Jones says, "I don't know whether our town has changed, or whether it's just me that's changed. I see people in a new way. For instance, I never cared for colored people before. Now I feel free with them." Mary Pratt is convinced that "we have *the* answer for any community." And Lottie

Chamberlain ventures that "at least Salem is aware that Jesus Christ is as much alive today as He was two thousand years ago."

Looking back over the past few years, one can see that the new life that has come to Salem has produced three stages of growth, much like the usual stages in a marriage. Just as the wedding is followed by a honeymoon and then by the serious business of building a family, so the new life that comes in response to the love of God in Christ, beginning with a definite commitment, is likely to be followed by a honeymoon of inexpressible joy and peace, but leads eventually into costly involvement through witness and sacrificial service.

This is what is happening in Salem. It began with a cluster of conversions and rededications that occurred almost simultaneously. The ensuing joy of fellowship created a true expression of the "Body of Christ," and many have been so overwhelmed by God's personal concern for them as individuals that they have just reveled in the joy of "Jesus and me." But for some the honeymoon is over, and they are responding to God's call to salt every area of their community's life in costly service.

The personal transformations that make up the story of Salem range from the spectacular to the scarcely noticeable— from Buddy Funk who "came to the Lord kicking and screaming on a horse's back and has been on a wild ride ever since," to "Mally" Jones who with painful deliberation learned to depend on someone bigger than himself.

Buddy's wife, Donnajean, was one of the eight who answered her minister's first call for women who wanted "a closer walk." She had been on a spiritual search for some time, visiting church after church, looking for some direction and purpose to her life. No children had come to bless her marriage, and this lack only accentuated the frail relationship that existed with Buddy, a construction man who lived for hunting and horse shows and seldom went to church.

When Donnajean visited the Presbyterian church, she felt she had come home to the warmth and reality she was seeking, and she stayed. She almost didn't get to that first meeting of "the eight" however. Called for grand jury duty that morning, she was excused only because the judge became ill. Running, relieved, from the courthouse to the manse, she arrived ten minutes late just as Nancy Murray was saying, "No, we prayed for eight and possibly there's another girl who's going to show up."

Donnajean recalls, "We were the most diversified group you can imagine. But each of us had a need, and knew it, or we wouldn't have been there. I thought all along that I was a Christian, but as we met each week I found out that I didn't know God personally."

Buddy was the first prayer project of the group. His experience with church had been limited to two or three courtesy visits, and Donnajean had jokingly remarked to Chuck and Nancy, "The only way ever to get him here would be to have a horse show in the sanctuary." Then an idea struck her. "Do you want to 'go fishing' at a horse show?" she asked.

Buddy was showing his prize horse, Bojangles, that weekend at the biggest show of the year. With dozens of trophies, Bojangles had been one of the biggest winners in the East, but as Buddy put him through his paces in the open class that night, everything went wrong. Bo was such a high-strung horse that it took all of Buddy's strength on the reins to slow him down to a walk, and he won blue ribbons because of his terrific parade gait, despite the fact that he "churned" on his walk. But that night Bo was "juiced up," and Buddy had to hold him so tightly that he wouldn't walk at all. Three times he froze in his tracks and finally was disqualified.

Buddy was in an ugly mood on Saturday—championship night—when Donnajean came bringing her minister and his wife. "I don't know if I'll even show him," he volunteered as he was introduced.

"Maybe we could sprinkle him with holy water," Chuck wise-cracked, but Buddy didn't think that was funny, and they went on to dinner, leaving him with his decision. Donnajean prayed that he'd at least show the horse, since she had brought Chuck and Nancy, but Chuck said, "We've got to pray that he does better than ever."

Buddy took Bojangles out of his stall an hour early, cross-tied and outfitted him, slowly and deliberately, and decided to show him. When his time came, he performed as never before. Buddy recalls, "I never had had such a sensation. When they called for a walk, Bo came down so flat-footed the reins were loose in my hands." Six times they called for a walk, he performed perfectly, and "walked away" with the grand championship.

"What the hell did you do to that horse?" someone asked Buddy afterwards.

"I brought my preacher with me," he chuckled.

After that it was only fair to say yes when Chuck and Nancy invited Buddy and Donnajean to hear Billy Graham in Washington, D.C., the following week. Buddy was taken immediately with Billy's straightforwardness.

When the invitation was given, Donnajean was praying that Buddy would go forward. Then it dawned on her that she had never made a public confession of her own faith. She felt Buddy's hand tighten on her arm like a vise as he struggled to make a decision. Then the two of them, hand in hand, bounded down the aisle. "So we came to the Lord together," Donnajean recalled later.

Buddy, who says he's still "a far cry from what I should be," was the one who gave Malcolm Jones the shove that moved him into the Kingdom.

Mally moved to Salem when he was twelve. His parents were Christians, but their beliefs did not attract him. As soon as he was given the chance, he made his decision—against religion.

He early developed a taste for independence. At fifteen, while he was still in high school, he learned his father's trade and worked as a mold-maker in the glass factory. He established himself as a popular figure among his peers, holding the position of president of his senior class. After graduation, he spent two years in the Marines—cut off from all family ties and living as he wanted to live—and Mally's sense of independance increased.

Then he returned home and enrolled in the state university. But he lacked any reason to want a college degree, so he just didn't go, returning instead to his old job at the glass factory. He "bummed around" with the boys, enjoying his carefree existence and their idea of a good time.

Not until Mally married, at twenty-eight, was he caught up short. Now responsible for someone besides himself, he found his zest for independence was turning into a problem. He knew that life demanded more of him than he had to give, and so gave in to his wife's request that he attend church.

The prayer groups were just getting under way, but Mally shied away from them. To him, it seemed "kooky" to hear men talking about Jesus as a personal friend, yet he sensed that he was missing out on something. He went far enough to join the communicants' class, but he wasn't ready to join the church.

After a year he came to the place where he was willing to give up the management of his life and learn to depend not on himself but on what Jesus Christ could do for him. Once Mally had made this commitment, Buddy Funk kept after him until he joined the men's prayer group.

Here he was expected to talk about himself, like the others who were taking little steps of faith and holding each other up in prayer. He knew that his first step was to get rid of evil thoughts and filthy language. He prayed that God would clean him up, but the process took time. For a while he'd get ready to say something, then realize it shouldn't be said.

"I didn't say much at all in the group for a good while," he recalls, "but now I can witness to people. I still get nervous, but I like to stand up and say a few words for the Lord."

The "independence problem" hasn't gone away overnight, however. Mally and his wife, Eppie, had been married three years without a child. Far from feeling bad about this, Mally liked it fine—he wanted to get the house, the car, and the furniture paid for before they started having a family. He liked things moving on his schedule, and he looked forward to being financially independent.

Then Eppie got pregnant and it upset all of Mally's plans. It was two months before he could accept the coming change in their family and in his schedule; and in the third month Eppie lost the baby. By then, Mally, too, wanted a child.

They prayed, and Eppie surrendered her hopes and her life to the Lord. Nine months to the day after she made her commitment their child was born. Mally says he never felt the presence of God so much as the night the baby came. The next morning, alone at the breakfast table where he and Eppie so often read the Bible together, he looked for a verse of Scripture for her, but nothing seemed to fit. Later that morning at work, where he keeps a Bible handy, he picked it up and it fell open at Psalm 104:30: "Thou sendest forth thy Spirit and they are created."

A honeymoon, as Mr. Webster defines it, is "the holiday spent by a couple after marriage"—that blissful interlude on Cloud Nine from which husband and wife finally awake to the responsibilities they have undertaken.

Salem has more than its share of "spiritual honeymooners," if one judges by the joy and hilarity of the new Christians when they get together. One evening fifty of them crowded into Jim and Hilda Galbraith's living room, brought together almost on the spur of the moment for what they called an "ingathering."

Almost everyone in the room, it seemed, wanted to tell his story—the story of a physical healing, of a restored relationship, or simply of the peace and joy of being right with God in one's inner soul. Some of the stories went back several years to their beginnings. Others were as fresh as yesterday. Finally it was time to go, but not before Johnny Bobbitt and his group sang some gospel music, with Johnny on the guitar and Mally Jones on the bass. Was it corny? Perhaps—if your musical tastes lie in other directions. But it was capably performed and as natural as flight to a bird.

Since new life has come to Salem, its spontaneous joy has bubbled over in an outreach that has sent individuals and "teams" to give their witness in some one hundred different meetings over a nine-state area in the first year. The music has been the icebreaker in many such meetings, whether in a church or at a luncheon club.

No one's witness has gone further than that of Jim Galbraith, who was given two minutes on David Brinkley's TV program in 1964—"Election Year in Averagetown, U.S.A."—to tell of his Christian faith.

A car salesman and part-time singer with dance bands, Jim gave his life to Christ at the age of thirty-five. "I saw Christ in these other people," he says, "and He was irresistible." On his knees in his living room, tears streaming down his face, he surrendered his will to "new management."

The next day Jim tried to tell his fellow car salesmen what had happened. They ridiculed him and rode him out of the business, and he wound up going to New York seeking a job as a TV model. "I was a social bum," he says today, "but when I met Christ my life blossomed."

"The agencies turn away up to a hundred men a week who try to get into the modeling business," Jim says, "and I had nothing to offer that others didn't have, but the Lord opened the door for me. I walked into an agency cold and within half an hour signed some contracts and began work that day."

Today Jim's sinuses are known from coast to coast through his Dristan commercials, and his sparkling good looks have made him one of the top male models on the East Coast and in Europe. In a business where six commercials a year are considered good, Jim landed eighteen during his first year as a model.

Jim has become an elder in the church and the teacher of a Sunday school class, and tells of witnessing to his faith even while he's working. "I've seen a TV studio turn into holy ground when two or three people begin to talk about Christ," he says. And commercials that had to be shot "on location" have given Jim a chance to bear witness at a governor's prayer breakfast in Alaska and at a church in Miami. Everywhere he goes his message is simple and direct. "Walking into a barn doesn't make you a cow," he says, "and walking into a church doesn't make you a Christian. A Christian is a person who has Christ inside. Don't get me wrong. I still have problems, but with Christ I know I can overcome them."

Such enthusiasm doesn't always meet with a welcome, however, especially among those who have "loyally served the church all their lives" and to whom such outbursts of emotion seem undignified and irreverent, especially for Presbyterians.

It is inevitable that in a church like the Presbyterian church of Salem, New Jersey, there should be "the other side"—those who for one reason or another disapprove of prayer groups or feel no need for them.

Lottie Chamberlain was one of these. For thirty-three years a member of the church, she remembers how skeptically she reacted to Chuck Murray when he came as the minister. Resistant to change, she didn't like his "dropping the Reverend" and calling people by their first names. Besides, he was "trying to do too much, and as for his bringing in all these young couples . . . well!"

Lottie held aloof from the prayer groups. *They should know that I'm a Christian*, she thought; *after all, I'm busy in the church.* She had heard criticism of the groups and had even helped to spread it. But she decided one day to find out for herself what they were doing that was considered wrong.

She joined a group and to her surprise she found nothing strange. There were no secret rituals, as she had been led to believe, just love and fellowship and deep caring. And praying aloud you couldn't help knowing each other as sisters. Perhaps that was what people feared—being known—and why they preferred to be undisturbed.

But others, like Ella Zaiser, a practical nurse, were longing to be known, and loved, and on her first contact with the prayer groups something seemed to say to her, *"This is real. Hang on to it."*

Spoiled as a child, Ella now sees that her life has been a long search for self-satisfying love, but only through the prayer groups has she begun to learn to *give* love.

She had been in a women's circle at church for thirty-five years and in the circle she felt a clashing of personalities, but in the prayer groups there has come, in time, a delight in God's work which brings leadership to the circles.

Every six months the membership of the prayer groups is shuffled to bring each woman into a new set of relationships. Ella has been in four different groups and each time has found herself thrown in with someone whom she resented—someone who dominated the study time, or in some other way irked her—and Ella has learned that the resentment can be overcome only by confessing it to the woman involved, and praying about it together. Then she is able not only to love her but to learn from her. "I grow in every new group," she says, "but I get humbled in the process."

Ella's ability to give love has been rewarded by appointment as her church's representative in "Christian Relations and Concern," a community group in which "social concerns are becoming Christ's work in Salem." For her, and for others, the "honeymoon" is over.

You can't salt a meat loaf by sprinkling a little salt on the surface. You have to stir it in. And the same is true of human society. If Christians are going to be salty, they must be mixed well into the whole "loaf" of human institutions and concerns.

In Salem, the big pinch of salt that has been added through the changed lives of some of its citizens is beginning to permeate every aspect of the community's life. This permeation takes the form of personal caring for individuals and involvement in matters of social concern, as the stories of Johnny Dague and Annabelle Tuthill illustrate.

Johnny Dague is a quiet, unassuming man with a warm heart and a winsome smile. His business—contracting home improvements—takes him into homes throughout Salem and the surrounding towns and provides many an opportunity to speak for Christ. "Each time I do it I find it easier," he says, "and there are several people who are active in church today because I met them doing some remodeling around their houses."

Until half a dozen years ago, Johnny and his wife, Doris, lived forty miles north in Haddonfield. Johnny was soliciting business in southern New Jersey and one Saturday night he stayed in Salem. On Sunday morning he attended the Presbyterian church, and afterward Chuck Murray invited him to a coffee hour. Johnny was so struck with the atmosphere of Christian love that he bought a house in Salem that very week and moved his family. "I've traveled a great deal," he explains, "and churches are usually cold and unfriendly. I've never known one as vital as this."

New life came to Johnny in a small group. He told Christ one day, in the quietness of his own heart, that He could have control of his life. But it was six or eight months before he actually told anyone else, even those in the group. "I didn't feel worthy," he explains. But now, worthy or not, he tells people whenever he can about his Lord.

"You'd be surprised," Johnny declares, "how in talking with customers about home improvements you get their ideas and feelings about things. It's easy then to talk about church and find out if they go anywhere. And I often meet people who have just moved to town and see that they're invited to church. Or I tell my minister, 'There's a new family that isn't going anywhere,' and he calls on them."

One such family were Puerto Ricans who were new in town and who felt isolated and unhappy. Johnny and Doris had them over for dinner. On the day they were to return the visit, Ida, the wife, was in an auto accident and Doris, who is a nurse, helped out as best she could while Ida was recovering. Others in the church helped, too. Now both Ida and her husband have responded, and Ida has offered to help the migrant Puerto Rican and Negro workers who flood Salem County at harvest time.

Annabelle Tuthill's spiritual adventure parallels the three stages of growth in Salem's prayer groups. When she enrolled her children in the Presbyterian Sunday school, she was met by a vivacious blonde. Not knowing that she was the minister's wife, Annabelle confided in her that she "didn't believe anything at this point."

Nancy Murray loaned her a book, *A Man Called Peter*, the story of Peter Marshall's life, and all alone Annabelle surrendered her life to Christ. When "the eight" came together to form the first women's prayer group, she was one of them, and three years later her husband, Jay, joined her in an all-out Christian commitment.

Jay had been growing in faith for some time. He dates the decisive beginning during his sophomore year at the University of Delaware. He and Annabelle were already married, they were both working, and a child was on the way. As his responsibilities piled up, Jay became obsessed with the fear that he wouldn't be able to finish college. He started cutting classes, jeopardizing his chances of passing. One day at the library he picked up Norman Vincent Peale's *The Power of Positive Thinking*. He wouldn't have touched a religious book ordinarily, but now it intrigued him, especially a quotation in it from the New Testament: "I can do all things through Christ who strengthens me." He began to read the Bible, and eventually resumed his studies.

Jay, who later became Technical Director at Mannington Mills, approaches problems scientifically, and so he decided to experiment in the spiritual realm. He began to pray not only for a way to finish college but that he and Annabelle would come to know God and realize the love for each other that neither had experienced in early life. One night he came home to discover that the personnel director at the mill had called and requested to see him. The company invested in Jay, paying all his tuition fees and providing a weekend and vacation job. Three years later he was graduated from the university second in his class.

It was at this point that Jay and Annabelle moved back to Salem. Because of Annabelle's ambition to know the right people and to get ahead socially, they attended the Presbyterian church. There they stumbled onto praying Christians and joined them. Annabelle jumped ahead of Jay temporarily. Jay went to church only occasionally, but when he did he sensed the power that was available. He could see the change in Annabelle, too, and he began to search more seriously.

Then their fourth child was due. It was in a breech position when Jay took Annabelle to the hospital, and thinking she wouldn't deliver that night he went home and back to bed.

In the middle of the night Jay woke up with the realization that his wife was dying. He dropped to his knees and prayed desperately that she would be spared, surrendering himself to God in the process. As soon as he uttered the words of self-surrender, he felt confident that Annabelle was out of danger, and he was filled with peace and tranquility. The

doctor called shortly after to confirm the fact that the baby
had come and that Annabelle's life had been in real danger.

In recalling the incident, Annabelle says, "I had prayed for
Jay to come to Christ. Finally I asked God to do it His way,
whether it cost my life or one of the children. It's strange,
but that's what God almost required."

Jay and Annabelle confess that the differences in their personalities still make openness and prayer difficult. "I have
always been a very selfish person," Annabelle explains: "as a
child, I got whatever I wanted, and never thought about
other people except those above me who could help me climb
higher. But we're making great strides. If it weren't for God,
I'm sure we'd have been divorced by now."

It is all the more remarkable, then, that when a senior
citizens' development began to be built outside Salem it should
fall to Annabelle's lot to organize the church women of Salem
in a program to help the new residents. During her first four
years as a Christian she had dropped out of all civic activities
and devoted all her considerable energy to "church work."
At a Mariners' conference she realized that she had cut herself
off from everybody but her Christian friends. There was no
area of her life where she touched the community as a whole.

Instinctively she knew she was wrong, and she went back
to the Great Books and Women's Clubs. Here she heard of
the senior citizens' home and as a result she was asked to be
chairman of "Christian Relations and Concern," a committee
of women from all the churches who were beginning to look
into problem areas in Salem, from the senior citizens to delinquent teen-agers, and from migrant workers to inmates of
the jail.

"This is a whole new way of life for me," Annabelle says
frankly. "It's a miracle. I, myself, can't feel for people, but
it's Christ's concern. In every prayer group there are people
with needs. You can't study and pray with them for long
without getting involved. I know some women who have

dropped out because they couldn't stand the involvement. This really tests your faith. Can I really afford to be this involved?"

Chuck and Nancy Murray have moved now from Salem to Oreland, Pennsylvania, but they left behind them a viable structure of prayer, study, and "sharing" groups which are led solely by laymen. Russell and Dottie Stewart, who followed them in the Salem ministry, were pleasantly surprised by this phenomenon. "This is the first church we've served," Russ declared, "in which so much initiative for prayer and Bible study has been shown on the part of the members."

The groups which, members point out, could be reproduced almost anywhere, began when the conversion of several young couples coincided. Their desire to grow in new life pushed them into weekly meetings, and trial and error experimentation evolved the present structure.

The women's groups—nine of them now—banded together under the name of "Followers," divide whenever they reach twelve members, and rotate leadership. Each group has a coordinator, a study leader, a prayer leader, and a sharing leader. The first few minutes, while the women are gathering, is spent informally over coffee, but the remaining time is divided into thirty-minute periods for Bible study, prayer, and personal sharing.

Everyone is expected to take part. The Bible leader encourages discussion without imposing her own views, and the resulting variety of viewpoints not only leads to a deeper understanding of Scripture but of the people involved. "We don't argue about Scripture," Regina Kiah explains, "and we are learning to love each other."

The groups are rearranged every six months and leaders cannot succeed themselves, so that leadership is eventually shared by everyone in the group. "It doesn't take trained leaders," I was told, "only *willingness*." But the minister makes himself available to the study leaders and offers his help. A recent development is that coordinators need not be Presbyterian so that leadership is now being shared among several of the Salem churches.

Each "Follower" commits herself to ten personal disciplines (such as church attendance, daily consecutive Bible reading, and prayer for each other member), and these are apparently the secret of the group's vitality and continuance.

"Prayer is the power—the most important resource a Christian has," Freda Kellow says. For the Followers, prayer takes several forms. Prayer requests are circulated in a monthly bulletin, though never without the knowledge and permission of the person involved. Emergencies dictate telephone calls to alert the "prayer chain." And whenever a need seems urgent enough, a prayer vigil is called for.

One such occasion arose when Chuck and Nancy announced their intention of moving away from Salem to another church. The new Christians in Salem felt hurt and abandoned until they called a twenty-four-hour vigil, and as a result they reached the conclusion that Chuck *should* go on to a larger opportunity.

The groups are linked to the church by a special prayer service that follows each Communion service. Elders face the congregation while those who wish prayer come forward and kneel, and the minister places his hands on their heads as he prays audibly for each one. Quiet dignity and vital receptivity characterize the procedure.

Four times a year a breakfast at the country club brings all of the Followers together. On these occasions outside speakers bring inspiration and invited guests are introduced to the possibilities that await them through the personal witness of two of the members.

Meanwhile men and women from the groups answer many requests from neighboring towns to share their witness or to help them start their own prayer groups. A field representative coordinates these activities.

One Follower says, "Everything we've ever planned has
ended in outreach. We planned to meet at the country club
so that we could see everybody from time to time, and it
turned into the best time to bring those who are uncomfortable in church. We've never been able to stay cozy. God
has us all doing things we never thought we'd be doing five
years ago."

So change has come to Salem as many of its residents have
changed—change so radical in many cases that the only fitting
symbol of it is the metamorphosis of the caterpillar that forms
a chrysalis and emerges a butterfly. When the Followers discovered that the Apostle Paul's word in Romans 12:2, "Be ye
transformed," was, in the Greek of his day, *metamorphousthai*,
and that the butterfly, with the fish, was an early Christian
symbol, they adopted it as their emblem. Many of them wear
a butterfly pin as a witness to the metamorphosis God has
brought into their lives.

And they tell the story of a boy who "helped" a butterfly
to emerge by cutting a hole in the chrysalis, only to discover
that he had been in too much of a hurry. The butterfly was
not ready, and could not fly. Emerging Christians, too, can't
be rushed, but must face their own inner struggles and grow
until their wings are strong enough to fly.

Questions for study and application:
1. What are this church's strengths?
2. In what ways can you learn from its experience?
3. What improvements would you suggest?

2

"The Day the Light Went On"

Lay witness at
St. Stephen's Church, Houston.

"Witness in the church isn't *everything*, any more than
yeast is the whole loaf of bread," says the Rev. Claxton Monro, but in St. Stephen's Episcopal Church, Houston, Texas,
where he is rector, it is what gives power to every other
activity.

And St. Stephen's is a powerful church, if judged by the
vitality of the witnessing laymen who are its heartbeat, and
by its influence on a dozen other Houston churches which
have joined to form an ecumenical "Laymen's Witnessing
Fellowship."

In July, 1965, St. Stephen's was chosen as one of six distinguished congregations by *The Living Church*, an independent Episcopal journal. Parts of its program were filmed by
an educational television channel for inclusion in a documen-
tary depicting the work of the Holy Spirit in the Church.

Asked if it would be possible to film his once-a-month Sunday morning healing service, Claxton Monro said, "Yes, but
what else are you going to report?"

"Speaking in tongues," the producer replied.

"You're passing over the principal gift of the Holy Spirit,"
Monro insisted, and went on to propound his favorite theme:
that the Holy Spirit empowers laymen to share their faith.
As a result his Sunday evening witness service in the sanctuary
was also filmed.

Claxton Monro feels that witness to "the living experience of those who believe" belongs at the center of the Church's ministry.

At St. Stephen's the witness of laymen is considered the primary power both for spurring Christians into action and for winning converts. "Ninety percent of the adults who join this church come to faith through the witness of lay people in a corporate setting," says Monro.

This "corporate setting" provides four opportunities for lay witness above and beyond the witness of individuals by their lives and their words outside the church. Every Sunday evening, in a service that has been held regularly since May 23, 1954, one man and one woman, each speaking for fifteen or twenty minutes, tell of the guidance and provision of God in their lives. Then men and women in the audience may go to separate rooms to discuss what they have heard or to add their own confirming witness.

A similar meeting, aimed at outsiders, has been held every Thursday evening since November, 1960, in the homes of parishioners. Again, a man and a woman speak, with a coffee break between and a leisurely time at the close for discussion and reaction. Often the speakers are invited from other churches.

On Sunday mornings a layman may speak briefly of his experience with a Christian discipline as a part of morning worship. Throughout the week in small groups for study, witness, and prayer, meeting in homes for the women and at the church and in offices for the men, church members share their faith as they report the insights that God has given them from their personal study or from the experiences they have undergone. At one point recently forty-two men and one hundred and seven women were attending some such group each week.

Out of the growing experience of these groups seven personal disciplines have been agreed upon and are urged upon all the communicants of St. Stephen's Church. Printed cards available in the narthex read as follows:

"St. Stephen's Episcopal Church, in Houston, Texas, urges on all its communicants seven personal disciplines to strengthen the Church, to help the world, and to grow in the Christian life.

"In the name of Jesus Christ our Lord, and as an expression of my love for God, I will do my best to:

"Seek God's plan through a daily time of listening prayer and Bible reading.

"Worship weekly in the Church, with emphasis on Holy Communion.

"Participate regularly in a weekly faith, study, and prayer fellowship.

"Give regularly a definite grateful share of my income to the spread of God's Kingdom through the Church and in the world.

"And as an expression of love for my neighbor I will do my best to:

"Exercise faithfully my particular ministry in the fellowship of the Church.

"Speak and act so that my daily life is a witness to the love of God in Christ as I have come to know it. So help me God."

The importance of these disciplines as the structure for Christian growth is frequently borne witness to by laymen and women who share their experiences from the pulpit or in small groups.

"Clax" Monro sees such witness as the cutting edge of evangelism and the matrix for mature growth. Its inclusion in the program of the Church corresponds to his own deep love for the Church. He was reared in a devout New England family, and his first memories are of worship services. For a time he stopped attending church, but he never completely lost his feeling for it.

At Massachusetts Institute of Technology, where Clax made the dean's list and earned a bachelor's degree in engineering and business administration, he realized he had become an agnostic, and set his goal at making a million dollars in five years. His ambition was a noble one as he rationalized it. It would make him secure, yes, but it would also enable him to help other people.

In New York, where he landed his first job, Clax found it harder to climb the ladder to success than he had anticipated. It was 1937, the nation was struggling out of the depression, and a lot of other young men had their feet on the bottom rung, too.

One evening Clax was taken by a friend to a church service "where people got right up in the pulpit and talked about their religion." It was Calvary Episcopal Church, where Samuel Moor Shoemaker was the rector, and Clax was intrigued. Laymen told their stories. "God has a plan for our lives," they said. "Day by day we are seeking His will, and when we obey Him He provides for us," and they had the evidence to prove it. Clax listened but made no response until he was invited to a Thursday evening meeting for young men. Fifteen were present and they were discussing God's guidance. "My heartbeat doubled," Clax recalls. "I can understand what Wesley meant when he said his heart was strangely warmed." A life-changing encounter with God was near at hand. Clax thought, *This is real.*

After his fourth meeting he took a walk with a friend down 21st Street to the East River. "Let's be quiet," his friend suggested, "and see what God says to us." After a long silence he asked, "What's He said?" Clax ventured that God was telling him to identify with Calvary Church. His friend seemed disappointed, as if he had expected some guilt-ridden confession. But Clax felt only a great need for direction, and this first tentative commitment was soon followed by the conviction that he belonged in the ministry.

Then began a battle that ebbed and flowed for almost two years.

Clax had begun at last to climb the ladder in a glamorous advertising agency. He loved the work, and as he faced himself in the mirror each morning he felt sure he was cut out to be a businessman. However, just as surely each night he went to bed certain that God wanted him in the ministry.

It was at this point that Sam Shoemaker urged him to read William James's *The Varieties of Religious Experience.* When he came to the chapter on "The Divided Self," he saw his own life—the new man in Christ seeking to be born and the old man seeking to hang on. God seemed to say to him, *I have a fulfillment for you which cannot be achieved if you insist on staying in the advertising business.*

His answer came reluctantly: *These last two years, since I began to pray and seek Your will, have been the best years in my adult life. I want to continue this way. I'll go into the ministry.*

Enrolling at General Theological Seminary, Clax became a lay reader at Calvary Church, then a deacon, and finally he was ordained to the priesthood. For five years he served Grace Church in Nyack, New York, in a quite conventional ministry. He did all the things expected of him. He preached the Gospel faithfully, administered baptism and holy communion, taught the doctrines of the Church. "I was baffled," he recalls, "everything I was doing was apostolic. Only one thing wasn't apostolic—the results. If the apostles had had as little impact on the pagan Roman world as we did on Nyack, they'd have gone out of business."

It was at St. Stephen's in Houston, where he went in 1950, that Clax's unrest reached the breaking point. He remembered the laymen's activity at Calvary Church where he had been converted, and in the fall of 1952 he called together several of his men for an experimental meeting. "Let's talk about what difference it makes to believe in God, to go to church, and

to pray—in our homes, our businesses, and our social life."
So unsure was he that such a meeting belonged in the church,
and so diffident was the response at first, that Clax held these
meetings in his home. The group grew—in numbers and in
depth—and when he went on vacation the laymen insisted on
continuing without him. Clax sensed that he had a tiger by
the tail. Then a crucial event occurred.

One Monday night, May 10, 1954, he had been in his office
helping Floyd Martin, who now edits the Chamber of Com-
merce magazine *Houston*, prepare for a Sunday school class
he was teaching, and discussing the Thursday night home
meetings. As they stood at the door, ready to part, with Floyd
holding an armload of books, Clax turned to him and said,
"This witnessing fellowship of laymen is destined to become
the focal point of power in the Church. And God is going
to speak in the decades ahead through this witnessing community as He spoke through the Bible at the time of the
Protestant Reformation."

He caught himself and asked, "What did I say?" because
the concept had never before entered his mind. He had known
that there must be a "koinonia," or fellowship of believers,
at the heart of the Church, but he had thought that the Bible
and the institution, with its theology and creeds, its preaching and liturgy and sacraments, were the means to nourish
such a fellowship. The thought that the spearhead of vitality
might come from the koinonia itself was shattering to him
despite his own conversion through it.

For two weeks Claxton Monro was "lit up like a candle."
He went through an experience which some would describe
as the infilling of the Holy Spirit. He knew now what God
had meant when He had spoken of a fulfillment outside the
advertising business. On Sunday, May 16, he shared this insight with his congregation, preaching a sermon which has
since been circulated in the tens of thousands: "Witnessing
Laymen Make Living Churches." He went to his bishop to

announce that, unless he was forbidden to do so, he would begin at once to invite laymen to witness in a Sunday evening service.

On May 23 the first such service was held with a full church. It coincided with the lighting of some beautiful new chandeliers in the sanctuary, and Clax used the occasion to announce, "Another light is going on in this church tonight that's going to go around the world." From that night on, St. Stephen's Church has never been the same.

"The day people quit witnessing in my church, I'll quit preaching," Claxton Monro says, and he means it, for he is convinced that most adults have been exposed to preaching but have dismissed it, and that they will only respond to Christ when they hear the preaching confirmed in the experience of their peers.

From the day in 1954 when this conviction first came to him, he felt that he must find a basis for it in the Bible, and that if he were ever to convince the leadership of the church, he would have to be able to speak theologically. He slept very little those first few weeks and spent much of the time searching the Bible for confirmation of his new insight. He looked up "witness" and "testify" in his concordance but found no suggestion of witnessing as a ministry within the church community. "There must be some other Biblical clue," he was sure, but he didn't know where to turn, until in a desperate prayer he cried, "God, you tell me where it is." The word "prophecy" came into his consciousness, though he didn't really know what it meant. He could think only of giants like Isaiah and Jeremiah thundering their warnings against disobedience.

He pulled Alan Richardson's *Theological Word Book* from the shelf and read what it had to say. There were several pages on the Old Testament prophets and then, tucked away at the close, a brief reference to prophesying in the New Testament. "This verb is employed," it read, "in the sense of (1) to an-

nounce as a revelation made by God, (2) to reveal that of
which the evidence has been hidden, and (3) to foretell the
future." The word, in the minds of most people, means only
to foretell the future, but here were two other meanings of
equal, if not surpassing, importance.

Claxton's mind leaped to a hypothesis: *If a Christian declared what he believed to be God's actions in his life, would
that not be to announce a revelation or to reveal that of which
the evidence has been hidden?* A witness to one's experience
of God, then, was prophecy in this New Testament sense.

Again he turned to the Bible. Soon he came to First Corinthians, chapter fourteen, and read it against the background
of his experience in his new insight. He saw that Paul was
discouraging the gift of tongues (except in private devotion)
and was urging the use of prophecy in the corporate fellowship. ("I want you all to prophesy," he said.) It was clear
what Paul meant—that to speak intelligently of what God is
doing in one's life is the best means for building one another's
faith and for convincing unbelievers. "If all prophesy," he
wrote, "and an unbeliever or outsider enters, he is convicted
by all, . . . the secrets of his heart are disclosed; and so, falling
on his face, he will worship God and declare that God is
really among you."

Paul did not mean "preach" when he said "prophesy,"
Claxton realized. He clearly said, "I preach," and, "you all
prophesy." He certainly wouldn't have encouraged every
layman to assume the preaching ministry to which apostles
were particularly called. Neither did he suppose that a room-
ful of laymen predicting the future would bring about the
conversion of pagans. But he was quite right in urging every
true Christian to stand up and witness to some victory, some
hope or joy, some release from sin, knowing that in doing so
he would speak to the condition of men's hearts.

In the twelfth chapter of First Corinthians Clax had found
prophecy listed as the second most important ministry in the

Church. The Apostle stood first, for he was the primary proclaimer of the Gospel and the organizer of churches. But next in importance was the prophet whose experience confirmed the proclamation. Only after this the teacher was listed. Again in Ephesians, chapter four, Clax found the same sequence, and also in Romans, chapter twelve.

Paul was saying that experience is more fundamental than concepts, that Christianity is not a theology but a relationship —an insight that the Church of the twentieth century is once again recovering, and without which it will fall again and again into the error of gnosticism, or "salvation by knowledge." To insist on the witness to daily experience within the Christian community will prevent people from making the fatal mistake of thinking that they can become Christians by merely ascribing to the right beliefs.

How appropriate it is that one of the strongest voices in our time calling the Church back to its true nature as a witnessing community should issue from a church named for St. Stephen, who was the first Christian to die for his witness to Jesus Christ.

Clax's newest project, still very much in the experimental stage, is a revolutionary one. He envisions an activity which might replace or at least radically alter the Sunday school. "Down deep in my heart," he says, "I feel that Sunday school is fundamentally wrong," and he says it despite the fact that St. Stephen's has an active church school, larger now than it has ever been. Clax's new idea, he feels, may "reconstitute the family spiritually, if not sociologically."

He has organized several family groups, with three families meeting together every other week in a home, and three generations represented, for a time of hymn singing, spontaneous prayer, Bible reading, and discussion of how Christian faith applies in daily life. The fathers take turns exercising spiritual leadership. Each group includes one family without a father, but the children are old enough to participate. Someone else's grandparents are included if none of the actual grandparents lives in the vicinity. Everyone, from the youngest to the oldest, is listened to respectfully.

"One thing that is wrong with Christian education now," Clax argues, "is that we take nine-year-olds and isolate them, then talk to them about Jesus, and He comes out a cardboard Jesus, meek and mild, whom they will have to discard when they grow up. Even when the curriculum emphasizes experience, I wonder how much children listen to and respect the experience of their own peers."

So Clax suggests that in its place we put children with their parents and grandparents, and let them share insights on a passage of Scripture. The children won't understand all they hear, but what they say will be appreciated, and hearing things beyond their own experience may save them from constructing—and later discarding—a cardboard Jesus. Fathers will assume their right role, worship will be restored to the home, conversation about God in the home will be prompted, and children will grow up in the atmosphere of a witnessing fellowship.

Will it work? Only time will tell, but in the first months of experimental meetings, Claxton Monro reports, "They have developed into a significant part of our work. All through my ministry," he adds, "I've tried to fit the new wine of witness into the old wineskins of the Sunday school. This may be one of the new wineskins."

Hustling, sprawling, air-conditioned Houston is the fastest-growing major city in the United States, a leader in oil production and refining, in chemical industries, in shipping, and now, with NASA's Manned Spacecraft Center nearby, the gateway to the exploration of outer space.

Each year Houston's expanding job opportunities and frontier spirit attract a host of young men and women, and by one circumstance or another some of them happen into St.

Stephen's Church, finding a new frontier—the exploration of *inner* space—and in almost every case the witnessing ministry is strategic in the process. Two typical couples—the Lubergers and Ellises—may help to explain the significance of lay witness.

Charles and Esther Luberger came to Houston from Cincinnati, by way of Washington, D.C. Both were raised in church but left it in their teen-age years and didn't return until they found St. Stephen's in 1954.

By this time Esther, who outwardly seemed to have everything one needed for happiness, was thoroughly disillusioned. Education hadn't brought happiness, nor had marriage, even though it was supposed to erase all self-doubt and inadequacy. Among her friends she began to see increasing failures—divorce, alcoholism, and mental breakdown—and she was frightened. Life was letting her down and she wondered if she and Charlie would be spared.

The move to Houston was a radical one into a new culture. For one thing everyone seemed to go to church, and Esther wondered why. When a new acquaintance invited her to attend St. Stephen's she went purely out of curiosity. She fumbled through the Episcopal service, but sat bolt upright when Claxton Monro preached. "He talked like a machine gun," she recalls, "and it was all about *me*. I wondered who had tipped him off that I was there."

"God has a plan for one's life," Mr. Monro insisted, "and He will communicate it day by day, if we listen." "But he's a clergyman," she said to her friend on the way home. "I don't think it would work for me, do you?"

"Yes, I do," was the straightforward reply.

The next day Esther made her first tentative experiment at prayer since childhood. She felt foolish getting down on her knees and didn't know if anyone even heard her plea for help. But she went through the ritual again the next day, and the third day she found herself repeating a simple prayer whenever she felt anxiety or pressure. Her prayers were heard.

A month later, as she was washing the lunch dishes and feeling the weight of the world on her shoulders, she repeated the prayer and, as she tells it, "was filled with the love of God from head to toe. I was so excited that I started out the back door to tell someone—anyone—that I had found God. But that didn't seem wise, on second thought, so I went back inside and waited to tell Charlie when he came home from work. I felt sure he would laugh in my face. But he didn't. He wanted to know all about it."

With the experience of God's love came a sense of sin—an unacceptable word until now—and an equal sense of God's acceptance which made it possible for her, for the first time in her life, to accept herself. She thanked God for this and asked Him what to do next. The answer came clearly, *Join the church and go to work.* So she entered the confirmation class and asked Mr. Monro for a job.

To her surprise he assigned to her attendance at the Sunday night witnessing services which had just begun. She was relieved to have no further responsibility, and nothing had ever impressed Esther as the laymen's talks did. For three years she never missed a Sunday night, and looking back, she credits most of her spiritual growth to the insights that came from these shared experiences. For one thing, the witness stressed the seven disciplines. She began to practice them one at a time, beginning with Bible reading and listening prayer.

Meanwhile she was reporting everything to Charlie, who listened attentively but showed no inclination to follow her lead. As she prayed about Charlie, God told her to stop talking—and to quit leaving those pamphlets around for him to read. When she obeyed, Charlie's curiosity got the best of him and he went to hear for himself.

Charlie is quiet and reserved. Behind the placid face it is easy to envisage a kindly, sweet man. Actually Charlie used to be smug and contented with himself, and extremely critical of others. When he spoke there was acid in his tone.

Proud of his background (his father taught law at the University of Cincinnati), holding down a good job (as an economist for a large oil company), with a wife and fine family, he felt no need for outside help (in spite of his inner alienation). And he was repelled when Esther invited him to the Witnessing Fellowship of Need (which the Sunday night meetings were then called). *Witnessing* and *fellowship* were bad words and *needs* were things other people had, not Charlie.

"Then Esther decided to clam up on me," Charlie recounts. "She stopped telling me what was happening, what she was reading and learning, and I had to go to church myself, at least to the worship services, to find out. I didn't participate. I just sat and listened."

But at last Charlie softened up to the point where he was willing to attend confirmation classes. There he heard laymen speak about their faith, and he was overwhelmed. "They came in all sizes, shapes, and ages," he recalls, "but they had one thing in common. They spoke of God without embarrassment, they told of His love for them, and how they were trying to fulfill His plan. They seemed to be busy, effective people, well disciplined, while I was totally undisciplined. I looked forward to each meeting and as time went on I wanted to be like these people. By the time I was confirmed I had made a commitment of my life to the Lord."

It was the other way around with Bob and Keadron Ellis, who came originally from Fort Worth. Bob went to church first and Keadron followed, perhaps because Bob's needs were so much more noticeable. As he tells his story, he makes it plain that "if it weren't for my new beginning at St. Stephen's, you couldn't drag this story out of me. Wherever else I've gone to church, my greatest fear was that people would know me and then not want me. But at St. Stephen's the witnessing takes care of all that. You feel a common cause with those who speak and find yourself pulling for them."

Keadron breaks in: "Where else could you go and be so intimate with the whole congregation that you could unload your sins and yet feel loved?"

Bob loves to quote Jesus' words, "I was in prison and you came unto me," because he feels that he was in prison most of his life, a prison he himself had built, but as real as any of brick or concrete.

As a child Bob was extremely timid, keeping his thoughts and feelings to himself. As he reached the early teens, he felt he had to prove himself to the other boys by some outward display of manliness, and he began a dual role, being one person at home and someone else with the boys, thereby reinforcing the prison walls he was building around himself. He could hold his own with profanity, smoking, and dirty jokes; in fact, he had a decided talent along these lines.

In his late teens Bob graduated to the bottle and found that it did wonders for his personality. He joined the Air Force, spending two years in India where mosquitoes and monotony made up the days, and there seemed to be nothing else to do but drink. But after all, he felt he had good reason to drink—it was merely making the best of a bad situation.

After the war Bob married Keadron, whom he had dated off and on since she was fourteen. Two girls and two boys were born to them, and for eighteen years he made life pretty miserable for everyone concerned, especially himself. Bob held a job and never failed to provide for the family, but weekends were usually spent in a horizontal position. He would reflect on whether life was really worth it or not, determining that next week he would finally straighten up and fly right, yet knowing that it wasn't going to happen.

Finally, when his self-respect was almost gone, he started home one evening from the bar where he had stopped after work and came across an automobile accident where a woman lay dying. She reminded him of Keadron, and for the first time he saw what he was doing to his wife and children.

Remorse and love hit him like a bucket of ice water. He hurried home and announced, "I'm going to quit drinking."

Keadron had heard this song a thousand times before and greeted it with raised eyebrows, but his younger son responded with, "Daddy, I believe you." Bob dropped on his knees before going to bed that night and prayed what was apparently his first prayer of genuine surrender, and two weeks later he realized that he hadn't had a drink and hadn't even thought of drinking—which, after three years of steadily "fighting it," day in and day out, could only mean that he had met God.

Two days later Bob, who had been confirmed in the Episcopal church but hadn't attended in a long time, was driving by St. Stephen's Church, which he had passed hundreds of times before, and thought, *Now, there's an Episcopal church I've never visited.* He felt, for the first time in years, a desire to attend. After one service he knew that this was the church for him, and his wife and children didn't need much persuading to join him.

One year and many experiences later, Bob had advanced to the point where he was leading a Wednesday night class on how to witness effectively (at the same time, other classes were being held on spiritual healing, personal evangelism, shepherding, and teaching).

"It's a funny thing," Keadron comments, "I majored in speech and drama, but I've never yet given a public witness, and Bob who was so bashful he'd blush at hearing his name called is the one who not only witnesses publicly but helps other people to do it." In the class Bob discusses do's and don't's. (Don't wash your dirty linen in public; don't preach a sermon; leave out extraneous details; make it clear you still have much to learn; and so on.) He also auditions new converts, hears their stories, and helps them to sharpen their impact before they witness in public.

"Two out of three people," Bob says, "will tell you that

their first reaction to witnessing was negative. It sounds like
bragging, or it seems too intimate, but in reality it exposes how
little they themselves have to say. The person who objects
that religion is too personal to share publicly usually has
nothing personal to tell, and is afraid he would be made to
look ridiculous if he were called upon to speak."

But after a while many people respond, just as Bob and
Keadron have, to public witnessing. "We grew up being
taught that Jesus *was*. Here at St. Stephen's, as people share
their experiences, we have learned that Jesus *is*," they explain.

Doesn't the exposure of needs and problems invite gossip?
Keadron, who hears a good deal in her study and prayer fellowship, insists, "I've never heard backbiting or criticism. Instead when people see a problem, they say, 'Let's pray,' or
they ask, 'What can we do to help?'"

Both Bob and Keadron are grateful for the new life that has
come to their home. "We used to be six people going different
directions, but now we're a family," Keadron explains. "The
children used to resent Bob's telling them anything because he
wasn't around enough to have any right to speak. Now he's
the head of the house, and we all talk about God freely."

Especially encouraging has been the response of their
eighteen-year-old, Debbie. She has given her life to Christ
and at St. Stephen's she has learned that she doesn't have to be
perfect or hide her imperfections. "I know I'll stumble and
fall," she says, "but I have a church that loves me and won't
give up on me." Houston has twelve hundred churches of all
varieties and sizes and St. Stephen's is not one of the larger
ones. The influence it exerts, from its location in an urban
neighborhood in the southwest section of the city, flows from
the revolutionary character of its inner life and the lives of its
members. This outreach, extending through individuals,
reaches into offices and schools and institutions, to local
churches, and to southside communities.

Eddie Kensinger's witness in his business office and at a

nearby prison is a good illustration of what can happen through one individual. Eddie's is one of the more dramatic conversion stories that one can hear by the dozen at St. Stephen's. He was led to Christ by the patient, persistent witness of Tommy Ross, and now he shows the same kind of persistent concern for others.

Eddie's life has been one long search for love which until recently resulted only in an increasing alienation from society. What he heard of Christianity in parochial school in Pennsylvania—which emphasized its doctrines and duties—did not prepare him to cope with the moral corruption he found in the world. At sixteen he rebelled against all authority and left home. At seventeen he was a delinquent and a potential alcoholic.

Eddie entered the armed forces literally "to keep out of the penitentiary," knowing he was headed that way. In Korea he found life at its rawest. It was kill or be killed, hate instead of love. He withdrew into a shell for self-preservation. Ending up in the hospital for a year, he breathed hatred against all who came near him, even the nurses and "gray ladies." And when he was released and went home to his wife in Pittsburgh, he resented the intrusion into his life of his two-year-old son whom he hadn't known until then.

He told his wife he loved her, and in this he was not insincere, but he simply had no capacity for love. She was cultured and good looking, and helped to satisfy his pride. But he had no concern for her. She was like the TV set; he turned her on when he needed her, but even her love could not satisfy his inner need.

For the next five years Eddie drowned himself in drink. He was in and out of hospitals and jails, and finally his wife had taken all the abuse she could stand and left him. Eddie remembers January 23, 1958, as the lowest point in his life, even through the alcoholic haze that fogged his mind. Alone in a hotel room, he looked at himself and hated what he saw. He

prayed his first sincere prayer, which expressed nothing more
than a desire to be different.

The very next day in a skid-row bar Eddie met a well-
dressed man who told him about Alcoholics Anonymous, and
over the next few months, with the help of AA, Eddie
achieved sobriety. But he noticed something interesting about
many of his AA friends. Taking alcohol away from them left
a vacuum, which some tried to fill by gambling, others by
other means. Eddie himself turned to clothes and a new car—
all that money could buy—but possessions failed to banish his
feeling of emptiness.

Eddie sensed that only God could fill the vacuum, and
began to search for Him. He went back to his boyhood
church, but it did not meet his needs. He went several times
to a men's discussion group, but when he was asked if he had
anything to say his hostility boiled over. "You're a bunch of
sanctimonious, self-righteous prigs," he shouted, and stalked
out.

Then Eddie met Patty, they fell in love and were married,
and he decided to move away from Pittsburgh and make a
new start. He chose Houston at random and landed a good
job there as manager of a warehouse. He bought a house and
a new car, thinking, *Now I'll find a niche in society and be
happy*. When happiness didn't fly in like a bluebird, Eddie
withdrew once more into his shell. For six months he spoke
only a dozen words to Patty, and finally she, too, left him,
and he moved in with Tommy Ross, an AA friend who was
active at St. Stephen's.

It was weeks before Eddie would go with Tommy to a
home witness meeting, but when he did he "heard Toni
Attwell talking about God as if He were her next-door neighbor who was concerned when her washing machine broke
down." And when Floyd Martin spoke, his God too was one
Eddie could understand. That night he met the God whom he
had been seeking blindly for thirty years. "I saw Him in these

people and wanted Him," Eddie explains. Eddie's first response was to bridge the gulf with his estranged wife. But when he tried to talk about God to Patty, she thought he had "flipped his lid." Finally she agreed to go to a noon Lenten service at the Cathedral. Bishop James Pike was speaking and Eddie thought his eloquence would get through to her. They were late in arriving and found all the seats taken. During a hymn the bishop came down from the chancel, pushed his way through the crowd that was standing at the rear, took Patty and Eddie by the hand and asked, "Do you know each other?" and led them up to his own seat in the chancel.

Afterward, Patty was angry. "You put him up to that, didn't you?" she asked Eddie.

"I never saw him before in my life," Eddie insisted, and called the bishop over to confirm the fact.

"God told me to come down to you," Bishop Pike assured them. "Now go to your parish priest and talk over your difficulties." Patty was overcome with tears.

When they talked with Claxton Monro, he didn't promise a quick solution. "You've both got to find yourselves spiritually," he said, "before your marriage will work." But from that moment on their relationship was changed.

Eddie joined a faith, study, and prayer fellowship, and as he grew in understanding he became restless in his job. He could no longer acquiesce to the unethical practices that went on there, so he quit his job and began to look for another. The men in his group prayed for him and the day he went for an interview to Daniel Orifice Fitting Company he told the group, "I'm going to work for this company." He was told by the plant manager, "I have a place for you, but first you'll have to learn the job as a welder's helper." The pay was sixty-five dollars a week. From warehouse manager to long hot days in the oil fields was a terrific comedown, but Eddie said, "I'll take it."

He worked up the hard way, moving eventually into materials control. Meanwhile he was speaking frequently at AA meetings but feeling guilty that he couldn't say more about Christ in his talks. If he were to talk freely of Christ, he felt, he wouldn't be invited back to speak, and when he explained this to his rector, Clax sensed his need for a ministry and said, "Go ahead and speak as your conscience directs. If one door is closed, God will open another." Three weeks later the opportunity came to begin a Bible study group at the plant. Eventually, fifteen men were meeting in Eddie's office every Thursday morning.

One day Eddie came to his group at the church with a prayer request. "I'm involved in a sticky situation at work," he explained. "If I do what I know is right, I may lose my job." As his friends prayed, Eddie went into a plant meeting and stood his ground, then waited for the axe to fall. Two days later he was summoned to the president's office.

"How would you like to be production manager?" he was asked.

Eddie couldn't believe his ears. "I don't know if I can handle it," he said at last.

"We think you can. And, by the way, we want you to know that we're offering you this because of the way you handled yourself in the plant meeting this week." Eddie had indeed come a long way since January, 1958.

For several years Eddie has been working in the AA group at the pre-release center of the Texas Department of Correction. Tommy Ross is now a paid counselor for the prison system, and together they are trying to help prisoners who will soon be put back into society. And who could help better than a fellow like Eddie who in Christian fellowship finds the love of God to meet his own daily needs and in the world finds opportunity to give God's love to others.

The outreach of St. Stephen's to other local churches is significant. Claxton Monro heads up the Department of Lay

Witness for the local association of churches, and under its sponsorship a recent two-day conference on the Laymen's Witnessing Ministry drew one hundred and fifty interested clergymen and laymen.

Ministers from four denominations—Episcopal, Presbyterian, Methodist, and Baptist—have begun meetings for lay witness, in one form or another, in their own churches, and meet together for fellowship and growth each month. Lynn Crossman, Associate Minister at St. Andrew's Presbyterian Church, had "just about written off the ecumenical movement" until he met these men and found them to be not competitive, but "helpful and unselfish."

Ralph Master, Rector of St. Philip's Episcopal Church, has held a home witness meeting each Sunday night for almost three years. "It has changed our church," he reports. "People find forgiveness. Now everyone knows church is the last place to go to for forgiveness—for advice and judgment, yes, but for forgiveness? Never." He says it with a knowing smile.

Dr. Walter Wink is Minister of the First Methodist Church in the outlying town of Hitchcock. Fresh from New York's Union Theological Seminary with a doctorate in New Testament, Walter came to his first pastorate in Hitchcock several years ago. It was not long before he found people in his congregation who needed more than minor reform.

"They needed a major overhaul," Walter says. "Nobody was being radically changed. I was preaching the Gospel, but little was happening. Finally I started preaching on conversion, then on the Holy Spirit. Everybody was agreeing with me, but still nothing happened. *Where was the key to make things happen?* I asked."

Walter had heard of St. Stephen's from one of his Union Seminary professors, so now he made contact. On the last Sunday in May, 1964, he visited the church with five of his lay people. They heard the witnesses, then participated in the men's and women's meetings that followed.

The speakers he had heard set him thinking. His members had been pressing him to schedule a week of revival meetings. He decided to structure them around lay witness. Accordingly, for five nights in August, a man and woman from St. Stephen's came to Hitchcock each night to tell their stories. "Afterwards, in men's and women's sharing groups our people interacted, and things began to happen," Walter recalls. "They began to be honest about their needs, and out of this beginning we formed two 'enabling groups' that meet each week at the church."

Looking back over his first few years in the ministry, Walter admits, "I can't point to a single person who has been converted through my preaching. Laymen don't really believe preachers, but they will listen to their peers." He has this to say about lay witness: "It provides the kind of variety of experience that reaches different kinds of people. Witness is merely a vehicle. You can put into it whatever content you wish—whatever your experience has been. In our church, witness stimulates a deep interest in reading. Those who are helped seem to be trying to find words to express the reality they have found. It stimulates honesty. Those who participate find their motives purified, and those who listen discover that one can afford to live openly before God and man without rejection. Lay witness is closer to New Testament evangelism than anything that has yet appeared in Protestantism. Witnessing laymen have taken the load off me. I used to carry the ministry all alone. Now I have a dozen assistants who share in it."

St. Stephen's is having an ever-widening ministry to the Church outside Houston and across the country. Claxton Monro gets an increasing number of invitations to share his vision with fellow clergymen. In one year he has spoken in such diverse places as California, Ontario, Pennsylvania, and North Carolina. But when he is asked to speak locally, he is likely to reply, "Ours is a witnessing church, and I think what you want is one of our laymen." Whereupon he will arrange for one of the laymen in his church to share his witness.

In October, 1964, when the Triennial General Convention of the Episcopal Church met in St. Louis, St. Stephen's, together with Trinity Cathedral Church, Sacramento, California, set up a booth that was the talk of the convention. Not only did it portray the various ministries open to lay people in the Church, but twenty lay people from Houston voluntarily made the trip to St. Louis to talk to clergymen and laymen who were attracted to the booth and to report their own experiences in this ministry.

Bishop Richards of San Salvador was so taken with what he saw that he invited Claxton Monro to send laymen to Central America to share the experience of St. Stephen's. Thus men and women, led and enabled by ministers who see their role as "coaches," fan out into the world bearing the brunt of the witness to the Gospel.

"I don't think I've ever seen a church the size of St. Stephen's where the rector has so little to do," someone observed to Claxton Monro.

He laughed, for he is on the one hand a very busy man, constantly on the go, but on the other hand relatively free of many of the usual demands on a pastor. He thought for a minute and then offered this observation, "I guess ours is the largest church in the diocese without an assistant. Last year the vestry asked if I didn't want an assistant, and I told them, 'Not right now. You people are doing very well.'"

Questions for study and application:
1. What spiritual principles in this story have the most to suggest to your own situation?
2. Where and how might you begin to apply them?
3. What questions does the story leave unanswered in your mind?

3

Send-off from Sioux Falls

First Baptist Church
"has teams, will travel."

It was a transforming experience for the seven laymen, members of First Baptist Church, Sioux Falls, South Dakota, when for four days they "teamed up" to answer an invitation from two small Methodist churches in Menlo and Jefferson Center, Iowa.

A variety of informal get-togethers—suppers, breakfasts, "coffees," and house meetings—had been arranged from Sunday through Wednesday by Ward Young, who serves the two churches. These meetings provided an opportunity for the Iowans to hear some of the ways in which their guests had experienced God, and then to explore together what it can mean to live—as a farmer, businessman, or housewife— in obedience to Christ.

Only Maureen Knight, who was the "team leader" from Sioux Falls, had done anything like this before. The experience was as new to the three couples who accompanied her as it was to the members of the two host churches. But this was its strength: it pressed into service ordinary "nonprofessional" Christians who only did what any committed Christian should be able and willing to do. Yet the scarcity of such an "exchange of life" between the laymen in different churches is so striking that this venture could be called a pilot project in creative communication.

Who can assess the results of putting seven ordinary Christians from two hundred fifty miles away into a local church for four days, mixing them well, so that what they believe, what they have discovered, and what they are struggling with can "rub off"? It is an open question whether the people in Iowa or their visitors gained the most.

The seven from Sioux Falls had never before been together—and probably would not be again—in just this manner. Thrown together by circumstance, they came to know each other at a deep level. "What do we have to give?" they asked, as they drove through Iowa in a station wagon. Before they reached Menlo, they were beginning to reinforce each other's faith, partly through discovering what they had in common.

Bob Scott had been reluctant to go. "I'll drive the car, but don't ask me to say a word," he warned. But once he got into a small group he "talked up a storm," the others reported.

Ask Oliver Clark what the trip meant to him and tears well up in his eyes. "The road to Menlo was to me like the road to Damascus for the Apostle Paul," he concludes.

Claudette Christensen looks back to a morning coffee hour where she described a tense family situation. "All of a sudden" she recalls, "it dawned on me that I was partly responsible, and Maureen was able to help me after I saw this."

The mission came to a close with separate meetings at Menlo and Jefferson Center on Wednesday night. At Jefferson the team got the meeting under way, then slipped out to start the long drive home. As they went out the door, Oliver heard one of the host leaders ask, "Where do we go from here?"

In Iowa individuals made new commitments of their lives to Jesus Christ, a group for personal growth was formed, and some of its members have gone out on similar visits to other churches.

In Sioux Falls each member of the team has fitted into the life of the church with a deeper sense of responsibility and

willingness to serve. Multiply this simple story by fifty and
you will have some idea of the power that in the past five
years has flowed from First Baptist Church. On the prairies
where Indians once sent out raiding parties, this remarkably
vital church now sends out teams of "life-changing" laymen.

Sioux Falls is a thriving city of 75,000, the largest city
in the state, and a center for distribution of manufactured
goods, for cattle, and farm produce. Predominantly Nor-
wegian Lutheran, it houses some forty other denominations.
First Baptist is a flourishing 1,800-member church with people whose hearts are as open as the "wide open spaces" they
call home.

Roger Fredrikson is an uncommon pastor. A native of South
Dakota, he grew up in a minister's home and felt God's call
to preach while studying at Sioux Falls College, just two
blocks from his present office. He was one of the early presi-
dents of the Baptist Youth Fellowship, studied at Andover-
Newton Seminary, and before coming back to Sioux Falls,
taught religion and philosophy at Ottawa University, Kansas.
The mark of the man is the seriousness with which he takes
his calling and the lack of seriousness with which he takes
himself. His eyes burn with love and integrity, but he ac-
knowledges his humanity with disarming candor.

Roger Fredrikson's deepest concern is for "life-to-life"
impartation of the Gospel. He remembers that on the day he
responded to the altar call to commit his life to Christ, an
older man buttonholed him afterward and said, "If you mean
it, start right away." He took Roger with him that afternoon
to witness at the local jail.

When Roger came back to Sioux Falls in 1959, he found a
church hungering for a deeper experience of faith. Edna G.
Roberts, a veteran member who was "born into" the church
and still has her cradle-roll certificate, recalls that just before
Roger came she was asked to organize the women into "friendship groups." Thirty-nine groups resulted, eighteen of which

continued as prayer groups which nourished the new minister's own desire to lead the members of the church into a
wider outreach.

In 1960, while on a visit to New York City, Roger met
Irving Harris and Bruce Larson of Faith at Work. "I was in
sympathy with their life-centered, evangelical theology," he
remembers. "We took to each other, and in 1961 Bruce came
to Sioux Falls with a handful of lay people—John Robie, Frank
Patton, Julie Harris, John and Mellie Mackenzie, Jack and
Louise Lamberts—and the church has never been the same
since."

Shortly after that Roger was asked to hold a week's preaching mission in Topeka, Kansas. "How would it be," he asked,
"if three or four of our lay people come and we set up a
series of coffees and women's groups and couples' meetings?"
The pastor in Topeka was eager to try it. Roger began preaching Sunday night and on Wednesday four lay people joined
him—Len and Arlys Perron, Lenore Bezpaletz, and Al Poirier.
"The excitement started," he recalls, "when they arrived and
began to relate to lay people in the Topeka church."

Since that time Roger has answered many requests for his
preaching by saying, "It's impossible for me alone to do what
you want done in your church. But we have something better
to offer you." As a result, dozens of teams have gone out
since 1961 to all kinds of churches in South Dakota, Iowa,
Nebraska, and as far east as Michigan and Ohio. When Roger
has gone as far as California or Pennsylvania to speak, he has
taken with him, at the man's own expense, someone like Merle
Brubaker, a wholesale grocer, or Del Greenlee, a meat packer,
to add the layman's punch. "My own role," Roger adds, "is
more and more to train the people who are going."

Since word has gotten around that First Baptist Church
has not only a gifted preacher but also willing witnesses among
its laymen, requests for teams have increased, and the deacons
have taken over the responsibility of deciding whether the

church can fill the request. A chairman for the Faith at Work teams, as they are called, confers with the pastor in choosing the participants, and at least two training sessions are held for them before they go out. In these sessions Roger Fredrikson or David Mallgren, his young associate, tries to kindle a great sense of anticipation. "Each team must expect God to do the unexpected. There are to be no prepared speeches, but just a willingness to do and say what God directs. It's the least likely guy who may be most effective, the person who doesn't speak all evening who may be most deeply affected."

To the host church Roger writes, "We're not coming to put on a program, but to share our lives. We hope that you will set up many informal gatherings away from the church building. And there must be a local team of people who will meet each day with the visiting team to pray and to plan the day-to-day strategy." "In addition to this" he adds, "we send a copy of *Groups That Work*, the helpful manual prepared by Faith at Work, requesting that the host team study it."

Before the team members leave home, they are dedicated to God for their mission and then upheld in prayer. "They need to know," Roger says, "that they'll be given resources in their moment of need. An amazing assortment of people have gone—the highly professional, the seeking, the unskilled laborer, the old and the young. When they get back, we frequently hear from them in an evening service."

The typical comment on such an occasion is, "I got much more than I gave," or, "I learned that God can use even *me!*" "Unready people find new levels of commitment from the experience," Pastor Fredrikson explains. "I know people think I'm brutal at times in pushing new Christians out on a limb, but I'd rather take a chance on failure—on a man standing up and not being able to say a word—than to wait and wonder when he'll be ready. The Church has waited and wondered too long." As a result, people in First Baptist Church are learning to take courageous steps and do daring things for God.

Bill and Janet DeWitt are an attractive young couple who point to the visit of the first Faith at Work team, some years ago, as a new beginning in their lives as Christians. Bill is a surgeon who came from Michigan to join the staff of the Veterans Hospital, and Janet came from Seattle to be Christian Education Director at First Baptist Church, where they met and were married.

When the team arrived, the DeWitts volunteered their home for an informal meeting, though they were apprehensive. Twenty of their neighbors came, but it was all John Mackenzie and Louise Lamberts could do to tell their stories. Their listeners kept interrupting and changing the subject, apparently in an attempt to avoid personal confrontation.

In the end it was Bill and Janet who profited most. Louise Lamberts sat next to Bill, and it wasn't long before they discovered they were from the same town in Michigan. "I knew your father and mother," Louise announced, and a flood of memories rushed into Bill's mind. "I felt my mother had walked into the room," he said later. "I couldn't understand it at first, but then I realized that the Spirit of Christ—the same Spirit I always felt in my mother—had walked into the room with Louise. I saw then that the Spirit comes to us on the horizontal as well as the vertical. And when I heard a lawyer like John Mackenzie talk about Christ, I said to myself, *If he can do that, so can I.*"

After the meeting was over, John stayed behind and they talked some more. Janet says, "I had grown up in a Christian home. I'd always considered myself a Christian, and tried very hard to follow Christ, but never before had anyone asked what Christ meant to me. When John asked, I couldn't put my feelings into words, and I went through a period of self-examination after he left. I'm grateful, because he helped me to stop trying so hard and to let God really take the reins."

Janet has found her mission since them in "program work," as program chairman of the Women's Mission Society of the

church, as president of the Sioux Falls chapter of the Association of American University Women, and in a community
study group. "Programming is the leaven that influences an
organization," she declares. "The whole trend a club takes
depends on what you study. We Christians need to make our
influence felt in this area."

Karen Swenson, who studied at Sioux Falls College, and
attended the church, comes from Mankato, Minnesota. "In
form I have always been a Christian," she says, "but when I
went on a Faith at Work team to Brookings, South Dakota,
my life took on deeper meaning."

Outwardly Karen has always been happy-go-lucky—a
"good sport"—even though she was hurting on the inside. At
college she got involved in every possible activity. She
wanted people to ask, "Who's Karen Swenson?" and meet a
barrage of answers: "Don't you know? Why, she's president
of this and president of that!" Attention, she thought, was
acceptance and love. She ran from one meeting to another,
not knowing herself who Karen Swenson really was.

Part of her rebellion was against the organized church. She
went to "bedside Baptist" most Sunday mornings, listening
in bed to a service over the radio. When she did go to church,
she chose First Baptist because it was so big she could hide
in the back and not be noticed—altogether different from her
small home-town church in Mankato. In the dormitory Karen
expressed her rebellion by forming a group to discuss Bishop
Robinson's *Honest to God*, hoping to unnerve the small group
of Christians who met down the hall for prayer—and who, she
knew, were praying for her.

One morning Karen was late for church and the ushers
seated her well toward the front. For the first time she felt
God speaking to her through the sermon. She kept coming
back irresistibly until one morning she "gave in" to God. The
need to put on a gay front began to fade, and she began, as
she says, "to be at one with the person I projected."

Soon after, Karen was asked to go with two middle-aged couples to the First Baptist Church at Brookings. South Dakota State University is in Brookings and it was felt that the witnessing team would be incomplete without a college student. For Karen the weekend was crucial. The church in Brookings reminded her of her home church in Mankato and revived all her inner resentments. In group meetings she found herself wanting to argue theology. But she kept her thoughts to herself and began to listen to what people were saying. Here were men and women whom she was inclined to think of as "old fogies," but they were relating experiences of God so real that they choked up trying to tell them.

Gradually it dawned on Karen that this was what Christianity was all about—this sharing of reality. Never before had she felt God moving in people's lives like this. She went back to Sioux Falls feeling that God had used her because she too had begun to open up to people. Letters followed her, letters from college students and from "the quiet people, the ones you'd least expect to hear from." The result of this experience was Karen's new discovery of people: "If you are open and put your feelers out, people will respond."

The following spring Karen was invited to speak at her home church in Minnesota. She welcomed this opportunity because she wanted to express to the people who had known of her rebellion how much her attitudes had changed.

Karen spoke from Luke, chapter five, about "launching out into the deep." "You don't have to know where you're going," she said. "You'll find out after you commit yourself." She quoted a good deal from Dietrich Bonhoeffer, which was a convenient way to speak about herself.

Lay witness teams are only one thrust in the total mission of First Baptist Church. An amazing variety of activities characterizes this healthy, vigorous communion. "We're in an area where attending church is the accepted thing," Janet DeWitt explains. "This we have going for us."

The church staff is capable and well-organized. David Mall-gren is Associate Pastor; Dan Holland ministers through Christian education; and Bob Veninga, recently graduated from seminary, works with college and high school young people. These men meet each Monday in a time of deep and honest interaction in which they share their dreams and longings for the church. This is an important time of growth following an hour for prayer and fellowship which includes the entire staff.

Dr. Lawrence Janssen from American Baptist Headquarters in Valley Forge, Pennsylvania, visited this church at the request of the church council to survey its total ministry and to make recommendations. "We find the church today very likely at the height of its strength," reads Dr. Janssen's report, which has been circulated among the members for study. "The church and its pastor are known throughout the nation. It has developed an outstanding program of lay involvement in traditional ministries."

The secret of First Baptist's effectiveness is that, from the ministers on through the congregation, it is a church that cares.

Committees of the Board of Deacons have been tailored to such vital needs as visitation, evangelistic "house parties," sponsorship of new members, and concern for the sick, the shut-in, and the bereaved.

Bible-study groups of various kinds are available in Sioux Falls. There is a men's breakfast group at the YMCA which has been meeting for more than six years. A number of groups meet in homes.

Sioux Falls is a college town with Baptist-related Sioux Falls College two blocks from the church, and Lutheran-related Augustana College two blocks farther away. Together the schools enroll twenty-eight hundred students and to each Baptist student First Baptist makes a unique offer: a married couple in the church will serve as "parents" to anyone desiring it during his stay in Sioux Falls. Parents are on call night or day if the student needs help.

High school students are welcomed to an informal "club meeting" in a member's home each Sunday night, and a "huddle meeting," related to the Fellowship of Christian Athletes, draws together young people from all the churches for mutual encouragement. An F.C.A.-sponsored banquet attracted four hundred and fifty men and boys to hear the Christian witness of athletes like Bill Wade of the Chicago Bears and Carroll Dale of the Green Bay Packers. The church has even held a "Festival of Religious Arts" to bear witness to the spiritual values in music, painting, sculpture, and drama.

First Baptist Church, in its pastor's own words, "has reached the point where it needs to be more involved." The Janssen report says, "The man on the street in Sioux Falls is relatively unaware of social needs." There are only about two hundred Negroes in town, and the Indians are out of sight on reservations throughout the state. Such problems as poverty and delinquency seem to be at a minimum here, but the church is discovering more need than was at first expected. An old fire station has been bought and converted into a coffee house. "The Fire House," it is called. A weekly meeting for honest personal talk and prayer, called "The Noon Spoon" has begun with the residents of a cheap hotel. Plans are under way for a community detention home and a program to assist school dropouts.

During one school year the church's study program focused on human problems. Basing their approach on Jesus' words in Matthew 25:35, 36—"I was hungry and you gave me food, I was thirsty and you gave me drink, I was a stranger and you welcomed me, I was naked and you clothed me, I was sick and you visited me, I was in prison and you came to me"—one sermon each month, the women's society program, and family discussions throughout the church membership took one of these areas each month for consideration.

In October, for example, the church raised money for an experimental farm in Japan. In January a mountain of usable clothing was shipped to Vietnam through Church World Service. In February church members considered how they might reach out in love to their neighbors. In March there was visitation in hospitals and in the mental institution at Yankton.

First Baptist Church is a healing community, a center of forgiveness and love. No one knows this better than Frieda Reimer and Don Ebert, who have found wholeness and motivation for their lives.

All her life Frieda Reimer has been looking for love. When she was a young girl in southern Illinois, the church was the center of community life. One went to church to meet his friends, and once there was fed on a steady diet of blood-and-thunder preaching and altar calls. Periodically one went forward to repent of his sins and make a new dedication to holy living. But there was little to help people grow strong in their faith. Not until years later, in Sioux Falls, did Frieda find a community that cared and a faith that sustained.

If it is true that a person must "hit bottom" before he turns to God for help, the road home for Frieda began in a Massachusetts hospital the night her youngest daughter, Lisa, was born. Frieda and Al, her husband, weren't getting along together. For two or three months Al hadn't even spoken. Divorce couldn't have separated them any further.

As Frieda lay in the delivery room she grasped at the only hope she could see. *I'm not going to come through this,* she thought, *and we'll all be better off. No one needs me and nobody cares.*

Just then Frieda heard a voice that seemed to fill the whole room. There were just two words: "I care." Where did the voice come from? Could it be that God cared?

Al, who had gone unsuccessfully from one job to another,

had a brother, Bill, who lived in Sioux Falls. Perhaps a move
would bring Al better luck. But Frieda decided, as he made
plans to leave for South Dakota, that she wouldn't be going
with him. She would stop off in Illinois with the children. She
and Al were through.

It was Bill and his wife who got Frieda on the phone and
convinced her that she and Al should try again. She boarded
the bus for Sioux Falls to make one last attempt. "After all,"
she says, "all I wanted was a home, a family, and for us to
get along. At my age if you can't find a meaning for your
life, what is there?"

For three months Al and Frieda and the six children stayed
with Bill and his family, who seemed constantly to be going
to church or to a Bible-study group—and getting joy from it.
Finally Frieda asked Delores, "What is it you folks have that
I can't seem to find?" Al wouldn't go to church, so Frieda
went alone. The church was too big to suit her—nothing like
the church of her childhood—and she felt lost in the crowd.
But when the pastor spoke, every word seemed to speak to
her. She signed a card asking for someone to call, and one
Tuesday night Pastor Fredrikson and a deacon rang the
doorbell.

Len and Arlys Perron started calling after that. Len had
pitched for the Sioux Falls baseball team. Now he was a hardware salesman whose home was open every Saturday
night for a group meeting. "Len and Arlys became our
friends," Frieda recalls. "They didn't make us feel, *These poor
people; they need our help*. They came as friends, as equals.
When we got to know them, we found they had the same
kind of problems everyone else has, but they were happy and
content."

Al and Frieda joined the church and kept searching for
more knowledge of God. In a small group one night someone
led off with a question, "What do you want most from God?"
"All I could think of," Frieda remembers, "was that I wanted

to be rid of my bitterness, to know how to love. How could I love my husband and be the kind of Christian woman I should be? That night in the group I said, 'I want love that will erase all hatred,' and it meant a lot to me that I had said it aloud."

Not long after that a friend at the church gave Al a job. He had seen how much Al needed help, so he bluntly announced, "You're either going to work for me or Lloyd. But you're not going to leave here until you take one of these two jobs." The job with Lloyd was the job Al held until his sudden death in 1965. During those months, Frieda says, "Al and I were happier even than we were at the beginning of our marriage. It was the prayers and the faith of our friends that brought us through."

It was that faith that put Frieda to work in the Sunday school, helping Arlys with the younger children. As she walked through the church she said to herself, *I'm not doing anything very important, but here I am and I'm part of this.*

"I've found a real family in the church," Frieda says. "When anything happens to you—like Al's death—it happens to them. You *feel* the love of these people when you're stumbling and questioning." And for their part the people at the church know that someone who has found the love Frieda has found has a lot to give to others.

A few years ago Don Ebert was a broken man. He had been a successful builder, but alcohol had reduced him to a shell of a person, sick in body and spirit. With his business gone, and his family about to leave him, he called Roger Fredrikson one night from a bar.

As Don opened his heart to Roger, he learned of Christ's forgiveness and power in their long talks together. But Roger is a busy man and Don felt guilty calling on him so often. After six months of sobriety, "I really let go and did some serious drinking," he says. "I was on the road and didn't have the strength to get home, so I called a local pastor for help.

He came and preached to me from the Bible and I almost threw him out. I didn't understand those words, and besides he seemed to me to be looking down his nose at me."

When Don came back to Sioux Falls, Roger introduced him to a group that could help him overcome his drinking. From this he made an easy transition to the Bible-study group which he attends every other Sunday night with equal faithfulness.

"Roger is a fabulous pastor," he explained, "but the real strength of our church is in the small groups. I've been meeting with six couples for two years, and I can't wait until the next meeting. Roger got us together and said, 'I don't know why I picked you guys. You're different ages, from different walks of life, but I know you're all searching for the same thing, and perhaps you can find it together.'

"We have a ball—I mean I laugh more at those Bible-study meetings than at any bar or night club I've ever been in. We all have problems, but we kind of make fun of our problems. We help each other. We're very open in what we say, and we talk about the love of God—and there are few places where you can do that."

To Don, God is love. "In order to have His love, you've got to give it away," he says. "If you take the love out of any man's day, his day is shallow. But if you can wake up in the morning and extend love to everybody—and mean it— to the people in your family, and even to the animals and the flowers. . . ."

Don's mind jumped ahead of his words and the sentence went unfinished as he tried to describe the gifts of God he had felt the day before. "I couldn't believe it! I was driving along the road in a new car, with money in my pocket, knowing my family wouldn't go hungry, and I began to see everything as alive with God's love—the green grass, the crops that were comin' up good, the cows with their calves, the birds, the trees. . . .

"I'm a miracle," he went on. "It's taken three years for me to become what I am, but if you were to make the change instantaneous it wouldn't be any more of a miracle. And perhaps three years from now the contrast will be even greater."

Don is worried about our world at this time in history. "I don't know why one individual should be so concerned," he says, "but I am. It may already be too late to reverse things —when you think of the Communists and the population explosion and the decay in the Christian world. I feel the battle's already lost, but for God. Now that's big talk for one little guy, but I believe there's something that can be done.

"Things are happening in our church. There are a lot of little guys like me who are like time bombs sitting in the shadow. One of these days we're going to go off, and this whole community is going to be lit up. We'll be a nucleus just radiant with God's love. People in other places will wonder, *What in the heck's going on over there? Let's go see!* Then there'll be other nucleuses (or is it nuclei?) . . . there'll be a blink here and a blink over there. Maybe the whole world will light up."

Questions for study and application:
1. What is the primary lesson that comes to you from this story?
2. What could your own church learn from it?
3. What might your church teach the people in Sioux Falls?

4

"Never the Same Again"

Mennonite youth spur renewal
by an "absurdly simple process."

They came to the church for five days, looking young and inexperienced. Three boys and two girls, their ages ranging a year or two above and below twenty, they talked about life in Christ—how hard it is as well as how much fun. They challenged other young people to try an experiment, then went on their way. But the church they left behind will never be quite the same again.

They were a LIFE Team—one of three LIFE Teams in successive years from 1962 to 1965—who made themselves available to Mennonite churches all across the continent. They brought a freedom and spontaneity that does not come readily to all Mennonites. And their work has revolutionized the Mennonite Church. These followers of Menno Simon, sixteenth century reformer, have been marked in popular imagery as a "horse and buggy" sect, due partly to the quaintness of such traditions as the head coverings worn by the women. But Mennonite families vary in their openness to change, from the ultra-conservative Amish on the one hand to the somewhat more open 80,000-member Mennonite Church on the other. And it is in this, the largest of some seventeen Mennonite groups, that the LIFE Team has been traveling from church to church, challenging the prevailing, rather grim pietism with an infectious abandonment to Christ.

It all began with Eugene Herr, who was at that time the denomination's Secretary of Youth Work. In looking back on the three years that the LIFE Teams traveled from one coast to the other, Gene finds it difficult to describe and define their ministry. "The whole thing was almost absurdly simple," he says. "It was a group of people who found a new quality of life in Christ and shared it with each other and with the congregations to whom they went in an altogether natural way."

But back of the simplicity was a depth of experience and vision and an intensity of planning and hard work that are staggering to recount.

The story begins with something of Gene's own story. He had been in church work for four years when, in 1961, he himself found "a new quality of life" and several forces from outside his church converged to shape his vision of the LIFE Teams.

When the Church of the Brethren in Greensburg, Pennsylvania—not far from Mennonite headquarters in Scottdale—held a Faith at Work conference, Gene's wife, Mary, went to the meetings, but Gene stayed home feeling no particular need for "one more inspirational meeting." Mary's reports were so enthusiastic that on Sunday morning Gene decided to go and see what it was all about. What impressed him were five laymen who opened their lives honestly to full view and told what it meant to live by God's guidance.

Eating together in the basement afterwards with these laymen, Gene sensed their freedom and spontaneity and wondered if it was related to the honesty they reflected. After they had gone, he righted some wrong relationships—with his pastor and fellow workers—and a surge of joy was released in his life.

Gene had been working for four years with the 18,000 young people in the Mennonite Church, praying, thinking, brainstorming new ideas, and trying new programs, but now he began to wonder what a group of released persons could do traveling from church to church and sharing themselves in an informal way as the laymen had done at Greensburg.

There is nothing new under the sun, as the writer of Ecclesiastes reminds us, but from the right combination of old elements it is possible to come up with something original. The structure of the LIFE Teams, though it owed its components to several sources, was in the combination of them genuinely original.

From Bill Bullard of International Christian Leadership came the challenge to formulate a vision—a five-year plan—for the young people of the church, and to think in terms of a team. From Addison Sewell and Harry MacDonald of Young Life came the inspiration to call it the LIFE Team (instead of an evangelistic team). "The Gospel is not boring," they said, "and God wants to give young people what they want most— life in capital letters."

From Don James of the Pittsburgh Experiment came the idea of presenting Christianity as an experiment—"something to jump into and get your feet wet, and give it a try in specific, concrete ways." From Sherry Day, who spent three days with the original team, came the wisdom acquired in forty years of life-changing ministry. From Irving Harris of Faith at Work came an inspiring challenge which kept Gene going even in times of discouragement: "Never in history has there been such an opportunity to live creatively for Jesus Christ."

And from his own denomination's Voluntary Service Program Gene borrowed some of the format for a traveling team: the strategy of selecting three fellows and two girls, each of whom had at least a year of college behind him, and asking them to give a year of their time to the adventure, for only ten dollars a month beyond their living expenses.

With his vision firmly in mind, Gene approached the Commission for Christian Education for approval and got their wholehearted backing. Then the process of selecting the first team and setting up their "missionary journey" began. At the August, 1962, convention of Mennonite Youth, the team was commissioned and began its travels.

A simple strategy developed. The team arrived on Friday to make their first contacts in a new church, in an informal activity such as a volleyball game or a party with the young people they had come to help, so that they could get to know one another. Saturday night they staged a formal dinner at which they shared their witness as to how Christ was working with them in everyday life. Sunday morning they attended church school and one or two spoke at the worship service, and in the evening they all spoke to the congregation. Monday night they met with the adult leaders of the youth program, outlining a thirty-day experiment, combining individual disciplines and small group meetings, to which they challenged the teen-agers on Tuesday night. On the last night, Wednesday, they ate supper with the youth group, held a commitment service, and the next day went on to their next assignment.

All the while team members were housed in a strategic way. One boy stayed with a boy who was in the local "in group" spiritually, and one with a boy who was in the "in group" socially. The girls duplicated this pattern, and the other boy stayed with the pastor or sponsor of the youth group. Things happened as a result. The team quickly got an insight into what teen-agers were really thinking, and their lives influenced those who were the strongest leaders in the group.

The thirty-day experiment centered around topics for each of the four weeks which demanded personal discipline and discussion in the group meeting. During the first week each young person had to discover from a normal conversation with a friend what was his purpose in life. In one town Jack Gross was in the football locker room when he remembered that he was due at the MYF meeting in half an hour and hadn't yet asked anyone, so he shouted across his locker, "Hey, Joe, what's your purpose in life?" He not only got an answer from Joe but enough curiosity from several other boys to lead to serious discussions of the Gospel that were still going on a year later.

The second week required each teen-ager to write his own spiritual autobiography. As they shared their writings, young people who had known each other all their lives met for the first time on a basis of honesty and found themselves drawn into a new fellowship.

Daily disciplines of prayer, of seeking God's guidance, and of sharing faith with others, rounded out the experiment, and after a month the LIFE Team returned for a second visit, from Wednesday through Sunday. These were exciting times as team members met with the MYF and each asked the other, "How are you doing?" On Sunday night the local young people shared their growth with the whole congregation.

In eleven weeks the team visited and revisited five churches, then took a one-week break before beginning another cycle. Each team completed four cycles, the first team in the East, the second in the Middle West, and the third on the West Coast. Now, sixty churches and 120,000 miles later, Gene Herr says, "For three years I gave the best of my time, my prayers, and my love to this pilot project, so that people could see in flesh its principles and ideas. We planted acorns, and now we'll have to wait for the oaks."

Gene sees seven results that have come out of these three years of "blood, sweat, and tears," from which other Christians, concerned for the Church's renewal, can draw encouragement.

The churches and the team members themselves experienced a new style of life. Naturalness and happiness blended with total commitment to Christ in a manner that many Mennonites were not accustomed to, despite the struggles and frustrations team members faced every week.

They were frustrated by what they saw of the weakness

of the churches. Staying in five different homes, they heard a cross section of the gossip and criticism that sapped the churches' strength. But they could absorb the frustration when their own relationships with each other were good, which wasn't always the case.

They struggled for leadership in the team, not realizing what they were doing until it was pointed out to them. Such a struggle was only natural since it was their evident qualities of leadership that led to their selection in the first place. But now one of them was designated as the leader and four were forced to follow, even when by natural gifts one of them was more of a "front-liner" with the crowd than the designated leader.

They were threatened in their inner security by the demands of living and traveling together, and even more than that by having to be ruthlessly honest with each other. Sometimes it was almost more than they could endure, and all three teams, somewhere along the trail, seriously considered abandoning the whole experiment. But they stuck it out and, as they sought to stay open to each other, they discovered the depths to which the life in Christ can go. Marian Kauffman of Oregon likens her year on Team One to a dentist's appointment. "God was the dentist," she explains. "The chair was the LIFE Team into which I stepped willingly, although I knew something of the surgery that would come. The prayers of God's people were the anesthetic that made the drilling endurable, and the drilling was the struggles that came my way. It was ironic: I didn't have to sit in that chair and endure the pain, but my absolute trust in the dentist made me willing."

Vel Gingrich recalls her year. "What has happened? There is a lack of the excitement which I had anticipated, and in its place lingers a wondering. It seems as if we ventured through a jungle together. The grass was tall on both sides. At times it covered our faces. At times it even covered Christ's face. Sometimes I wanted to turn and run. I wanted to be free, and yet I continued. Why? Sometimes, even now, I find myself praying, 'Father, lead me through more jungles.' " Of her teammates she writes, "I was convinced that they needed me, but I was not convinced that I needed them. But strangely, God had chosen them to help me become aware of myself. My teammates were the Clorox that helped clear away the grayness of my life. The day Marian told me at the laundromat that I was not as independent as I let on was the beginning of the Clorox treatment."

Jim Helmuth describes how honesty became a way of life and changed his relationship with his parents, his brothers, and his sister. "I am the root of all my problems," he writes, "and many of the struggles I entertained that year were brought on by my own flesh and not by carrying the Cross."

Denton Wyse, from Team Three, summed up his experience in this way: "I can only use one word to analyze the year —revolution. There were significant changes and there was a general movement. The roof has come off my house. God has moved from the unknown through people to me."

The team and the churches caught a new glimpse of what God is like. Team Three summed up the concept they found almost everywhere they went: "God is an angry man upstairs who wants absolute perfection, and the main thing wrong with us is that we don't read our Bible enough or witness enough." Many young people in the churches seemed never to have seen the unconditional love of God as Jesus lived it out.

When team members tried to share their excitement about Christ by retelling stories from the gospels in contemporary terms, it was often the "religious kids" who had the hardest time understanding, and the "outsiders" who responded most readily.

But many "insiders" did respond, and their understanding of God grew.

Dennis Cressman, of Ontario, says, "The team made me aware that Christianity is exciting because Christ is an exciting person." "I found God as a real person," Dale Beachy, of Illinois, recalls. "It was the sharing we did which meant so much to me."

The team and the churches learned that Christianity must be lived in fellowship with others. For this reason five people could communicate what no single person could. They did not just give talks on fellowship. They lived in fellowship, even though they sometimes found it exceedingly difficult.

"Some weeks we'd bat only four hundred," they were frank to admit, but their audiences caught the fact that they were frank about it and were learning to be open and honest with each other. As a result the officers of local youth groups began to see themselves as groups that were to live out the same quality of life, and that meetings were to be planned for *people*, rather than that people were to exist for the sake of meetings.

Some churches have begun to reproduce the team idea in sharing their witness with other churches. This was Gene Herr's goal all along and it explains why the experiment with a traveling team has not been continued. Once the teams had offered themselves across the nation, it was felt that local churches should take the responsibility of reproducing the pattern, and in several places they are doing so.

One church in Ohio, under Eldon King's leadership, has sent teams to six other churches, starting them on thirty-day experiments and going back a month later for a second contact.

From Roanoke, Illinois, Rosemary Imhoff went with a team of young people across the state line to a town in Indiana where Negro Christians were trying to withstand organized prostitution, and together they gave their witness. Rosemary says, in retrospect, that the coming of the LIFE Team was a high point in her spiritual growth but that this chance to minister was the highest point of all.

The Mennonite Church is discovering new ways of renewing and communicating its faith. The traditional revival meetings and spiritual life conferences are being supplemented by lay witness teams, and other forms will no doubt be developed as people are free to experiment.

The LIFE Teams reported through "Life Partner Letters" to adults all through the Mennonite Church, who saw them announced in church publications and asked for them. Through this reporting many a church member caught a glimpse of the freshness of their witness and began to think in new ways about how he could share his own witness.

Some ministers have gained a new concept of preaching the Gospel. True, there were ministers who criticized the teams' openness. "I'd prefer more emphasis on God's historic acts," one minister told Gene Herr. "These kids are too introverted and I don't know how they stand it week after week."

But many a minister learned to speak from experience and to make "the Word become flesh" with illustrations from his own life that week. And one minister learned to trust God with the naivete of youth. The team was standing in his kitchen one night discussing a boy who seemed hopelessly resistant to Christ. "Let's just believe God for this guy," Jim Houghton volunteered, "that he'll really commit himself to Christ." In the thirty-day experiment he "came through," and the minister confessed to Gene Herr later, "My experience with the team was a revolution!"

But the biggest result of the three years, perhaps, is the development of key lay leadership among the Mennonites. The fifteen team members promise to bring a new kind of leadership to tomorrow's church. They have been through a demanding, but rewarding, period of training. They know the pitfalls, and they know their resources. A few will no doubt go into the ordained ministry, but most will be laymen who can take the kind of responsibility tomorrow's world will demand.

Gene Herr has unconsciously followed a pattern remarkably like that of our Lord, who took twelve men and lived with them a quality of life that is still the key to transforming both individuals and society. Gene has poured his own life—and God's—into the three LIFE Teams, and he sees his investment paying higher dividends each year.

"The kids on the teams are living what they talked about better now than they were during the team experience," he feels. "It seems to take them a year to analyze what they've been through."

What are the basics of the team ministry? Gene feels there are three: *relating, communicating,* and *"disciplining."*

The teams learned first of all *to relate* to others. The definition they liked best was "laying down your life alongside somebody else," and this meant for them "winning the right to be heard" by spending long hours with young people just listening and showing an interest in what they were thinking and doing.

They tried not to play favorites. Everyone was to them a "key person." When Team Three reached Los Angeles, they heard that Dr. Paul Tournier (whose books they had been reading) was speaking downtown and they wanted to hear him. But by then Suzie Yoder, who was as excited at the prospect of hearing Dr. Tournier as anyone else, had agreed to go shopping with the girl with whom she was staying, and the opportunity to be with this girl was too important to put off to satisfy a personal desire.

Jim Helmuth found his host, Ken, already in bed when he arrived at his home, but they began to talk. Soon Ken was out of bed showing Jim his ham radio, his chemistry set, his hamsters, and his security box. Finally, he asked, "What are you interested in, Jim?" This talk led to others and it came quite naturally to Jim to share his love for Christ.

The teams learned *to communicate.* They talked honestly about conflicts in their relationships at home and of their experiences in dating, and when they led small group Bible studies, they made them intensely practical.

Vel Gingrich was the only team member who, in the cycle of ministry, came to her own church. As she witnessed Sunday morning, she says, "I discovered I was speaking to people who didn't really know me. I had sat where they were sitting for years but never removed my mask. These were the people who had helped me to be a Christian, but I had never told them why I needed them."

Marian Kauffman says, "I had always played it cool with people, watching how they operated, and then I knew how to play my cards. But on the team you lay your cards out on the table the first evening. I found out that in myself I couldn't care for people. Only Jesus could fill my emptiness and love them through me."

Finally, the teams, learned *to discipline* those who wanted to grow. They met with pastors and youth sponsors, learning from them, and passing on their own growing knowledge. On their second visits to churches, particularly, they instructed young people in how to "continue in the faith," and worked with them in removing impediments to this end.

Although each team imposed on itself a rule against dating during the year, it was natural that young people drawn to a common ministry might be drawn to each other. John Shearer and Vel Gingrich shared the Team One experience and fell in love. It was difficult for them to abide by the team rules but they did so faithfully, not permitting their feelings for each other to intrude into their ministry to young people.

Today they are married and, under Gene Herr's supervision, have directed a ministry to youth at Laurelville, the Mennonite Church Center in Pennsylvania's Laurel Mountains, encouraging the same freedom and honesty among campers they learned in their year on the LIFE Team, and witnessing the same results they saw all through their year of visiting churches.

One summer's highlight at Laurelville, as John reports it, was a week in July with fifty-eight campers. One night, in the cabin where Ed Moshier was counseling, the boys had a time of prayer together before going to bed. Danny, a handsome sixteen-year-old holdout, broke into the prayers to say he was sorry for the way he was living and wanted to become a Christian. Spurred on by this breakthrough the fellows began to pray for other boys in the camp, especially a rugged Negro named Gary. "Gary is a big man with a big mouth, Lord," one boy prayed, "and he's the kind of guy the Kingdom of God needs." The prayer meeting broke up at one, but just as the boys were crawling into their sleeping bags they heard Gary yell from the next cabin, "Hey, you guys in Cabin A, wanna rumble?" and over they came.

What they found amazed them. The boys in Cabin A didn't want to roughhouse. Instead Danny told them what he had just done and the prayer meeting started up again, interrupted from time to time as boys asked forgiveness of each other and of God.

At breakfast next morning Gary asked permission to talk to all the campers. "We went over to Cabin A to rumble but accepted God instead," he explained.

And so one life touches and changes another as in freedom and spontaneity God is given His chance to release the fearful and guilty and empower them with His love. They can never be the same again.

Questions for study and application:
1. What elements of this story challenge you the most?
2. What are its limitations?
3. How could you adapt some element of it to the ministry of your own church?

5

Freedom at Fox Lake

Prison walls prove no barrier
to spiritual breakthrough.

Prisoners are traditionally the loneliest people in the world.
Condemned for their crimes, they are shut away from society,
often ignored or forgotten by friends and relatives, humiliated
and depersonalized by a punitive prison system, and left to
fend for themselves in an atmosphere that amplifies suspicion
and hostility. But in Wisconsin a group of such men have
found in Christian fellowship a dignity and freedom they
never knew was possible.

One hot night in August, a group of men met in the administration building of Wisconsin's newest, most progressive
correctional facility. The meeting began in a familiar manner,
with a prayer, followed by discussion of a Scripture text.
The men were working their way thoughtfully through the
beatitudes from week to week, and on this particular night
the ending of the fourth beatitude struck them: "Blessed are
those who hunger and thirst for righteousness, *for they shall
be satisfied.*"

"We sure aren't satisfied in here," one of them said.

"No, but we weren't satisfied on the outside either, or we
wouldn't have gotten ourselves in here," another added.

"Being in this group is satisfying," a third man volunteered,
and then, for an hour or so, they went around the circle, each
taking his turn to describe what had brought him the deepest

satisfaction. Almost to a man they spoke of their recent discoveries of God's love and forgiveness, and of the human
relationships of trust that had developed between them.

This group and several others like it got started through
the efforts of a policeman by the name of Earl, who three
years before had shot and killed his wife and was imprisoned
for second-degree murder. Tonight he was the group leader
and he spoke deliberately and quietly about his own experience of the recent past—of the enormous guilt that had tor-
tured his mind and conscience, of the love two neighbors had
shown him, and of God's forgiveness which he had only recently been able to accept. "At last," he said, "I can stand up
straight and feel like a human being once more."

The neighbors Earl referred to were a couple who lived
around the block from him in Madison. They had known him
as a quiet man who passed them occasionally, walking with
his children, and they had met his wife several times at neighborhood social functions.

When the tragedy occurred, they discovered that he was a
Presbyterian minister's son. They too were Presbyterians and
at Westminster Church had discovered a dimension of honesty
and openness which enabled them to face themselves and find
healing for their sins and shortcomings.

The young couple felt bad now that they had not come to
know Earl as a person. The wife particularly had struggled
with her own repressed inner anger and had been finding
release through the grace of God. She wondered what pent-up
emotions had burst their bonds in Earl's sudden act of
violence. She wrote him an understanding letter which led to
permission being granted for them to visit him, and take his
three little girls to see him. Many visits followed, and they
tried to communicate their growing experience of the love
of God even when they found Earl in deep remorse and
depression.

In May, 1964, the first Faith at Work regional conference

was held at Green Lake, Wisconsin, and under the provision of a recent law which permits prisoners to leave the grounds under staff supervision for purposes of education or rehabilitation, Earl was permitted to attend in the custody of the institution chaplain, Orwoll "Oz" Anderson.

Here Earl confronted a difficult test. People in the small group to which he was assigned were introducing themselves, telling their names, where they came from, what they did. Should he expose himself? At first he decided against it and said nothing that would give him away. But as the members of the group talked about their own needs, he sensed that here were people whom he could trust. The second time around, he told them frankly that he was an inmate of the correctional institution, and looked around for signs of shock or withdrawal. Sensing only acceptance, he settled back in relief and surprise. From that moment on he began to experience God's love and forgiveness in a new way.

Chaplain Anderson was as surprised by the conference as Earl. In his pietistic Lutheran past he had encountered "testimony meetings" that seemed to him unhealthy "bragging sessions," and he had come to Green Lake as a "reluctant agent" —only because it was necessary if Earl was to attend. But he found a quite different attitude at Green Lake from what he had expected, and he went away enthralled.

"My wife asked me how it went," Oz Anderson recalls, "and I started telling her. Suddenly I realized I had been talking and gesturing excitely for forty-five minutes and hadn't even taken off my coat."

What surprised Oz most was the release people gained through the simple openness and love that prevailed at the conference and from the power of spontaneous prayer. Oz had been thoroughly trained for his position as prison chaplain. As a Lutheran minister, he had had clinical training in psychology, serving internships both in hospital and prison chaplaincies, but his training had equipped him only for "profes-

sional therapist to client" relationships. He was unprepared for
the power of laymen ministering to each other which he found
at the Green Lake conference. Oz Anderson had been over-
joyed at his assignment to Fox Lake when the progressive
institution was first opened.

Wisconsin has two traditional penal institutions, the prison
at Waupun and the reformatory at Green Bay for younger
men. The correctional institution at Fox Lake, which opened
in September, 1962, is unique, and is the result of enlightened
thinking on the part of the state legislature and the Wisconsin
Department of Public Welfare.

All adult male offenders, upon conviction, are sentenced
either to the prison or the reformatory, but after a six-week
period they can be transferred to Fox Lake if they appear to
be good risks with no severe emotional or sexual problems. At
Fox Lake they find a minimum of security and a maximum of
opportunity.

From Warden John Gagnon down to the last staff member
they sense an attitude of trust and helpfulness. For men who
have not been able to make wise decisions or who have a
degraded image of their own worth, the usual prison routine
only compounds the problem and makes them less able to
move back into society once their sentences are served.

But at Fox Lake men find a climate which respects their
dignity, which refuses to do for them what they can do for
themselves, and which provides abundant opportunity for
self-improvement. Men are known by name, not by number;
there is no group marching, no "lights out" rule; and individual room doors are never locked by staff members. Each
prisoner has his own key.

The educational program permits men to take five hours
or more of schooling every day, with classes in English, mathe-
matics, social problems, marketing, arts and crafts, as well as
excellent vocational training opportunities. There is work to
do on the grounds, which includes a 1200-acre farm, and men

are paid nominal amounts for their efforts. Evenings are taken up with art classes, recreation, visits to the library or the chapel, and a wide variety of counseling groups, led by trained social workers and others on the staff.

Wisconsin, along with California, New York, and the federal government, is a leader in prison reform. The Huber Law, for example, permits men who are guilty of non-support of their families to live in county jails at night, work outside during the day, and contribute their wages to their families' support. In 1963 a law was passed allowing men to leave the prisons under suitable escort for purposes of rehabilitation. In 1965 Chaplain Anderson took out twenty-four groups for various purposes, including choir appearances and the Faith at Work conference. The Roman Catholic Chaplain has used the law to send scores of men to spiritual retreats known as "cursillos."

Earl's visit to Green Lake on May 1, 1964, was the first overnight use of the law, however, and he and Oz Anderson came back excited by the possibility of continuing small groups. Oz had always felt that when deep feelings and problems were aired in a group and someone simply said, "Let's pray," rather than launching into a discussion of the problem, it was an evasion. But now he saw that it brought a new resource of power from the Holy Spirit.

Warden Gagnon was hard to convince when Oz asked permission to take four men to a group meeting in Madison. "Don't we have a good counseling program?" he asked.

"Yes, but this is different."

"What's different about it?"

"Well, in the first place, no staff member will be present. Men will be freer to talk and less likely to turn the meeting into a gripe session. Besides, two things will be added—the Word of God and prayer."

The warden gave his permission and Oz took four men— of his own choosing—to meet with six men in Madison. After two or three meetings outside, they began to meet Friday nights at Fox Lake, with several men driving the one-hundred-and thirty-mile round trip from Madison to participate.

That was February of 1965. Soon the group grew to ten men, and when the second Green Lake conference was held in May, all ten men attended. This time there was no secrecy about their presence. All who came to the conference were informed that ten prison inmates would share it with them, each of the ten rooming with one of the conference leaders. They came back with new enthusiasm for the opportunities in Christian living.

Since then several more groups have begun with no urging from the chaplain. No record is kept of attendance, so that a man's chances of being paroled are in no way influenced. Though a man's motives are always difficult to assess, and there is no doubt that some men join the groups, just as they attend the chapel services, "to get God on their side," it is difficult to stay in such a group for long without talking honestly and openly.

And being honest opens the door to what every man wants most—though he may also fear it—the deep interpersonal trust of other men. And when this door stands ajar, it permits two-way traffic. In one direction it leads to an authentic encounter with God, who seeks men through truth and love, and in the other direction it opens into the world, the world where most of these men will some day have another chance to prove themselves worthy of trust.

What is really happening at Fox Lake? How deep and how lasting are the transformations of lives?

Chaplain Anderson says, "I am enough of an idealist to believe that *every* man can be salvaged, but enough of a realist to know it isn't going to happen to all of them. I've been in this work long enough to know that the religion a man gets in prison may not last beyond the gate."

The Wisconsin Parole Board watches all this with more than ordinary interest. On their judgment rests the decision to hold or release hundreds of men.

Several men from the first Faith at Work groups have already been paroled. One went to Michigan, one to Milwaukee, one to Madison. Will they discover the kind of Christian fellowship they found at Fox Lake on a continuing basis? Ken C--- has found it in Detroit with Faith at Work friends who have helped him to get work. Leslie P --- has found it in Madison where Bucky Lippett has hired him as an accountant. Les meets with the Madison men regularly and joins them on the visits to Fox Lake. He has, in fact, become the coordinator for the ten or twelve men who regularly participate in the Fox Lake meetings.

Here is part of Les P - - -' s story, past and present, told in his own words:

"Four years ago, when I was twenty years of age, I was married, the father of two wonderful kids, and in business for myself. I was one of the youngest members ever accepted into the National Society of Public Accountants.

"But I was having a great many problems. I was suspicious of my wife, I was disgusted with my home life, and I was having trouble with my business partner. My business was failing and I could see it coming, but couldn't do anything to stop it. I didn't tell anyone about my problems, but kept them inside of me where they ate and gnawed at my 'innards.' I didn't want to tell anyone because I wanted everyone to think I was a big shot. I didn't want to lower myself in their eyes. I thought I could work my problems out for myself.

"My problems finally got the best of me. One night after a day when everything seemed to go wrong, I went out and committed a crime, and was arrested. While I was in the county jail awaiting sentence, I prayed diligently every day. 'O God, give me probation and I will do whatever you want me to do.' I was telling God that as long as He did what I

wanted Him to do or gave me what I wanted, I would do
what He wanted.

"I went to court and the judge sentenced me to four years
at the Wisconsin State Reformatory at Green Bay. God had
let me down. He didn't help me when I needed help so I
had no use for Him.

"On October 22, 1963, I was transferred to the Wisconsin
Correctional Institution and started to go to church, not
because of God, but because I thought it would look good
to the parole board.

"In February, 1965, I was asked by Chaplain Anderson if I would like to join the Faith at Work group. I still can
remember my first meeting. Three men came up from Madison to help us and to guide us. I listened to these men tell of
their experiences with God. I remember thinking to myself,
*What's with these men? What angles are they trying to work?
What do they want from us?*

"The other inmates told them about Eddie M - - - - who had
gone to the University of Wisconsin Hospital for an operation. They said they would visit him in Madison. I thought,
*Yeah, they will go and see him once, and that will be it, and
then they'll come and tell us how much they did for him.*
Later, when Eddie M - - - - came back, he told me that they
were up to see him, not once, but every day, and sometimes
two and three times a day.

"I had built up a barrier between myself and other people.
I would never let people get close to the real me, because I
was afraid they would hurt me. Yet these three men, and
especially one of them, got through my barrier. It was like a
hand coming through the dark to help show me the way. I
couldn't forget the things these men said.

"For the next two days I was filled with questions that I
kept asking over and over again. I was utterly confused, and
as I lay on my bed Sunday night, I realized why. These men
had something I wanted. They had found God. Then I realized

why God never helped me. The only time I called on God was when I was in trouble or when I had a big decision to make. Otherwise, I didn't need Him. I used God as one uses a water faucet to turn the water on and off.

"That night I found myself on my knees. I asked God to forgive me and to show me the way to live my life according to his will. I asked if I could become like the men from Madison. I can't express the exact feeling that came over me, but I felt very calm, as though I didn't have a care in the world.

"Since then many things have changed in my life. The biggest change is my feeling toward my wife. She had filed for divorce in December, 1963, but in the meantime had moved into a new apartment and registered as the wife of another man. She sold the car, signed my name to my checking account, and overdrew my account. I was bitter, hateful, and resentful. I wanted to get even with her any way I could. I wrote to the district attorney, the judge that granted the divorce, her attorney, and my attorney requesting that a warrant for her arrest be served on her, but I never got an answer.

"These letters were written about a week or two before I found God. After that the bitterness, the hate, and the resentment against my wife started fading. I found myself being concerned for her and the children's welfare. I asked God to watch over them, to guide them, and to be with them. One day I wrote her that I didn't want to press charges.

"I have come to realize that even when I had no use for God, He was watching over me. I thank God that I was sent to prison. I could have gotten into other, more serious trouble. But God has given me a chance to start over. If it wasn't for this time in prison, I might never have taken the time to find God."

"I've found freedom in prison."
One hears this statement again and again at Fox Lake. Her-

man P - - - - said it in a group meeting. "I was up for parole last year, but I'm glad I didn't get out. I would have missed the Faith at Work conference. And I wasn't ready for parole. I see that now. I could have gotten into worse trouble and been right back in here."

Later Herman was paroled and given work in the construction firm of his Madison friend, Doug Madsen.

Richard S - - - - goes even further. "I've found freedom in prison, and more than freedom. I've found a new life, an inner peace, and an understanding of my fellowman which I had never experienced before.

"Every time I've been in jail I've turned to Church, not because of my belief but because it was good for a parole. It was a way I could tell people that I was a different person, completely rehabilitated. The funny part is that it always worked; I guess I must have been a pretty persuasive liar. But a series of events turned me to the Church this time for other reasons.

"I am presently serving a two-year term at the Wisconsin Correctional Institution. Five months ago everything began to happen at once. I was up for parole. I had secured a trusted position of attending to the chapel on Saturday nights, and everyone thought I was sincere. Things were going along nicely until I was confronted with more crimes that I had committed, and the possibility of several more years being added to my sentence. I ended up in the chapel, not for forgiveness but to steal the chaplain's wine. Soon afterwards I was asked—not accused, but asked—if I had taken the wine. For the first time in my life I couldn't look someone straight in the eye and lie to him. Before I knew it, I was telling the chaplain all my problems. He let me keep my job on Saturday nights and didn't report the incident to the front office.

"I had joined the Faith at Work group as part of my front, but I saw something in the men of this group and in the outside men who drove all the way from Madison because of their concern for us. I thought there was something wrong with them until this incident. Then I saw that I had betrayed a trust, and that these people had in turn turned the other cheek. That was when I saw something in them that I had to have, though I couldn't describe it.

"Our meetings drew me a little closer to God. I stopped worrying about myself, put my concern to work toward helping others, and was surprised to find that they had as many problems as I did. In May we were allowed to attend the Faith at Work conference at Green Lake, for a complete weekend, and it was the greatest experience of my life. A very cheap but proud person came to be one of God's humble children.

"I can't begin to describe the emotions you feel when willing people, each with his own problems, drop all barriers and masks used to protect themselves from hurt, and then tell people they haven't known for even two days everything that troubles them, and try to help each other.

"People say that this feeling I have now will go away, and that I'll come down off cloud nine, and that my barriers will come back again. I can't believe it. In just two days, these people have shown me a new life, something I had been fighting to find for the past twenty-one years. I can no longer live in my own past, or my own future, but live for today and for God in my life always. There is a lot of work to be done for God in this institution, and I've just begun to live my life for Him. I see that He has put me here for a purpose, to help as many of the men here as I can."

One of the most beautiful examples of new life at Fox Lake, according to Oz Anderson, is the change that has come to Donald S----. Not long ago he was described as "a walking dead man." Today he is a dynamic, triumphant Christian, an inspiration to those around him. Here is his own explanation of what has happened:

"Some of my first memories are of pain, because I had to wear a brace around my chest holding my right arm in a rigid upright position from the time I was about a year and a half old until I was four. When I was seven, the doctors decided that I should wear this brace again. I wore it until I was nine. Many, many nights I cried myself to sleep because of the ache in my arm.

"I wasn't left in doubt long that I was different from other children, and couldn't join in many of their activities. This caused me many unhappy hours until I finally learned to depend upon myself for ways of spending the free hours after school. I started getting into trouble when I was eleven or twelve, and pulled my first hold-up at sixteen. To make up for the lack in myself, I used a fast car and a gun. This made me feel equal to everyone and gave me an added sense of power.

"I was sentenced to the reformatory just short of my eighteenth birthday. I was forty years old this past June. Between my eighteenth and fortieth birthdays I have had less than two years of freedom.

"I lost both of my parents while in prison. I couldn't even go to my mother's funeral. As the years passed, I gave up hope and was just doing time, becoming very sorry for myself. I wanted to change, but the wall I built around myself was higher and thicker than the prison wall. Going to church had become a habit with no meaning in it outside of the hymns, which I loved to hear. After being transferred out here to the correctional institution I went to church as usual. But because we have a beautiful chapel and a wonderful minister whose sermons can be applied to everyday living, I became really interested and tried to learn about Christ and His teachings. I started praying for guidance and God's help to change my life.

"One day Oz Anderson called me in and told me about a Faith at Work group in Madison. He was going to take four men down to one of their meetings and asked if I wanted to be one of them. I agreed, and what an experience it was!

"After sitting down in a circle we opened the meeting with a prayer. Then, working around the circle, we introduced ourselves, told about our lives and where we were spiritually at this point, and how with God's help we could become better individuals. All the time this was going on I was wondering why these men from Madison had asked us convicts to come. What did they want from us or expect to gain?

"In the weeks and months since that meeting I have received my answer. They are not trying to·gain anything from us, but to serve God and spread His message to those who need it along with the love and joy of Christian fellowship. At Green Lake I saw in practice more of this love and concern and willingness to help that I first saw in the men from Madison. This conference truly helped me give my life to Christ.

"Saturday morning I wanted to go up in the bell tower to observe the view. It was locked, and I was disappointed, so instead I decided to take a stroll. As I walked away, the chimes inside the tower rang out, filling my ears with beautiful music. I strolled around a curve in the path a little while later and a deer—one of God's most beautiful and graceful creatures— bounded across the path, I realized later that in turn for the one disappointment, God had given me three blessings: filling my ears with a joyful blend of chimes, filling my eyes with a wonderful sight, and because of these first two, filling my soul with wonder and peace. He taught me that I don't have to climb a tower to see His beautiful world. Just open my eyes and look. Also, if I open my heart to Him, He will share His love with me.

"I have always stayed in my cell or my room, keeping to myself, not wanting to be bothered by other people's troubles. Christ's coming into my life has changed this. I am spending my time trying to help other men in here and, by letter, people on the outside. I have found the wonder and beauty He can bring into the life of a person who will turn his life over to Him to manage."

The men at Fox Lake are a help to outsiders as well as to
one another. Since attending the Faith at Work conference
they have written hundreds of letters to encourage those with
whom they shared spiritual discoveries and decisions. Priscilla
Medler's experience is a dramatic one. She met the men from
Fox Lake at the conference, and like them was released from
an institution in order to attend.

At first she felt out of place, but after hearing Les P - - - tell
his story in a public meeting, she spoke to him. "You and I
have something in common," she said. "I'm also institu-
tionalized, at Mendota State Hospital." She talked to Eddie
M - - - -, too, though briefly, and during her first week back
in the hospital, letters came from both Les and Eddie.

Then Eddie was transferred to Madison for surgery on
his eyes. By now Priscilla had been released and had found a
wonderfully suitable job as secretary to a medical researcher,
but she was panicky at the responsibility. She went to the hospital at lunch time to cheer up Eddie before his operation, but
he sensed her anxiety and prayed with her that she would
find the courage she needed.

Through all her search for serenity and faith, Priscilla says,
"The biggest help was the letters from those men." Her faith
has grown by leaps and bounds under their encouragement.
"I used to wish I had the faith in God to say, 'Heal Eddie's
eyes,' but I didn't have it," she confesses, "but the confused
thinking that has been a part of me for a year and a half has
cleared away. Now I have really come to the place where I
can say with real faith, 'God, heal Eddie's eyes.'"

The men in Madison, meanwhile, aren't certain who has
been helped the most—the men at Fox Lake or themselves—or
whether any distinctions should be made between the two
groups for that matter. They have gotten to know God together and are part of one indivisible fellowship.

As one of the Madison men puts it, "We have developed a
rare kind of fellowship over this past year. I really think there

is more freedom and personal integrity developing inside those 'prison walls' than is usually in evidence on the outside."

But Dick Pritchard's experience at the Faith at Work conference in 1965 expresses it best of all. As minister of Westminster Presbyterian Church, it was he who several years ago brought the Faith at Work concept of lay witness and small groups to Madison, and paved the way for both the Green Lake conferences and the ministry at Fox Lake. "The ten men from the prison were a benediction to us all through the conference," he recalls. "It was uncanny how God worked in and through them. Saturday night the chaplain referred to them as convicts. I remember shuddering at the word. I was inwardly angry at him for hurting their feelings, as I thought.

"The men were asked to sing as a choir at the Sunday morning service and since they needed some extra help, Dave Stewart, Bucky Lippitt, and I were asked to sing with them, 'Lord, I Want To Be a Christian.' But when our time came and the worship leader said, 'The convicts from Fox Lake will now sing,' I almost didn't stand up. *Will the congregation know who I am?* was my subconscious question. And then, with shame, I realized how shallow I still am, and I jumped up, proud to stand alongside these men. For I too am a convict. I stand convicted, as much as any man, of sin. The bars that confine me aren't made of steel. They're made of pride, prejudice, lust, self-centeredness, and the like. But any man, wherever he lives or whatever he may have done, is truly free when he asks for and accepts the forgiveness found through Christ.

"I am humbly grateful to God and to these men for showing me that we are all convicts together, and that we can all be free together."

Questions for study and application:

1. List the positive forces at work in the situation described here.
2. What opportunity have you for a comparable ministry?
3. Do you sense problems inherent in the program at Fox Lake? How might they be avoided?

6

"We're Sticking with the Church"

Nine New England pastors
find a pattern for growth.

One of the tragedies within the Church is the isolation of so
many of its clergymen inside the closed walls of an "image"
which robs them of their common humanity with laymen
and precludes their ministering with integrity. They are set
on a pedestal, expected to live by a higher standard than
others, then unduly criticized when they fail.

Can clergymen be as open and honest as laymen are supposed to be? Can they afford to take off their masks and expose their human foibles and struggles? One place to begin
this perilous but liberating journey is with fellow clergymen.

Every Tuesday noon in a plainly furnished office in downtown Boston a group of young ministers has been meeting
to work out together a style of life. For two hours these men,
most of them in their thirties, report the significant experiences
of the week just behind them, prod each other into an honest
facing of their problems and their potential, then fan out to
their suburban pastorates and specialized ministries renewed
for both the difficult tasks and happy privileges that await
them.

---

*This story was written in 1966. Since then the group has divided into
several groups, enlarging the ministry reported here. Howard Keeley has
joined the staff of Faith at Work as Development Director.

In many other places across the land, "angry young men" are denouncing the Church for its irrelevance or as "Young Turks" are plotting ways and means to overthrow its existing structures and move it into new channels of activity and influence.

What distinguishes the young men in Boston is their common admission, "I am what's wrong with the Church"—a discovery that has deepened in the group—and their determination to do something about themselves.

One of the unpublicized trade secrets about ministers is that a suprising number of them want to move. In this they are no different from the rest of us who feel that we could be happier or more successful somewhere else, in some other situation, and who tend to blame our circumstances for our troubles. Grass is always greener on the other side of the fence. Somewhere there must be a situation tailor-made for me where I could fit hand in glove and function happily without friction.

At any rate, these young men have come to terms with reality. They share many of today's concerns about the Church, but they believe it is renewable because they have experienced renewal in themselves and see the way in which it can spread. The greatest result, perhaps, is their willingness to stay right where they are—for the rest of their lives, if necessary—and let God work His renewing power through them.

There is in New England an evangelistic association, now in its eightieth year of activities. Howard Keeley is its Executive Director. It is in his office that the group meets and it was right there, in 1961, that in frustration over the seeming fruitlessness of much of the association's efforts, Howard decided to resign from his position. But before "throwing in the towel," he consulted his board of directors and they encouraged him to investigate those organizations where he sensed that "things were happening" and to ask for their help.

He went first to Doug Coe of International Christian Lead-

ership in Washington, D.C., who challenged him to gather a
corps of men around him who shared his concern for New
England and who were "of one heart." Doug kept referring in
his conversation to Jesus and His "corps group" and to the
Apostle Paul and the band of men who traveled with him,
stressing the power of a team committed to each other in a
common cause.

Visiting a Faith at Work conference in the Pocono Mountains, Howard began to see that the key to effectiveness in
such a group is honesty and integrity. He and his assistant,
Bill Udall, determined to make openness the basis of their
relationship, and with two other men who were willing to
pay the price, they began meeting in a small group. Others
joined them and together they worked out common disciplines
to guide their relationship—such as promises to attend each
meeting, to pray regularly for one another, to be ruthlessly
honest when speaking of themselves, and to read both the
Bible and other provocative books with regularity.

Honesty, in certain areas, came hard for Howard. Outwardly he exuded strength and self-sufficiency, but his seeming strength was his greatest weakness. He resisted criticism,
but when he could no longer hide his sense of failure in the
evangelistic association and admitted it openly, he found courage to face other areas of insecurity and discovered that the
more honest he became the greater freedom he found. New
power infused his work.

The tensions Howard thought he was successfully covering up came out in physical symptoms, such as the seemingly
insignificant but annoying habit of scratching the calf of his
leg. One day at the group meeting the reporting time began
with Howard's announcement that this habit had left him,
and a chorus of voices confirmed the fact. The others had
noticed what was probably a true sign of release from tension.

Howard's personal freedom has led to a new dynamic
throughout the work of the evangelistic association. Con-

ferences for ministers that used to put big-name speakers on
the platform, who in turn put ideas and sermon illustrations
into preachers' notebooks, have been supplemented by men
who share themselves openly and by small group encounters
where ministers are encouraged to discard their defenses. "For
the first time," Howard says, "pastors and laymen write to
tell us how God has changed them." One of the most
promising forms of ministry that has resulted is that of witnessing lay-clergy teams going into churches on weekends,
spending most of their time in home meetings, and encouraging people to be open and realistic in examining their lives.

"I'm experiencing a whole new level of living," Howard
concludes, "as an individual, as a husband and father, as a
neighbor, and as a minister, and all of this is an outgrowth of
the new relationship I have discovered with other men who
are dedicated to Jesus Christ and are seeking to be authentic
in that relationship."

Robert Heskett, pastor of the Baptist Church in Roslindale,
Massachusetts, one of the regular members of the group,
strikes one as a typical New Englander. He is quiet and reserved. His emotions only seldom come to the surface but
he speaks with deep sincerity.

When he moved to the Boston suburb of Roslindale, he
joined the Tuesday group "as a part of my continuing search
for renewal." As a result, he feels free to be himself among
the members of his congregation, and to absorb their hostility
when the need arises.

Another aspect of Bob's new freedom is a deliverance from
"get whole quick" panaceas. "I've gone down many dead
ends," he explains, "from healing conferences to handwriting
analysis that promised to change your character by changing
your handwriting. But I don't believe God works in these
ways. My fundamentalist tradition taught me that God works
only suddenly and dramatically. That's a myth I have dis-
carded. God works slowly, patiently, and lovingly."

One of Bob's disappointments is that he has been unable so far to reproduce the experience of the Tuesday group in his church. But renewal may come, he thinks, together with outreach. In a community very largely Roman Catholic, he and his church have been through a time of deep discouragement.

They reached a low point in 1963. Membership and financial pledges were unpromising. In spite of this there was concern for social action. "We don't have much here in the way of resources," Bob announced, "but we have a building. Let's give it to the community." There are now three neighborhood clubs for children and young people, a cub scout pack, a mother's club run by Family Service, and desire has been expressed for a club for elderly retired people.

When Bob was asked, "Where would you like to be ten years from now?" he replied unhesitatingly, "Right where I am." Though he feels Protestantism in New England is in crisis, and though his own church numbers only one hundred and fifty members, he sees the possibility of its being a reconciling community. "Because of the clubs many people will come through our doors who are not members of this church," he explains. "But we are willing to serve the community, regardless of whether people become members."

Bob believes that three elements are essential to the renewal of the Church: honest preaching from the Scriptures, renewal groups, and service to the community. "Renewal has not yet come to our church," he concludes, rather wistfully, "but we go on waiting for the working of the Holy Spirit and expect that it *will* come."

Delwin Schneider is a man who knows what it means to involve himself and his church in an authentic ministry to the neediest people in the community and to be crucified for his efforts.

Del's struggles were within an historic downtown church which no longer served its neighbodhood but whose members drove in from forty outlying suburbs. Del himself, when he came to the church some years ago, settled in fashionable Wellesley, but he could not stay there long. His social conscience, supported by the Tuesday group, led him to move into the parish house in Boston's Back Bay section. The "disreputable characters" he began to befriend and lead into the church caused such serious opposition from one or two church officers that Del finally resigned to accept a teaching post in world religions at Gustavus Adolphus College in Minnesota.

In describing his own Christian growth, Del says: "In my circles one never talks about his personal faith. Most of one's friends are church members. Such a thing as faith is taken for granted. We speak of the organizations of the Church and their activities, of the Church's statements on birth control or automation, but it just isn't cricket to speak of what is involved in the day-by-day renewal of one's baptismal covenant or one's daily commitment to the Lord."

From his first parish Del went to Tokyo as director of "The Lutheran Hour," and while there he earned a Ph.D. degree in theology, studying under Shinto theologians as "an attempt to appreciate an old faith for the understanding of the total complex of contemporary Japanese life and culture."

Coming from such a cultural confrontation to a church in Boston which seemed to him unwilling even to confront the alienated and non-conformists at its own doorstep was an almost unbearable burden to Del Schneider. But in the Tuesday group he learned to live with himself and to see his own rationalizations and shortcomings. "Our group," he writes from Minnesota, "came as close to the New Testament concept of fellowship, of being transparent to one another, as anything I have known. Jesus Christ liberated us from our masks. He did it on a day-to-day basis through people who really knew us as we were."

Del learned in the group that "in tension there is growth," and this prepared him for conflict in the church. "Every church in America," he says, "is faced with new and trying times. The church in Boston was no exception. The civil rights movement, the campus revolution, our new understanding of the Church and its theology are causing much unrest. Every forward-looking church is asking hard questions—questions that often generate more heat than light—but together we can find strength to seek out God's activity in these turbulent times and even to be grateful for the growth because our times are turbulent."

Dick Doss, pastor of the three-hundred-fifty-member Baptist Church in Whitman, Massachusetts, admits to quite different interests from Del Schneider's. "I'm personally afraid of involvement in social and racial issues," he says candidly. But even such candor is a sign of growth.

Life in Dick's earlier years was playing a game. He grew up in the playland of southern California, went to UCLA with nothing in mind but to play tennis. Then, in his senior year, Bill Bright of Campus Crusade spoke to the men of Dick's fraternity house. The claims of Christ were presented and Dick responded, because Christianity offered a purpose in life which he had not had.

He went at once to the college department of Hollywood Presbyterian Church, where every serious Christian was challenged to enter the ministry. Dick did. But looking back he can see that one strand in his motivation was to become an "answer man."

"One thing tennis does for you," he confesses, "is to teach you to act cocky and self-assured. Even when you're down five to one in the third set, it's forty-fifteen and your opponent's serve, you must walk up to the baseline like you've got the world by the tail. It's an air you put on. You have to if you're going to win."

From being the center of attraction on the tennis court Dick made an easy switch to the center of attraction as Minister of Students at Boston's Tremont Temple. He learned "to play the game" theologically and vocationally—to say, "I

don't know," or, "Tillich says this, but on the other hand
Barth says that," to college students. Always he was the professional, informing the other person and enjoying his role.

When Howard Keeley invited him to the Tuesday group—
which met just two floors down from his office—Dick didn't
come for answers. "I didn't even know the questions that were
being asked," he admits today. But the result has been a realistic search to find himself as an authentic person. As a doctoral
candidate at Boston University he is making an investigation
of theology. In the group he is investigating himself as a
Christian. The disclosures are painful at times (such as his
admission that his doctoral studies are chiefly to satisfy his
desire for prestige), but they are liberating as well.

And since Dick has moved out to Whitman he has carried
with him a spirit of optimism. "The Church is renewable,"
he believes, and as evidence he reported to the Tuesday group
a deacons' meeting when "from seven-thirty to eleven-fifteen
we talked only about people, their needs and how we are
ministering to them." His wife Barbara greeted him later with,
"It's great to see you come home from a church meeting feeling so good."

A sub-committee of the diaconate (nine people in all) have
been calling with Dick on their inactive members. "We find
people who had a perfect attendance at our Sunday school for
twelve straight years," he says, "who now couldn't care less.
So we are asking, 'What's wrong? Where did the church fail
you?' or, 'Where did *you* fail?' " The results? "Things are
happening both to those who are called on and those who do
the calling. It's a two-way street."

Peter McClelland is also finding himself, but traveling a
different road from Dick's. Peter, who at the time of writing
was pastor of the Baptist Church of Hingham, Massachusetts,
and who has lived in New England all his life, finds it difficult
to relate easily and casually to others. He blames his rigid
family and church in part. When he was a boy it was unusual

to have guests in his home, and when people were invited they were usually from the in-group at the church. "For years," Peter says, "I felt like a fish out of water on social occasions."

Peter's experience in the Tuesday group has been both disturbing and releasing. His thinking has been stirred. Some of the "absolute truths" of earlier years are open to question. Alternately he wants to go on into greater freedom, then is tempted to run back to safe and familiar patterns. Being in flux is sometimes hard to live with.

His ministry has become more personal and more rewarding. Some months ago he was pushed into deep water, and he has been swimming ever since, more and more successfully. He had preached a sermon on loving people, and one lady said to him afterward, "I'd believe what you say more readily if you'd visit the lady across the street from me."

It turned out that the lady across the street was a member of the church, in her eighties, and Peter had visited her only once in four years. He was irked by the criticism, but on Monday morning he called on the old lady.

"Well, it's about time you came," was the greeting he received.

"Yes, it is," Peter said humbly, and then added, "I want to say I'm sorry I haven't been here before. I have no excuse. But here I am."

"You don't love me!"

"Well, probably that's true. But I don't intend it to stay that way. I'm your pastor and I want to love you and I want you to love me."

They talked a while. Before Peter left he offered a prayer. He could still sense the old woman's hostility, and so he said, "I want to ask you a question: Do you think the Lord has forgiven me?"

"I suppose so."

"Do you think you could find it in your heart to forgive me? I can't see the Lord, but I can see you."

That was the beginning. Peter started going by every week. Soon he had a list of shut-ins, half of whom weren't church-related, and to each of them he offered, "If you'd like me to, I'll come every month to see you." It was the start of a happy ministry among the elderly.

Bill Udall had spent twelve years as Howard Keeley's associate in the evangelistic association at the time this story was written, but until the group began he found little satisfaction in his work and kept wanting to move. Invited to preach in a church, he would invariably ask himself, *Is this an opening I'm being considered for?*

Then the Tuesday group was formed and in it both Bill and Howard shared their inner struggles. The group helped them to understand their motives and to come to terms with them. "I find it hard to be reflective about myself," Bill explains. "I get involved in the mechanics of organization. My own time with God isn't what it could be. But in the group men pin me down and ask probing questions. Although I may resent the questioning at times, as the others minister to me and pray for me specifically at the point of my need I find myself solving problems I couldn't handle independently.

"I used to live in an 'if only' world," Bill goes on. "If only I lived somewhere else or worked somewhere else. . . ." One evening his eight-year-old daughter Debbie climbed onto his lap and they talked for a long while. When Bill tucked her into bed she smiled up at him, "Daddy, I'd rather be *me* than anyone else in the world."

God spoke to Bill through Debbie's words. He has come at last to feel the same way about himself—grateful to be who he is and where he is.

Bill is most optimistic about the witnessing teams who have visited members of churches in the past few years and have elicited a warm response, especially in Massachusetts and Maine. Even board members of the evangelistic association are being recruited for the visiting teams. One man, after his first such experience, sent a check for one hundred dollars to the association. "Some men may think they should get paid to go," he wrote, "but I want to pay for the privilege."

When Bill speaks of what the Tuesday group means to him, he keeps going back to the change of focus it has brought to him. "Our dissatisfaction now centers in ourselves," he says, "rather than in our situations. Solutions to problems come as we get ourselves out of the way so that God can use us."

Ken Curtis—the newest member of the group—for several years occupied Dick Doss's former position as Minister of Students at Tremont Temple. He regularly drew more than one hundred students from such schools as nearby Harvard, M.I.T., and Boston University into his college and career group.

Ken developed a fascinating weekly TV program, "Turning Point," to interview Christians and air their witness over Channel 5 in the Boston area. On his way to the studio one night he stopped to meet with a small Protestant student group on the campus of a college of accounting. Only four or five students showed up to add to their existing discouragement about witnessing effectively on their campus. Instead of giving the talk that had been announced, Ken chatted freely about their objectives and hopes, feeling his way for an opening whereby he might both challenge and encourage them. The opportunity came in response to a question.

"What's the biggest gripe on your campus?" Ken inquired.

"The commons room," was the quick reply. "Kids eat lunch in there and leave it a mess!"

"Perhaps this is a way-out idea," Ken countered, "but have you thought of taking responsibility for cleaning it up each day? What would happen if, without any publicity, you just quietly took turns cleaning up the commons room?"

The beleaguered group of persistent Protestants thought about that for a minute. It was obviously a new idea, and not a comfortable one.

"There are other religious groups on campus," one of them ventured at last, "the Newman Club and the Menorah Club. Maybe we could involve them, too."

The meeting broke up just as one of those clubs was to get under way a few floors below, and the Protestants trooped down the stairs to visit their Jewish counterparts and propose a joint service venture by campus religious groups that might implement their witness.

As Ken Curtis walked out into the chilly night air of Boston, this gesture seemed to symbolize the possibility of all the evangelical efforts toward renewal in New England. The forces seem small and in many cases isolated, but as they link up with one another and take on the character of servants, who knows how far-reaching may be their ultimate influence?

Questions for study and application:

1. What problems are inherent in an ordained ministry and are common to all pastors?
2. What pastor's situation in this story most clearly parallels your own?
3. How can you help your pastor find new release and freedom?

7

Today in Bethlehem

New life in First Presbyterian Church
radiates from the center.

The Church throughout America is filled with religious
people who don't know God—for whom the forms and activities of Protestantism, such as its worship, church school, men's
and women's organizations, have provided a religious orienta-
tion for life without leading them into a deep and personal
relationship with Jesus Christ.

This is the conviction of Lloyd Ogilvie, a vital young
minister who came to First Presbyterian Church, Bethlehem,
Pennsylvania, in 1962, with a vision for a new style of life
which he felt could revitalize any church. A quiet revolution
has been going on under his leadership since then, one which,
in the words of many of its members, has made the church
"come alive."

The key to its power seems clear and communicable. The
driving force is a quality of openness and honesty—both with
God and with one another—which radiates from the staff
and official boards through the entire congregation, and on
out into the community. The church is like a launching pad
and its life like a three-stage rocket, only in this case the
stages are inverted, beginning with the smallest unit and opening out successively into larger, broader stages.

First Presbyterian Church, Bethlehem, was ready for take-
off in 1962. Lloyd Ogilvie succeeded the outstanding preacher

and writer, Dr. Elam Davies, who had given a firm call to commitment and had guided the congregation through a dynamic building and expansion program. The church moved in the 1950's from downtown to a 54-acre tract on the north edge of town, and the erection of a three million dollar building added both to the membership rolls and to a sense of satisfied security.

Once the building was completed and the resources for a wider church program were prepared, the question arose, "What kind of church do we want to be?" First Presbyterian had the reputation of being a prestige church in the denomination and in the community. It was "the thing to do" to belong, and many people did just that.

All that is changing now, however, as a surge of new life envelops the congregation, and as newcomers, along with many who have been members for years, find Christ as a living power. Dr. Carey Joynt, chairman of the Department of International Relations at Lehigh University, has watched it happen, and in the process it has happened to him. "I was a slumbering Christian," he says. "I learned the faith at my mother's knee and never left the Church, even when I was wrestling with God over the nature of belief and the validity of the Christian claim. But I had never tested the promises of God until I was chosen to be an elder. Here my commitment to Christ took on a new quality.

"Our pastor, Elam Davies, had left, and during a long interim while we looked for another pastor, the session (the ruling body of elders) was thinking through the hard questions of where we were going. I kept asking, *What am I doing here?* and then I began to realize that I had been called to help contribute to unity. The session had to become a fellowship before we could find God's will and do it.

"Lloyd Ogilvie came, at the appropriate time, and led us into the stream of life. At first some of our members were suspicious. We were on our guard against letting down our

masks. Gradually our resistance was broken, and by the end
of the first year we had learned that God wanted us elders to
be the Church in microcosm, putting fellowship with Christ
at the center of our business.

"The session, and the church, must be a place of forgiveness, where we are fully known to each other and where a
spirit of forgiveness has replaced the spirit of condemnation.
But we must first of all be individually committed to Christ,
and set our own houses in order. We must be reconciled to
our families, our friends, and our neighbors.

"Session problems become difficult when personal egotism
interferes with calm, reasoned judgment. But when session
members are committed to Christ as persons, they surmount
tensions and feelings to a remarkable degree. Cutting remarks
are at a minimum. Power struggles don't develop. Brothers
are treated with respect. Even when problems aren't resolved
—and some problems are intractable—they become livable."

Spiritual growth in the session, as well as among the trustees
and deacons, fulfilled the first part of Lloyd Ogilvie's dream
for the Bethlehem church. He had learned from previous
experience and observation that authentic, lasting renewal
must take place through the leadership of the church. Too
often new life comes only in some corner, and may result in
a divided church.

"It was my dream in coming here," he says, "that I could
spend enough time with the officers, with individuals first of
all, then with the official boards, that deep relationships of
mutual caring and love could be born, so that the congregation
then would begin to sense what Christian relationships were
meant to be—to look at the session and be able to say, 'That's
what the whole church is meant to be.' We've experienced
this, so that as the session has faced controversial issues, the
congregation has known that they are so deeply committed
to Christ and to each other that they cannot be separated or
split or disturbed."

To accomplish this goal, Lloyd took the elders, the trustees, and the deacons on a series of overnight retreats. Here they analyzed their own relationship to Jesus Christ and together asked the question, "What does God really want of us as a church?" They came to see that the Church needs to be four things: a worshiping congregation, a healing communion, a training center, and a missionary sending-station. To focus more specifically on their calling, they divided into six departments—worship, koinonia, nurture, evangelism, outreach, and stewardship—to reevaluate all that they were presently doing and to seek new directions.

In all of this, Lloyd Ogilvie's function has been not to project a program onto the church, but to lead its elected officers into the kind of fellowship and concern where they discover together the forms their life should take and the mission God wants them to fulfill in the world.

"The reason the Church has become so impotent to deal with the crises of the times in which we live," he argues, "is simply that it is filled with people who have not been able to take an honest look at themselves and admit that they lack the resources of the Spirit. Once they receive Christ with humility and openness, they get excited about what God can do with others. Up to that point it's sheer drudgery.

"During those early months," Lloyd goes on, "I was in deep fellowship with several of the elders. When I was open and honest, sharing both my needs and discoveries and visions in consistent get-togethers, God sustained and guided me. The difficulty with most of us is that we are afraid to be known as we really are. And it is the session, because the session is a focus for our egos as leaders, where many pastors are reluctant to be known. If I were faced with a resistant session, I would ask for one man. I would let him know me as I am and seek to know him as he is. I believe a quality of life would grow between the two of us, into which a third, a fourth, and a fifth could be drawn."

In the case of the Bethlehem church, the men of the session were ready for such a quality of life, and they responded.

The most distinctive feature of life in Bethlehem's First Presbyterian Church is its multiplicity of koinonia groups, or "K groups," as they are called, beginning with its staff and official boards, and encompassing all of its members who wish to experience this inherent power.

Koinonia is the word for fellowship, but "fellowship" conveys so little of its meaning that in the Bethlehem church people prefer to use the word that appears so frequently in the Greek New Testament. Koinonia groups are the answer to the question, "How can a church of nineteen hundred members know and care for each other?" Some method must be discovered whereby the church can be experienced in miniature. K groups are the answer, and there are dozens of them in Bethlehem.

Bryan Jay Cannon, the pastor whose primary responsibility is to develop koinonia groups, renewal conferences, and the church's ministry of healing, believes that "everything that comes to us from Christ can be experienced in a small group within the church—study, the sharing of our concerns, prayer, and the discovery of missions."

The first K group began when Lloyd and Mary Jane Ogilvie invited a few other couples to share such an experience with them. "We feel it is important to be in such a group," Lloyd explains, "so that the things we call the congregation to do are things in which we ourselves are involved. Something wonderful happens when you see the Holy Spirit working in the lives of your people, and you're involved with them in the discovery. The loneliness of the preaching task is gone. You preach from the edge of your discovery and you watch the faces of people in your congregation light up because they are discovering the same things."

Lloyd feels that for a minister to deny himself the fellowship of such a group because he may arouse jealousy or be accused of playing favorites is "to contradict the fact that the pastor is a human being and must be sustained in his spiritual life as much as anyone else."

One of the principal ways of getting into a K group at the Bethlehem church is through an inquirers' group, an essential step in joining the church, even when one simply transfers his membership from another church to this one. No one can join without going through a six-weeks course of instruction with B. Jay Cannon, in which everyone pursues certain prescribed studies, submits in writing a spiritual autobiography and statement of "The Creed by Which I Live," and experiences the interaction of a small group. At the end of the six weeks, if one has made a sincere commitment of his life to Christ, he may join the church and continue in the same small group under the leadership of one of the lay couples especially trained for such leadership.

All phases of the church's life—preaching, the choir, the church school, a weekday nursery school, the baptism of infants, the men's and women's organizations—serve as doorways through which people walk and are intrigued into uniting with the church. In the inquirers groups, most of them are united vitally to Christ and come to share the excitement of Bethlehem's new style of life. These are examples:

Bruce and Helen Whitmore are "PK's"—preachers' kids— from Canada who withdrew from church until children came —not in open antagonism but simply bland neutralism, as they describe it. When they moved to Bethlehem, where Bruce is a research metallurgist for the Bethlehem Steel Corporation, they tried to enroll their oldest child in a nursery school but found them all full. Even at First Presbyterian the registrations were closed, but an exception was made and Michael was accepted. As a result, the Whitmores came to church, but when they saw all the "steel names" among the church officers it threw up a mental block. They had no intention of "apple polishing," going where they might be seen and benefiting from it. But the friendliness and sincerity of ordinary members wouldn't let them go. They were intrigued, too, by the fact that they would have to go through an inquirers' group to join the church—there was no automatic "rubber stamp" membership—but that they could drop out at any time.

"Inquirers' was a totally new experience to us," Bruce recalls. "We brought out questions and prejudices we'd been sitting on since childhood. We asked Nick and Lillian Dinos over to dinner one night—they were 'planted' in our group, I'm sure—and they talked freely of how they had found Christ. 'It can happen to you, too,' they said. We knew that night we were never going to be the same again."

Helen says, "One Saturday morning I was standing in the shower. I *love* hot showers. I can run the tank dry! I was very relaxed—not thinking about anything—when all of a sudden I was positive that Jesus Christ was with me and always would be, and I knew this would never change. It just happened." Bruce's conversion followed swiftly, in a long talk with B. Jay Cannon.

Ken and Sara Bollman moved several years ago to Bethlehem, where Ken works as a sales engineer for Ingersoll-Rand. They attended the Presbyterian church. "I wasn't interested in joining," Ken says, "but we wanted our daughter baptized. I called B. Jay Cannon and he told me we had to be members first. I was upset. I thought it was automatic—that you just called a church and they told you what Sunday morning to bring your baby.

"Sara went to the inquirers' group, but I didn't. Then she volunteered our house for the second meeting—which was a sneaky thing to do—and I was forced to sit in. I liked it. Religion to me had been memorizing the catechism and learning the ritual. It was one hour on Sunday and had nothing to do with the rest of your life. But here were people discussing their problems, who admitted they felt lost at times the same way I did. Their faith was an active, living thing."

Ken missed three of the six meetings of the group because of business trips, but he was "hooked" by now and ready to let God run his life. But before joining the church he felt he should take "the full treatment." Sara waited for him while he went through another series of six group meetings, then they joined the church together. Now they're busy pointing other young couples to the church. "Many couples are just like us," they insist. "They simply don't know what Christianity is all about."

How involved is the Presbyterian church in Bethlehem in the crises of its community and of the world? Everywhere among its members one senses a feeling of expectancy—a premonition that the church is being prepared for a larger mission than it has known. No one seems to know quite what form its mission may take, but the feeling is in the air nonetheless.

Under B. Jay Cannon's leadership, the women's association has been considering the church's relevance in a secular society. Already the church has actively promoted an open-housing covenant in the community, and Lloyd Ogilvie has served as president of the Civic League, which concerns itself with racial justice. Several women are active in a program to relocate slum dwellers from a deteriorating neighborhood on the south side of the city.

Members of the church are also involved in resettling Cubans, working with the Puerto Rican neighborhood, and assisting the South Terrace ministry in an underprivileged area of the community.

But two strong convictions undergird the pastors' convictions about the church's mission. First of all, they believe *individual church members need to relate what they believe to the tasks to which God has already called them.* "Some of our people are in strategic positions of leadership already," Lloyd observes, "in social organizations, in institutions working with the troubled and the indigent, in groups working toward racial integration, in educational agencies, in the power

structures of industry and civic government. Our people have
infiltrated every corner of the community. Our task is to
equip them to communicate the love and forgiveness and
lordship of Jesus Christ to the world of business and society.
I still think the way the world will be changed is through
changed people who take seriously their witness in the community and become involved in changing the laws, regula-
tions, housing conditions, or whatever binds or debilitates
human beings in discovering their full heritage as children of
God. In a time like this a Christian must spend time in prayer
and study to know the mind of Christ. He must also be in
fellowship with others for encouragement and correction, and
he must discern what Christ is doing in the world. In other
words, we are not to work to win the world for Christ; it
already belongs to Him. We are to allow Him to work in us
and through us.

"When you're in a town like this with a large major industry," he goes on, "it's wrong to spend your energy complain-
ing about its influence in the church. Our men are steel men
and God loves steel men. I think it's my responsibility to be
with these men in the stream of life as well as in the church—
at their jobs, at breakfast and lunch, asking them the question,
'What does your faith mean to you here, in the responsibilities
and ambiguities and conflicts of this kind of life?' "

A second conviction underlies the mission of First Presbyterian Church, Bethlehem, in the world: *no social action can
be authentic unless it has a solid base in redeemed individuals.*

"I envision the layman," Lloyd Ogilvie says, "out in the
stream of life, in the situations and crises of our community,
equipped with a personal relationship to Christ, empowered
by His Spirit, knowledgeable with the plumb line of His will,
in fellowship with other Christians so as to withstand the
pressures and ambiguities of life. In the church, I ask what we
must do to provide all the resources to train and equip that
person. I see everything in that light—worship, fellowship,

study—and it provides the basis to judge what should have priority and what should be eliminated as irrelevant."

It is obvious what has priority in the Bethlehem church. At the circumference of its life is the insistence that all who join it come through the experience of koinonia in an inquirers' group. And at the center is the insistence that its staff and its official boards live out a koinonia that is observable and communicable to others.

One of the church's more obvious missions is what Lloyd calls "the Macedonian exchange." Any number of individuals in the church—seasoned veterans and young Christians who have taken their first step of commitment—have gone out as lay witness teams to share their faith with neighboring churches.

A unique feature of the Macedonian exchange from Bethlehem is the teams of elders who have gone, with one of their pastors, at the invitation of churches and presbyteries to share with other ruling elders their convictions and experiences.

Al Thurn is a good example of the kind of man who sees in all his relationships an opportunity to be a channel for God's grace. Al is a recovered alcoholic who made a shambles of the first fifteen years of his married life, as he tells the story, "losing jobs and moving from one place to another—from Michigan to Iowa to Pennsylvania with smaller moves in between, always letting someone down, feeling guilty about it, and finding the only relief I knew in drinking all the more. I didn't know that I had a compulsive illness. It never dawned on me that I needed to learn to live without drinking. I kept searching for a way to drink without getting drunk.

"When I was let go by the bank in Bethlehem where I was working, we decided—my wife Betty, rather, decided, because I was no longer able to decide anything for myself—that we would stop running and stay in Bethlehem. God had His hand on us, though we didn't know it at the time, because staying in Bethlehem was the best thing we ever did.

"The outlook was bleak. I was way in debt and needed grocery money. But I went down to the steel office with my hat in my hand and was lucky to land a job as a clerk. It paid less than my first job. For several years longer I went on trying to get my drinking under control—using all my willpower —with Betty screaming threats to leave and take the children.

"One day the company sent me to New York. I left in the morning and was to be back that night. I stopped at a hotel for just one drink, and three days later they were still looking for me. I don't know to this day where I was, but sometime in those three days I called home and told Betty I needed help. It was the first such admission I had ever made, and when I got home I found that Betty had done some investigating and had located a doctor who offered some help for alcoholism. Betty was ready to leave me, but she suggested holding off our separation until I could see Dr. Fisher.

"He was kind but firm. He explained that I had a disease for which there was no cure, which sounded like a death sentence, but he threw me a lifeline at last. There was a man in Bethlehem who had recovered—the only one he knew of, and that was eighteen years ago—in a way Dr. Fisher didn't understand, but it had something to do with an organization called Alcoholics Anonymous. He sent me to that man, who surprisingly enough was a senior official at Bethlehem Steel, a man I had held in respect and awe. He greeted me as if he'd known me all his life. He shared his own experience with me, then asked me two questions: 'Do you really want to quit drinking?' I did. 'Do you believe in God?' I mumbled that I wasn't sure, but at last I blurted out, quite emotionally, 'Yes, I believe in God!' 'Good,' he replied; 'If you really mean it, the rest is easy.'

"As we attended AA meetings, I saw how powerless I was to lift my burden, but I found a power that helped me, a power I later came to see was Jesus Christ. I learned to forgive myself, so that in turn I could be forgiven, and as I did the

need for alcohol diminished. With my new freedom came a
desire to share it with others. I began helping a fellow alcoholic to recover.

"Meanwhile I returned to the church, and when Lloyd and
Mary Jane Ogilvie came, I sensed they had a vision for the
church not unlike the fellowship of AA, where people would
be willing to share their experiences, their knowledge, and
their hopes, just as the early Church must have lived its life
in small groups. We have seen our church come to life."

Betty Thurn has also "come alive" as a result. "I had
thought I was a Christian," she explains. "I had certainly become a different person as a result of Al's recovery from
alcoholism, but now I encountered a new type of Christianity.
I heard talk about spiritual rebirth and small groups, and then
at a Lenten service Bruce Larson, of Faith at Work, spoke and
something struck me between the eyes. I was churning inside
the next day, and after a hairdresser's appointment my car
just wouldn't take me home. It headed for the Ogilvies."

" 'I don't know what's happening,' I told Mary Jane, and
started to cry.

" 'Why, it's the Holy Spirit that's got hold of you,' she
replied. I spent the day with her and decided to turn my life
over to Christ. That was the beginning for me. Everything
has become more real and alive since then, especially my consciousness of people and their reactions."

Today Al Thurn is a purchasing agent for Bethlehem Steel
and an elder at First Presbyterian Church. "But my ministry
is to alcoholics," he says. "On the job, people with drinking
problems are sometimes referred to me. We talk them out
and often the process of recovery is begun." In the last two
years Al has watched the steel company introduce a generous
and farsighted policy whereby any employee with a drinking
problem is given an opportunity through the medical department to find a means of recovery. The seriousness of his
illness is explained to him. He is urged to affiliate with AA. In

this the company, of course, has unique leverage, and already more than a hundred and fifty men have made significant progress who otherwise might have been discharged. Bethlehem Steel has joined a pioneering group of industrial corporations who are finding that alcoholism is a costly illness not only to employees but to employers as well.

The outstanding example of Al Thurn's personal ministry is the redemption of a Bethlehem ear, nose, and throat specialist who lost his practice through alcoholism and addiction to pills. As one of his patients, Al was able to share his experience with the doctor and to get him into AA. From there the doctor went back to one of his medical school instructors, a Philadelphia psychiatrist, who helped him so much that he decided to study psychiatry and devote the rest of his life to working with alcoholics. He has been given a grant and a few old buildings at a state mental hospital where he has been experimenting in rather spectacular ways, through the use of new drugs, with men who heretofore have been considered beyond redemption. His first forty-eight cases have added up to forty-eight successes, and it may be that he is on the verge of a significant breakthrough in medical treatment.

Questions for study and application:
1. In what ways is this church like your own?
2. How does it differ, and what ought you to learn from it?
3. What could the Bethlehem church learn from your own?

8

The Church That Stayed

Calvary Church, Cleveland—
"where the action is."

Many churches, aware that they should be involved in today's crises, are trying to go "where the action is." Not so Calvary Presbyterian Church of Cleveland, Ohio. Calvary Church is already there.

For eighty years the imposing sandstone church building has stood on Euclid Avenue at East 79th Street while the neighborhood around it has suffered successive changes and deterioration. Euclid Avenue was once one of America's finest streets—"millionaire's row," it was often called—and the Hough area fashionably housed many of Cleveland's first families. Hough (rhymes with rough and tough), a two-square-mile section, was the scene of violence, looting, and burning during the riots that broke out in July, 1966. It is the home of many of the poorest of Cleveland's three hundred thousand Negroes.

Calvary Church has not only weathered the storms of change, it has grown in membership, in spiritual strength, and in relevant ministries. Long ago it elected to stay and to meet the needs of its new neighbors. Today it is a truly integrated church which is discovering dimensions of the Christian Gospel which elude some Christians who have fled to the suburbs.

The Hough area was beginning to change when Dr. John Bruere, with his wife Nancy, came twenty-two years ago to serve as Calvary's pastor. At the time, Dr. Bruere, who had held a fellowship in theology at Oxford, was Professor of Religion and Dean of Men at the College of Wooster. He declined the offer of a college presidency to come to the Cleveland church long before inner-city work had become fashionable.

While other churches on the avenue moved away, Calvary chose to stay. Dr. Bruere, with Floyd Begin of St. Agnes Roman Catholic Church (in an association formed many years before ecumenism became popular), coined the slogan, "You can live in a better neighborhood without moving." With the exodus of whites and the influx of poorer Negroes, the two men helped form the Hough Area Council to do battle with landlords and city commissions to maintain living standards in the fine old homes that were now being subdivided into apartments.

Through the years Dr. Bruere has seen building codes enacted that require hot water in every house, rule out "community kitchens," and require a private bathroom for each apartment. He has headed campaigns for clean-up and rat extermination. He has served on the Cleveland City Planning Commission and at one time, had he chosen to leave the ministry, could have been Cleveland's Housing Director.

John Bruere is remarkably talented, a man of unswerving convictions and a leader of men. Though conservative theologically, a Republican and a former Rotarian, he has a keen social conscience. As Horace Williams, who for thirty-two years has been clerk of the session at Calvary Church, says, he is "a trend setter, a news maker, one who anticipates a problem and attacks it early."

Dr. Bruere is also a man who believes deeply in prayer. He and his wife felt strong guidance from God in coming to Calvary, though to many of their friends it seemed an unwise choice. They have never considered leaving. "I get more excited all the time," John says with a laugh. "I wouldn't be anywhere else on the face of the earth. I have never had the slightest interest in the strictly conventional church, for I find nothing that corresponds to it in the New Testament. There I find a fellowship of sinners who believed that Christ lived and died for them, and who were willing to go the limit for Him. The Church is the group of those who in every generation have appeared to many as fanatics because they believed that nothing in the world is as important as Christ."

At Calvary, prayer and God's guidance are paramount. Prayer is part and parcel of every activity, and God's will is earnestly sought in order that the church and its members may do God's work in God's way. A prayer group started years ago by Nancy Bruere and others is the spark plug for much of the church's spiritual power. "The Church is Christ's Body," Dr. Bruere explains. "No matter how inadequately, we are attempting to represent Christ in every situation."

The result is a church which Horace Williams describes this way: "Aggressive, conservative; changing, stubborn; urban, suburban; rich, poor; diverse in cultures and occupations, but united for service and worship—Calvary Church is a Christian fellowship with broad dimensions and strong convictions."

No record is kept of the members' racial backgrounds. One third of them live within walking distance of the church, another third are members of long standing who have moved out of the neighborhood but continue to come to Calvary, and the rest—both whites and Negroes—live some distance away but have joined Calvary because they prefer to worship in an integrated congregation and feel that this is where they ought to serve.

Roger Shoup, the church's young associate minister, is cut from the same cloth as John Bruere. Nine years ago, as a student at Western Reserve University, he joined the staff to coach basketball and assist in the youth program. In high school he was headed toward the ministry but his studies in college, together with the politics he observed in some churches, had soured him. "I wasn't going to go into the

ministry if little people were going to rip me apart and have
me for dinner," he says. But Calvary Church was looking for
help and Roger needed the money.

It took exactly two weeks to convince him that he had to
be active in the church, in this kind of church, and in the
ministry. As he worked with boys and shared the gamut of
their experiences, he became as attached to them as a father
to his sons, and he saw how the Gospel of Christ held the
answer to their needs. Roger has been at Calvary Church ever
since. After college he attended theological seminary in the
area so that he could devote his weekends to the youth program. He has grown up at Calvary, and today he shares with
Dr. Bruere every phase of the church's ministry.

One of the convictions that John Bruere and Roger Shoup
hold is that any effective inner-city ministry demands long-
term commitment from both ministers and laymen.

"The Church must be one place," Roger explains, "where
continuing relationships can be built that aren't going to be
shattered. Almost every institution in the inner city experiences a tremendous turnover of personnel—the schools,
the settlement houses, the welfare services. People must be
able to come to the church confident that teachers and
ministers will be there this year, next year, and the year after
that. An inner-city church cannot afford to be merely the
training ground for young men fresh from seminary to 'learn
the ropes' before they move on to bigger things."

Calvary Church discourages hobbyists who would like to
serve in some capacity for an hour or two a week. "Every
week ten or fifteen people call and ask if they can help on
that basis," Roger says. "We say, 'No, we're sorry, but if you
are willing to become a member and commit yourself all the
way, you can have the privilege of working here.' All too few
really want to make that kind of an investment."

So Calvary Presbyterian Church has stayed where the action is all these years. In so doing it has drawn together a re-

markable team of dedicated men and women and young people and has built a ministry with a strong spiritual base that serves the diverse needs of Hough residents. Where these team members concentrate their efforts and the kinds of response they engender will be evident in the pages that follow.

One hundred twelve youngsters form a circle on a vacant lot in Hough. As the last toddler finds his place, Roger Shoup barks instructions on a bullhorn. In a moment five teen-agers will reenact the story of the Good Samaritan as part of a two-hour program that includes instruction periods, small groups for discussion at different age levels, crafts, an opportunity to slip into the prayer tent to pray, and a free ice-cream bar.

It is a July morning in 1966. Each morning for a week a staff of some forty teachers and workers will convene at this vacant lot to hold vacation Bible school. Each afternoon they will repeat the process on another vacant lot, with as many as three hundred in attendance. Each week until September, they will move to two more lots until they have served in eighteen neighborhoods and registered 4,650 youngsters.

Through role-playing and discussing the parables of the Lost Sheep, the Good Samaritan, and the Ten Talents, young people will be taught how God works in the world—how He loves, forgives, and guides those who obey Him.

To make the parables live for youngsters from the ghetto, the lost sheep becomes a junk car which has been stolen and which the car dealer makes heroic efforts to recover. The parable of the Good Samaritan becomes the story of the milk-man who is beaten up by hoods and left in an alley. A "hood" and a "squeak" pass him by, but a "cool square" stops to care for him. From this is taught not only God's loving care for us, but the care we ought to show our neighbors.

The content of the teaching may eventually be forgotten, but it will be a long time before the teachers are forgotten, or the quality of caring and acceptance they represent, and because the church has come to them, some of these youngsters, now or later, will come to church.

Calvary Church focuses its greatest efforts on children and young people. Of fifty-five thousand residents of Hough, thirty thousand are under twenty-one years of age and on Sunday no more than one in ten is in any church.

It all began early in the fifties when token integration came to Calvary. Two retired Negro school teachers attended and were invited to join. The word got out and on any given Sunday after that as many as fifteen or twenty Negroes might be present at the worship service, checking to see if the welcome was sincere.

No more adults joined for some time but they began sending their children to the Sunday school, and gradually some of the parents followed.

In 1956 Dr. Gladys Foulke Goodwin, Calvary's gifted organist and choir director who died in 1966, invited her youth choir, which rehearsed on Saturday mornings, to stay for lunch together with Dr. Bruere's communicants class. They not only stayed but began to invite their friends, and soon, like Topsy, a full-scale youth program developed which now draws as many as three hundred youngsters to the church for a full Saturday morning program and four hundred on a Sunday morning.

Since Dr. Goodwin's death, Tim Wagner, a high school physics teacher, has directed the weekend youth program. For him, as for the forty other leaders who assist him—and who are paid a nominal sum for their labors—it is "very, very hard work." It means working seven days a week, with never a morning to sleep in.

The program begins on Saturday and Sunday mornings at eight with a prayer and planning meeting of the staff and Youth Service Council. Meanwhile, youngsters are arriving at the registration desk where each has a card to insert into a time clock. Checking in and out helps to teach the children punctuality. The reason for the early morning start, as John Bruere explains, is that "these kids are on the move. There's nothing much to keep them at home. We've learned that if we're going to get them, our doors have to be open when they get up and ask, 'What are we going to do today?' "

Calvary's youth program is one of Christian education. "We try to make the Christian faith relevant," Tim Wagner affirms. Mrs. Corinne Bryant, who teaches in the primary department, elaborates: "The main thing we teach is love. Parents in Hough aren't able to give their children much, financially or personally. You can't, if you're worrying about where the next meal will come from." But love is tough. It doesn't simply accept. It sets standards, it disciplines, it expects honesty and responsibility. Thus, young people are taught the importance of cleanliness. Sometime on Saturday morning every boy and girl is given a shower—his only complete bath, perhaps, that week. In small classes they are taught what it means to respond to God's love in prayer and commitment. They are taught to obey their parents, to do a job well, and to be Christian citizens. The day begins and ends with prayer. At the close of the Saturday program every young person files quietly into the sanctuary for a period of silent prayer.

Children at Calvary are taught to give. "We started out," Roger Shoup admits, "by saying, 'Let's not talk about money because these kids don't have much.' We came to see that we were teaching them to be irresponsible toward the church. We weren't giving them an opportunity to help pay for what was provided, thus continuing the kind of dependency people learn on welfare. Now we make a strong effort to have every kid tithe. If he gets a dollar a week, bring a dime; if he gets only a dime a week, bring a penny. And in turn we take half of what they contribute and give it to Korean orphans, the John Milton Society for the Blind, a mission for lepers, as well as our missionaries abroad. This gives the children a world-wide concept of Christianity and a sense of being part of it."

Miss Helen Evans, a retired school superintendent, gives this evaluation: "I know no other church that does what Calvary Church is doing for young people." Warren Battle, a deacon, adds, "It is a home and a school to the kids of Hough —teaching religion in the everyday living situation."

When young people enter their late teens, they learn what is expected of them on a job and how to make a job application. If they need work, someone in the church will help them to find it. As they qualify they may join the Youth Service Council and work for minimal pay in the youth program. If they plan on college, their pay will go into a reserve fund toward scholarship assistance.

Carl Hunt, a criminal lawyer, joined Calvary Church when he "walked through the Sunday school, saw kids I knew from the courts, and the advancement they were making." Another attorney, Charles Russell, says, "I never felt the Church was getting anywhere until I found here a program of action." Russell is on the board of directors of two settlement houses in Cleveland, but he concludes, "What Calvary is doing is fairly unique. And it works. Two of the kids from Calvary have worked in our office. They've learned to show up on time, to put themselves into their jobs, and they've developed a Christian faith I wish I had had at their age."

Other advantages accrue to the youngsters who come to Calvary. On Saturday noon a free meal is provided—all the "sloppy joes" and milk and ice cream they care for, which for some is their best meal of the week. For those who need shoes and clothing there is the Clothing Corner, presided over by Mrs. Mary Willett—"Mrs. Floppy Hat," as the children all know her.

Mary Willett lives in Shaker Heights. "I joined here," she says, "and decided to work out of gratitude for all I have. I began by teaching three-year-olds and arranging for the flowers each Sunday in the sanctuary. I was putting up the flowers one day when I thought, *What if Jesus walked in and saw this? Wouldn't He wonder if it would be better to spend our money on shoes for the children?*

From clothes that are donated to the church Mrs. Willett tries to meet the children's needs as she sees them. If she doesn't have what's needed, she'll shop for it the next week and on the following Saturday or Sunday a brown paper bag with the needed items will be waiting for each child.

Mary Willett likes to tell of the "coincidences" she experiences time and again in her work. "One day I said to a girl, 'Does anyone in your family need a pillow or a blanket?' To my surprise she replied, 'My mother does.' Then she told how a man who had stayed at their home had stolen her mother's pillow and blanket."

Recreation has its place in the Saturday program and for the older boys there are athletic teams, like the basketball team, coached by Tom Flewellyn, which has lost only two games in the past two years. Tutoring is available in English and math for those who need it, and when a young person gets in trouble, a lawyer like Carl Hunt is quick to come to his assistance.

Perhaps the most challenging aspect of the youth program is the integrity with which the Christian Gospel is applied to teen-age delinquency. "Too often," as Roger Shoup puts it, "the Church is soft and slipshod. It says to a boy in trouble, 'You're really a good kid—your home's just bad—and you won't do it anymore, will you?' We let him off easy, trying to buy his allegiance.

"Here at Calvary we see the application of the Gospel as tough and yet compassionate. When a boy has done something wrong, like stealing a car, we tell him, 'You're going to have to stand up before all your friends and tell them exactly what you did, why you did it, why it was wrong, and why you aren't going to do it again.' Then you're going to have to meet with us regularly in conferences, and you're going to have, to stay in school.' " If the boy expects the church to

stand with him in court, he has to stand up and be counted
with the church.

"This gives a boy a chance to get everything out in the
open honestly without fooling anybody, and the rest of the
fellows learn from the experience. He doesn't lose face because it takes a lot of guts to do it. The other guys are compassionate and have real understanding. They pray for the
fellow who has come clean, and there's never any monkey
business while we pray."

Roger tells how it works: "Recently one of the fellows—
let's call him Bo—drove into another car. Without a driver's
license, he got scared and ran. When the authorities caught
him they 'threw the book' at him. Carl Hunt went with us to
court and we managed to get a suspended sentence from a
correctional institution on the basis that Bo would follow the
Calvary Church program faithfully. He told the other fellows
just what he had done and how stupid it was to run. He described the pain that it had caused.

"Later that summer I got a phone call from another boy
in the group—let's call him Rip. 'Mr. Shoup,' said a very apprehensive boy over the phone, 'this is Rip. I just hit a parked
car. I got no driver's license. The cops are coming.' When I
got there Rip said, 'I remembered what happened to Bo, and
I stayed.' "

As Roger Shoup sums it up: "It works. And nothing else
works. Among the boys who've gotten into trouble and have
come clean with the group and prayed together, we've had
no repeaters. Rip, the boy who stayed, is now one of our
leaders."

To Thelma Tucker, Calvary Presbyterian Church is a
twentieth-century equivalent of the Church in the Book of
Acts. "I could bring any kind of person here," she says. "I
can't think of anyone who would be rejected."

Bill Tucker, Thelma's husband, is a mechanical engineer
doing research in nucleonics for Republic Steel Corporation.

He was a student at Case Institute when he and his wife heard John Bruere's radio broadcast, "Religion That Works," and his announcement that "Calvary is a church that has decided to stay in the city. If Christianity won't work in the city, it won't work anywhere." The Tuckers came and joined. Then they went to Ghana for three years to teach. When they came back, Bill took over Nancy Bruere's adult Bible class.

Bill finds that belonging to Calvary gives integrity to his Christian witness. "It encourages me to talk about my faith. I can talk about social problems from firsthand knowledge. I'm constantly finding an opportunity to speak about Christ. It stems from the fact that I'm at Calvary Church."

There are three principal reasons why all kinds of people come to Calvary—Negroes, whites, and Orientals, the educated and the uneducated, the affluent and the deprived, suburbanites and people from the inner city. (A bank president and an unemployed truck driver once joined the same membership class.)

Some come because they live nearby. Mrs. Patricia Salo calls the church "a big heart in a big city." She lost her husband Charlie last year and now lives on public support. "Roger Shoup preached at the grave," she says, "and as he walked me back to the car, I swear he disappeared and God took me by the hand." Mrs. Salo sits side by side at Calvary with her good friend Mrs. Fanny Frackelton, widow of a bank president and head of a large industry.

George Wilson was a juvenile delinquent at thirteen when a friend talked him into joining the Calvary youth program. "The people here—their personal interests," he recalls, "made me see I was worth more than I thought. I decided to make something of my life." From D's and E's his grades at school shot up to B+'s. He began to help his mother at home. He came to know God personally as he prayed aloud with the boys at Calvary. Today George is a technician at Glidden Paint Company, married to a practical nurse named Margaret whom he met at Calvary, and teacher of the junior boys in the Saturday-Sunday program.

John Glaefke also grew up in the neighbodhood. "71st and Hough was my old stomping ground," he says. "At seventeen I got into trouble, but a Judge Merrick and Dr. Bruere came to my rescue. I had a badly disfigured face and the judge helped me to get plastic surgery. It was my face that had started me on the wrong course. I felt, *People don't care for me; why should I give a damn about them?* The judge could sense how I felt, and he saw to it that I got the surgery. And I got spiritual help at Calvary Church.

"They put me in charge of the coffee at the coffee hour. One day Dr. Bruere said, 'Since you get here so early, we might as well give you a key.' I wondered how people who knew my prison background could place such confidence in me.

"Then the newspapers got wind of my operation. The next thing I knew I was on my way to New York to appear on 'We the People.' And when I married Angie, a Cuban girl I had met in Miami, they flew me to New York again, and as a wedding present the judge canceled half of my remaining probation."

Today John Glaefke works for a pharmaceutical concern manufacturing vitamins and drugs. He works with Evangelist Gil Sheridan in a ministry to crippled people. And he is an elder at Calvary Church.

George Wagner, like many Negroes, grew up in a very religious home. But when he went into the armed forces he dismissed the Church from his life. It was in a hospital in Japan that George found the reality of God. A seventeen-year-old soldier was flown in from Korea who couldn't walk and wouldn't even try. One day the two soldiers got to talking about home.

"Have you written your mother?" George asked.

"No, I can't even pick up a pencil," Charlie retorted.

"A Red Cross lady will help you. By the way, your mother
is a Christian, isn't she?"

"Yeah."

"Then she's praying for you to walk."

"My mother doesn't even know I can't walk."

"Well, if she knew you couldn't walk, she'd pray, wouldn't
she?"

"Yes."

"Well, then, why don't you walk?"

At that, Charlie got up and walked like a child taking his
first steps. And ever since then prayer has been a big part of
George Wagner's life. When he came back from the war he
lived near Calvary Church. He joined it in 1956. Today he is
a real-estate broker and a church elder.

Some come in order to work. Bill and Christina Banks left
a middle-class Negro church which, in reacting against the
emotionalism of some Negro congregations, had swung to the
opposite extreme of cold intellectualism. What they were
looking for was a church that was practical. "Here at Calvary," Bill says, "you find warmth, practicality, and intellect—
homogenized. This is where we want to work" And work
they do: Bill as a deacon, Christina as a counselor. During the
week Bill works for the Cleveland Transit System and Christina teaches a child development class in the public schools.

Mary Force came three years ago to be Dr. Bruere's secretary, leaving a church ten minutes from her home where she
was paid better and where she was "bored to death."

"Calvary Church has made me grow," she affirms. "In a
prayer group I came to know the power of God, and Dr.
Bruere has made me face all the weaknesses which I have
rationalized for so many years."

Mary is deeply involved in the Saturday-Sunday program,
in addition to her other work. "You'd think I would be ex-
hausted working seven days a week. But whenever I reach
my limit I ask God for strength, and I'm no longer tired."

Some come because Calvary Church is integrated. "We've never talked integration as such," Nancy Bruere explains. "We've just been Christians together." Her husband says, "Having all kinds of people on an equality basis is a very enriching experience." Roger Shoup adds, "You think of people here more in terms of function. What do they do and where can they fit into the ministry? I'm uncomfortable talking about race."

Nevertheless it is the fact that people of all races are accepted at Calvary that draws many to its membership. "Racial crises have revealed the Church's true nature," Dr. Bruere feels. "But we need to avoid being self-conscious about race. Let's learn to say, 'I am a Christian first, an American second, a Negro or white man third.'"

Mr. and Mrs. Robert Kimmel came to Calvary because of such sentiments. "I've made friends here I couldn't have made elsewhere," Bob reports. "In our former church I used to wonder what we'd do if Negroes wanted to join. Now I wonder why I wondered. All of us are accepted here on the basis of our personal worth.

"The Gospel is preached here with greater integrity," he goes on. "In the atmosphere of Christian love bars go down more readily than anywhere else. God has something to do with the dissolution of those bars, and we can experience it best in an integrated situation."

He explains that on Worldwide Communion Sunday members with fifteen or more national backgrounds extend the invitation to share the bread and wine from the pulpit, each in his mother tongue. "We have worldwide communion right here at Calvary," Bob concludes. A lawyer who heads the legal department of Cleveland Cliffs Iron Company, Bob Kimmel is also a trustee, an elder, and chairman of Calvary's Christian Education Committee.

As this story was written the newest members to join Calvary were Leonard and Sally Lybarger. The Lybargers are a young couple who, "as racial problems arose, looked to the Church to tell us what to do. But the Church seemed slow to speak. When it did, members of our former congregation objected. That's why we came to Calvary. They'd gotten past the stage of talking and were acting. We live in Ludlow, the first area of the suburb of Shaker Heights to be integrated. We felt it would be wrong to live where we do and not attend an integrated church."

It was a strange sight to those who came to Calvary Church on December 13, 1964, and found it picketed by placard-carrying marchers from the United Freedom Movement asserting that its minister was obstructing civil rights. Probably no one—white or black—knows the Hough area better than John Bruere or has stuck his neck out more often for community improvement.

Though he shares the goals of such militant civil rights groups as CORE, Dr. Bruere sometimes disagrees with their means of achieving those goals. Late in 1964 he disagreed with a boycott of the public schools, sit-ins at the Superintendent of Schools' office, and deliberate slowdowns of the construction of new school buildings, in the process of which a young Presbyterian minister got himself killed by lying down behind the wheels of a bulldozer. "We have seen nothing gained by this type of protest," Bruere insists. "Such methods lead to madness and chaos. One blocks whatever doesn't meet with his approval, but this approval isn't *needed* for people to perform their lawful work in a free society.

"We thought it a great mistake to call a boycott of the schools. We are everlastingly trying to get the kids to go to school and then these leaders tell them to stay home. Or are they leaders?" he asks. "A leader is a person with followers who leads in the right direction."

Privately, Dr. Bruere says that he is misunderstood by extremists on both sides. The conservatives ask what he is doing down at city hall arguing for better housing when he ought to be preaching to people. And the militant humanists think he is a theological fossil who can't keep up with the times.

What should be the Church's role in social action? John Bruere answers the question this way: "The Church has had nineteen centuries of experience and knows that the roots of material poverty are intellectual and spiritual poverty in rich and poor alike. Only in the Church is the answer to be found through the disciplines of prayer, worship, and fellowship. . . . Conflict can be worked out only in an atmosphere where intimidation and vindictiveness are absent. The role of the Church is to provide that atmosphere.

"Sooner or later our people have got to have jobs and decent housing. The Church's function is to find out who can provide these things—whether it's the government, or industry, or certain individuals—and motivate them with Christian incentive. A Christian experience is what people have to have if the problems are ever going to be licked.

"The Church is responsible for more than its members. It is responsible for all those people who have no church. And the Church speaks with authority when it tells the community it is responsible for the living conditions of its citizens. Just *how* conditions ought to be changed may be a matter of disagreement. Within our own church there are very different points of view, but we worship together and we find it absolutely impossible to feel hatred in our hearts. We know that God has the answer, and when enough people begin to listen to Him the answer will become apparent.

"So far as I can see, little has been accomplished in Cleveland by resorting to lawlessness; much has been destroyed. A young man's life was lost. Property has been damaged. Respect for law and order has been diminished. There is more hatred among us than there was a few months back."

There are many in Cleveland who agree with this position—Miss Evelyn Barbour, for one. Miss Barbour, who is trained in social work, came to Cleveland twelve years ago as a branch executive of the YWCA. Concerned about the racial situation, she joined a middle-class Negro church, only to be disillusioned. "It was an eye-opener for me," she recalls, "to discover how much discrimination there is against their own people in some Negro groups. I wanted to work in Hough. But I like to work more creatively than to carry placards and protest. I am interested in reconciliation, in person to person confrontation." So she came last September to Calvary Church. Now she works with girls in the Saturday program.

Dr. Donald Hadley, a school psychologist, echoes these feelings. "I was distressed with the problems of the inner city," he says, "and disgusted with the solutions of the city administration. It seemed to me that only at Calvary and churches like it were people getting at the heart of things—dealing person to person, especially with the children." Dr. Hadley contributes to the program through tutoring and counseling. "If Jesus were picking a church," he says with a twinkle in his eye, "I think He'd be comfortable here. I know I am. I've worked through my prejudices and I think I could look Christ in the eye now and tell Him I understand what He was talking about."

The cross atop Calvary Church stands both as a symbol of hope to all who see it and as a symbol of sacrifice for its ministers and members. Strange as it may seem, the area in which this aggressive, outspoken church has labored all these years is still the most blighted area in Cleveland.

Not only has the Hough area deteriorated. It has been virtually abandoned. Time after time redevelopment programs have ground to a halt amid political bickering. Houses have been bought and torn down to make way for new apartments. But the new buildings have not come, and today there are four thousand vacant houses and hundreds of vacant lots scattered throughout Hough.

Last July violence erupted at a bar just five blocks from Calvary Church, and for four days riots swept through Hough,

until National Guardsmen slowly restored order. Hundreds
of fires were set. White-owned stores were looted. Today,
wherever you go in Hough, burned-out buildings and board-
ed-up stores still remind its residents of those days of destruction, while a feeling of despair and entrapment shrouds the
area.

Mrs. Jewel Cummings remembers seeing the National
Guardsmen, as she came home from work, and being puzzled
by their presence; she remembers turning on her television set
to pictures of the rioting and wondering, *Where is it this
time?* But not until her roomer, Smitty, ran in and she asked,
"Where is it?" did reality dawn on her. Smitty shouted, "Are
you crazy? It's here!"

Kathy Force, another staff worker, recalls, "We were met
at the church by National Guardsmen patrolling the area. I
was frightened, I guess. But what ran through my mind were
the children with whom we had worked, and how petrified
they must be."

To Donna Sneed, who was on the staff, the riots seemed to
destroy everything the church was working for. "I felt sorry
for the children," she recalls. "They saw grown-ups looting
stores and asked, *Why shouldn't I?* But that's when we were
needed most, because the kids were confused."

Each morning John Bruere and Roger Shoup toured the
area near the vacant lot to see if it was safe to proceed that day,
and the program went ahead without interference.

Calvary Church carries a cross. It can point to changed lives
here and there in Hough, but it cannot point to any sweeping
transformation of the neighborhood.

Roger responds to this philosophically. "We can't afford
the luxury of looking for rewards," he says. "If we weren't
here, it would be a lot worse."

John adds, "When we get so discouraged we can't go any
farther down, either Roger or I will say to the other, 'Well,
we're where we're needed, aren't we?'"

Meanwhile at Calvary Presbyterian Church the young people pray every week for their city, in a prayer written long ago by John and Nancy Bruere:

"Heavenly Father, we pray that this may be a city that has foundations whose builder and maker is God. May we have just laws, citizens with love and righteousness in their hearts, neighborhoods of friends of every race and creed, young people preparing for a better future.

"I pray for the power of the Presence of God in this city and in every city in our land. I pray that I may do nothing to fan the flames of fear, suspicion, or hatred, but that my every thought, word, and deed may increase a spirit of Christian love and understanding; through Jesus Christ our Lord. Amen."

Questions for study and application:
1. What are Calvary Church's strengths?
2. What untapped resources do you sense in their situation?
3. To what specific action does the story challenge you?

9

Renaissance in Pittsburgh

"Get changed, get together, get going."

Pittsburgh, Pennsylvania, is the city where two rivers meet. There the Allegheny and the Monongahela merge and become one—the Ohio. It is also the city in which businessmen are finding that two other streams—personal faith and daily work —can meet and become one.

A dozen years ago the Pittsburgh Experiment came into being out of two concurrent sources: a sense of men's need and a vision of the city's potential greatness. A young steelworker, Dave Griffith, felt these tensions acutely during the long, hot summer of 1952 when a costly strike idled thousands of workers. Talking it over with his pastor, Dr. Sam Shoemaker, then rector of Pittsburgh's Calvary Episcopal Church, he concluded that Christian faith must somehow be relevant to the day-to-day situation. When work resumed he started a prayer group at the Homestead Plant of the United States Steel Corporation where he worked.

At the same time, Sam Shoemaker met another group. These men were up-and-coming young businessmen—the "golf club crowd," he called them—and they began a weekly luncheon meeting in which they discussed how to become a Christian. In Sam's mind was the vision of a "city under God": a spiritual renaissance to match the incredible physical renaissance that was going on all around.

147

Pittsburgh, the dirtiest major city in America, had long been plagued by smoke and floods, paradoxical by-products of its two greatest physical assets, its vast coal deposits and its magnificent rivers. A smoke control program and a flood control network were beginning to bring these culprits to book. In the triangle at the confluence of the rivers acres of slums were being replaced with a magnificent park and new skyscrapers, which since that time have entirely remade the central business district. Today Pittsburgh boasts of its Golden Triangle, while the men of the Pittsburgh Experiment point others to a second triangle—one that shines like gold to the hundreds helped by it.

This second triangle, which expresses three aspects of a new way of life, was articulated in December, 1961, when Dr. Sam Shoemaker was honored on his retirement from the ministry by a huge crowd of friends. For five years men had experimented with prayer for their personal needs, had formed small groups for discussion and prayer in steel mills, offices, and restaurants, and had sought to share their faith with others. Now, as Dr. Sam bade them an affectionate goodbye, he summed up what they had learned together, and closed with a ringing challenge. "Let me give you three nails to hang these thoughts on," he concluded in his rapid-fire, staccato style. "Get changed; get together; get going!"

How conscious was Sam Shoemaker of the implications of his words? His three admonitions can be seen as three aspects of a style of life that brings wholeness. *Get changed*: make a sincere commitment of your life to Jesus Christ. *Get together*: find fellowship and growth in Christian understanding. *Get going*: show forth God's love through concern for all mankind and for the problems which plague them. Here is life in its wholeness: individuals rightly related to God, rightly related to one another, and rightly related to the world.

Such wholeness can be depicted by a triangle, for each concern is linked naturally with the other two, while each lacks integrity by itself. Enter this life at any of its three points, and you will be led inevitably into the others. This is the experience and the witness of the first dozen years of the Pittsburgh Experiment.

Dr. Sam's "parting shot" in 1961 captured the imagination of some of the men in the Experiment. Don Rehberg and Kirwan Flannery went away from the meeting stung by the challenge to "get going." It was as if they had never heard it before. Their own commitment to Christ was secure, and they were being "fed" regularly in group prayer and study. But what did it mean to *get going?*

The need they felt immediately involved several of their friends who were unemployed. Inviting these men to lunch one day, they initiated what is now known as Employment Anonymous, a Tuesday noon meeting at the downtown YMCA where men out of work can find the resources of faith to help them seek employment with a new attitude. In the past five years more than four hundred men have found work through participation in this program while finding spiritual renewal as well. The Tuesday luncheon meeting has become the best-known of a dozen small groups functioning within the Pittsburgh Experiment, popular probably because it focuses on a problem specifically tied to one's sense of well-being. A man and his job can hardly be separated, for without a job a man is as vulnerable as a peeled banana.

Dave Craig, a lawyer who found Christ in Sam Shoemaker's golf club crowd years ago, is now Director of Public Safety for the city, responsible for police and fire protection. He draws this parallel:

"The lucky people in terms of personal regeneration are those who hit bottom and find out they are human, fallible, and dependent on God. For the person who is open to God's grace, hitting bottom can be a real advantage. Pittsburgh as a community went that way. After the war we opened our eyes and saw that it was a squalid, smoky mess. This gave us a head start over other cities on urban renewal. We hit bottom as a city, and it gave us the impetus to get together and do something—to start almost anywhere to improve things."

As civic leaders in Pittsburgh have sought to improve things in almost every area—physical redevelopment, race relations, education, the arts—so the men of the Pittsburgh Experiment have been drawn into many areas of need: unemployment, poverty, racial discrimination, crime, delinquency, spiritual impoverishment.

As Dave Craig puts it, "There's some kind of inexorable law that spiritual development comes only on a person-to-person basis. It has to operate through individuals as the molecules of the structure, and this necessitates creating an atmosphere of trust such as small groups provide. From personal experience I know that the Pittsburgh Experiment works."

The heart of the Pittsburgh Experiment is a practical, gut-level experience in prayer. Sam Shoemaker believed that the way to find out whether things work, in the spiritual realm as in any other, is to try them.

Perhaps no one exemplifies the dynamic of the Pittsburgh Experiment better than its executive director, Donald T. James.

During World War II Don enlisted in the Marines, "wanting to die and figuring that was the best way to do it, since I hadn't much use for life." But though sixty percent of Don's bomber squadron died in the Pacific, Don survived. He came back to his native Pittsburgh, became an insurance salesman, and worked his way up to a position of responsibility in recruitment and training. His death wish gave way to a search for life. With his wife, Joan, he began to visit churches, and in due course he found his way into Calvary Episcopal Church. Here he met Sam Shoemaker, who guided him into one of the first groups being formed under the Pittsburgh Experiment.

Don's first reaction was one of extreme skepticism. Introducing himself, he described a log-jam in a relationship with a business associate which was blocking the flow of normal life.

"Have you prayed about it?" one man asked him.

"Are you out of your mind?" Don snapped back.

"Not at all. Why not pray about it whenever you think of it for the next thirty days? We'll pray with you and see what happens."

Don acquiesced to the plan, but it wasn't until two days later, after a phone call or two of assurance that men were thinking about him—men who had been strangers until a week before, that he realized, "Gee, they really mean it." Long before the thirtieth day, Don had found a new relationship with his supervisor and had begun to open other areas of his life to God. Now, thirteen years later, he speaks with conviction when he says, "No matter what the problem, we feel that if a person will pray every day, seeking the will of Almighty God, he can expect to find help toward its solution." Hence, the "thirty-day experiment."

For Don James the experiment led him, after thirteen years in the business world, to an Episcopal seminary and the call, upon his graduation in 1960, to head up the Experiment. To this work he has brought a strong concern for cooperation with churches and community organizations. As a diocesan missioner, he preaches nearly every Sunday in some Episcopal church. During the rest of the week he works to bring together those who are concerned about spiritual renewal.

Don believes that when men meet to talk and pray, they "stay alive" by finding other men who will begin to share their experiment in faith. One such group meets each week around a table in a room in the Jones and Laughlin Steel Company offices in the beautiful new Gateway Center. This group is sparked by Don Rehberg, the company comptroller. Two of its recent "products" are Jerry Klein and Wayne Pascuzzi. Jerry is in sales and service with J&L. Wayne is a percussionist with the Pittsburgh Symphony.

"I was with an investment firm that went bankrupt," Jerry Klein explains. "I lost my own money and some that didn't belong to me, and was deeply in debt. I made a list of forty-one people I thought could help me get a job, but after going through the entire list I still wasn't employed. I couldn't figure out why. Some time later a friend suggested I see Don James.

"Don took me to Employment Anonymous, and he also got me back into my church. I'm a Roman Catholic, but I hadn't been a practicing one for five years. Even before that it didn't mean much to me. It was—well, like being out at Forbes Field when the Pirates are away.

"When I began to turn my problems over to the good Lord, I learned to cope with them. I once thought my basic problem was financial. That wasn't so. Everybody has financial problems. Then I thought it was the people who didn't understand me. But that didn't add up. When I finally realized my problem was *me*, I was able to turn it over to the Lord.

"I joined this group after I came to work at J&L. The fellows are interested in you, not as they would like to see you, but as you actually are.

"I stop by St. Mary's Church every morning to thank God for my blessings. When I get dressed I remember that you can always find some reason to be thankful. When a siren screams, or I see a handicapped person, I pray for the one who's in trouble, and thank God for all He's given me."

Wayne Pascuzzi admits that he came to the group for selfish, personal reasons. "I had an alcohol problem, a job problem, a resentment problem—even a skin problem, which is bad in the music business. My self-confidence was gone. I was playing with the symphony but at times my hands shook so badly I didn't think I could get through the concert.

"The version of Christianity I grew up with, where preachers yelled and threatened you with hell, was no help to me. I never got anywhere so long as I thought God sent punishment. I've found out God isn't like that.

"In Alcoholics Anonymous I licked my drinking problem, but even though I was sober I couldn't catch the spiritual angle until I came to this group. Here, all of a sudden, I've got my confidence back. I played recently with the Bolshoi Ballet. There were forty-five musicians from New York, and they hired sixteen of us from Pittsburgh. The music went well. I had no more trouble reading the score than reading 'one calorie per serving' on this Tab bottle! And that hasn't happened in a long time. One month ago I couldn't have cared less if I never saw another drum or piece of music. Now I'm playing well again, and even teaching in a new way."

Wayne sat thoughtfully resting his head in his hands and leaning over the table. "I've gotten to think a lot of this group," he went on. "I drive fifteen miles back and forth to come here—it takes a big chunk out of the middle of my day. But something has happened to me that I'm just beginning to understand. I committed my life to Christ here two years ago. Then I went out of town, got away from this association, and slipped backward. I have to be around where the rays from these guys hit me, I guess. But I'm learning to get things out of the Bible. I've been reading the book of Romans in the Phillips translation and understanding it."

There was another pause. At Wayne's left sat his brother, who is newer to the Christian "experiment." Suddenly Wayne spoke up again. "It just occurred to me that things started happening in a hurry when I tried to help someone else. I made very little progress until I tried to help my brother here."

When Sam Shoemaker said, "Get together," he meant primarily Christians meeting face to face in small groups to work out the implications of their faith. "This is almost *the* characteristic way in which the Holy Spirit is breaking through in our time," he said in his farewell address.

Already a dozen groups of men were meeting in and around Pittsburgh—in offices, restaurants, and factories—studying the Bible together, reporting their successes and failures, and praying for each other. In the years since, some of these groups have outlived their usefulness and died. In their place have come others, like the group which meets on Thursday noon in Monroeville. George Kemp, a park and recreation consultant, tells how and why he began the group.

"Don James came to talk to a dinner group at our church— First Methodist Church in McKeesport. I was struck by the honesty of his personal witness and arranged to have lunch with him. He took me to the Employment Anonymous meeting in downtown Pittsburgh where men were learning to cope with the same human problems I had. They could smile and not be eaten up by fears and resentments.

"Over a period of three months I gradually committed my life to Christ and decided to try a thirty-day prayer experiment. The first thing God did was to guide me into a job change. Six years before I had changed jobs and, although we had no children at the time and my wife was working, I got so stirred up I landed in the hospital. Now, although I was leaving a salaried job and going out on my own, I made the change without hesitation. The difference lay in my fellowship with other Christians.

"When I moved my office to Monroeville and found the drive to Pittsburgh—a twenty-five mile round trip—too much of a hardship, I looked up several other men in my area and we decided to start our own group. We've been meeting since March."

One of the members of the Monroeville group is John Hormel, a meat-cutter who is Secretary-Treasurer of his local in the Amalgamated Food Employees Union. John comes from "the other side of the table" from the Hormels of meat-packing fame, as he phrases it. He administers his union's affairs, negotiates contracts, and follows up on complaints with retail stores in western Pennsylvania. An elder in Memorial Park Presbyterian Church, John has learned that "getting together" may involve one in a series of widening circles like those created by a stone dropped in a tranquil pool. In addition to the once-a-week meeting in Monroeville, he occasionally goes to laymen's conferences, like the ones held each fall by the Pittsburgh Experiment, to which the men can bring their wives. Last spring something unusual happened to him at such a conference. Here's how he tells the story:

"On Sunday afternoon, as I was going to my small group, I learned that a man with whom I had ridden to the conference—I'll call him Al—resented me very much and had said so in his group meeting. I was disturbed because we had greeted each other cordially and nothing at all had been said about it earlier.

"It seems that eight years before, Al had managed a store somewhere in my area where conditions of a contract hadn't been fully met. I had represented the union in pressing for changes. Though I had never dealt directly with Al, some of his decisions had been reversed by his superior, and he had been harboring a deep resentment against me all these years.

"I told my group about the situation and once our meeting was over I went looking for Al. It was seven hours later—eleven that night—before I found him. We sat down to have a cup of coffee and I started to say, 'I hear you have a resentment against me,' when he interrupted. 'You've been looking for me, John, and I've been looking for you. When I told my group the story it began to burn in me like fire and I had to find you and ask your forgiveness.'

"We talked until three in the morning while Al told me about his conversion to Christ and his involvement in a small group in North Hills. He told of how my name had been mentioned in the group one day and he had wondered if this person they were talking about, this John Hormel, who had love and concern for other people, could be the union official he had resented. He apparently didn't feel that a labor union official could be a Christian. But as we talked we were united in the love of Christ. Nothing I've ever experienced has touched me so deeply as this reconciliation between a store manager and a labor representative."

There are still wider circles "getting together" in Pittsburgh —circles of ecumenical friendship and cooperation between the Pittsburgh Experiment and a dozen other agencies, each formed to meet some of the needs of the city.

Before you're with these men very long you'll hear about Dom Orsini and what he's doing for delinquent teen-agers through Grubstake; Jim Leckie and Youth Guidance; Tom O'Brien and his St. Joseph's House of Hospitality; John Garvin at Bethany House in the Northview Heights housing development; Reid Carpenter and John Patak and their Young Life ministry to high schoolers; and Don Gross and Everett Campbell of the Pastoral Institute, where three counsellors offer psychological help to these agencies and to the churches of Pittsburgh. Nor can you be with Dom Orsini, or Tom O'Brien, or John Garvin, on the other hand, without hearing of the Pittsburgh Experiment, and especially Employment Anonymous, for everyone, it seems, at one time or another has brought an unemployed man to the Tuesday meetings at the downtown YMCA.

Meet one of these men and before long you meet them all, and sense the camaraderie which exists between these committed Christians, each of whom is serving a particular need and asking the other, "How can I help you?"

This is as it should be, and as Don James likes it to be. "We need more interrelatedness," he affirms. "It doesn't make sense to duplicate efforts any more than for members of the same company to compete with each other."

The Rev. Dom Orsini is pastor of St. Luke's Episcopal Church in suburban Bloomfield, Pennsylvania. This is Dom's first charge and in it an unusual ministry has unfolded.

"Three years ago," he says, "Norm Cowie, a lawyer whom I had met casually through the Experiment, called me. He had a problem. A young man whom he was defending needed a home while awaiting trial. Though the boy was accused of murdering his father, the judge had high hopes for him and didn't want to put him in jail.

"What promised to be thirty days stretched into nearly a year before Jimmy's case was heard. By that time we had come to love him as our own son. When the trial was finally held and Jimmy was placed on six years' probation, the judge released him to our custody, feeling that we had already done more for him than was possible in any institution. This past June Jimmy became our legally adopted son.

"Meanwhile, as I followed his case through the court, I felt the coldness of the courthouse and the lack of concern on the part of the Church for these young fellows who had never before faced trial. I realized as I saw youngsters brought in handcuffed that they had 'reached bottom' early in life, and that they might respond readily to help.

"After Jimmy's case was over, I got to know the judges and the staff, and explained my concern to them. I talked to probation officers and to people in the behavior clinic. I talked to Norm Cowie constantly and to Don James. Then Judge Henry Ellenbogen sanctioned a courthouse ministry and Grubstake was born—an organized effort to stake boys to a better chance in life in the hope that they will pay it back to society. As judges gained confidence in me, one by one they began to turn over young men to my jurisdiction. We now have twelve fellows.

"From nebulous beginnings we have hammered out the Grubstake program bit by bit in hour after hour of conversation. I had no knowledge of what to do, though I grew up in the slums of Albany, New York. I stole and vandalized as a boy, but never got caught, so I knew nothing of court procedures. But I knew these kids, their type of life, and the areas of depravity and poverty. To hammer out a program for rehabilitation, however, was strange to me. Even the ministry was strange. I had been a priest only three years.

"I came into the ministry by the back door. As a drug salesman in Akron, Ohio, I had married, and my wife—a wishy-washy Congregationalist—and I—a Catholic turned atheist—felt we should join a church, one that would help me in my business. The doctors and druggists I dealt with went mostly to St. Paul's Episcopal Church, the wealthiest church in town, so we joined it. But what happened? We drew a really great Christian for a pastor and bit by bit, through private discussions, my own intense admiration for the man and his sermons which beat at me constantly, God won me! I gave up everything I had and entered the ministry. So God took even my lousy motives and redeemed them.

"In Grubstake we hope eventually to build a house for twenty-four young men, and to give ourselves enough time— two or three years at least—to influence them in depth, to deal with their character disorders, their educational and vocational deficiencies, and to reorient them socially and spiritually.

"One call from Norm Cowie got me into all this. He—and Jimmy—have turned my ministry upside down. And one remarkable thing is what it has done to our congregation. St. Luke's is made up of many old people who never get out of Bloomfield and who, for all I know, feel that men and boys in trouble ought to be bullwhipped and locked up for life. But they took to Jimmy and because of him they've permitted me the time and given me money for a courthouse ministry, without a dissenting voice."

Chet Samson, a teacher in a public junior high school, has caught a vision of what it can be to "teach with Christ." "It's a funny thing," he says, "how the Lord guides some people gently while He clobbers others with a heavy hand. He whomped me a good one!

"I was a card-carrying Christian who hadn't been going to church except on occasions like Mother's Day. But one Sunday I was sitting in St. David's Episcopal Church and Jim Baker, a licensed lay reader, spoke. Instead of preaching, he told his experience and I thought, *He's talking about me.* Then he announced a Faith at Work conference that was going to be held in the church. I'd seen the posters and thought, *Big deal! A hymn-sing or something.* But Jim's talk intrigued me.

"Do you know how it is when you catch the mumps? Well, at the conference I 'caught' Christianity. That was in the spring of 1965. I grew slowly in a small group—through the patience of that group, I should say, because I'm one of those guys with a mouth big enough to keep right on talking when my foot's in it. But they put up with me, through weeks of questioning and doubting, while I began to see that my life— which I had always thought of as a series of accidents—was actually following a plan. Finally it dawned on me that when I asked prayerfully that problems be resolved, and stayed out of the way, things did work out.

"Then came the Oglebay Conference in November. At the time I was immersed in the toughest teaching situation I had ever faced, with some pretty rough kids. Soaking wet I weigh under 140 pounds, but I could have put together a forward line from my classes averaging 200 pounds! Add to that the facts that we had 879 students crowded into a building meant for 450, and that my classes averaged thirty-seven, and you can see why 'Blackboard Jungle' wasn't my favorite movie.

"At the closing meeting at Oglebay, a teacher from West-minster College, Bob Galbreath, wondered aloud if there weren't some way teachers could get together to encourage each other in implementing their faith in the classroom. We know we can't teach Christian faith directly, but we also know that we teach more by example than by word. Bob's concern, anyway, was not to teach *about* Christ, nor even *for* Christ, but *with* Christ. Some of us met afterwards and formed 'Teaching with Christ' to try to help us get going.

"Well, I got through the school year, and I can see where

Christ helped me. My only recourse before, when I got in trouble with a class, was to call the principal. But now, with the new confidence that Christ's presence has given me, the barriers between me and my students are breaking down. I find I can talk to them and teach them, and the trouble vanishes."

Bob and Jane Carter are a couple who, in obeying Christ's call, have been led down a path few white Christians have been willing to follow. Bob is an engineer with the Aluminum Company of America. Since 1957 the Carters have been in small group discussions, but not until 1963 did they hear the call to costly involvement.

"John Garvin had just begun the Bethany ministry in Northview Heights, a new integrated housing development," Bob recalls. "He called on men in the Pittsburgh Experiment, with their wives, to start study and prayer groups in the project. Jane and I told John we were already 'taken' because we had agreed to help our church custodian, a Negro named Charles Graham, begin a group with his neighbors just outside the project.

"The following summer our daughter Marjorie wanted to attend the New Wilmington Missionary Conference at Westminster College. We decided the whole family should go, and it was there that Marjorie and Marian, our younger daughter, had their first social contacts with Negro youngsters. After the conference, Margie visited in their homes, and we opened our home to her Negro friends, a practice that was frowned on in racially segregated Mt. Lebanon.

"The next year Margie began to attend SCORE meetings in the East End. Our whole family got involved in civil rights, participating in a program in which we visited Negroes in their homes and got to know them personally. Meanwhile, in our Bible study group, we learned that our intellectual approach to faith was not the most meaningful one for our new friends, who responded to life on a more intuitive level.

We were glad when Harold Fowler, a Negro who had committed his life to Christ at Bethany House, joined us. The Holy Spirit gave him the kind of perception the group needed.

"By the fall of 1965 most of our close friends were Negroes, and we were uncomfortable in Mt. Lebanon. We had tried to arouse social concern in our church, but without results. There was a social action committee, but little action.

"There seemed to be nothing to hold us in Mt. Lebanon, and we were driving ten miles every time we went to meet our friends near Northview Heights. So in January we moved up there to a house a hundred yards from the project.

"In the meantime Margie began dating a Negro she met in the SCORE meetings. By then we had become well aware of the indignities Negroes have to live with in our society. Margie has come to know them especially, as people have spat at her on the streets. Yet when these two young people decided to marry, we felt we had no grounds on which to say, 'This can't happen in *our* family.'

"We've gained from the move. Marian is in an integrated school where the 'book learning' is not the best, but where she gets good lessons in human relations. The Negro community has much to teach us—and Christ has much to teach us together. We went 'where the action is' and we heard God say, 'You are all one.' But this really hasn't been our doing. Once we opened our lives to God, we felt Him pushing us in this direction."

In and around Pittsburgh men are discovering this style of life, so aptly summarized by Sam Shoemaker—"Get changed; get together; get going"—and are passing it on to others. For some this leads to quiet witness on the job and to one's neighbors. For others it means volunteering to go for a few days with a traveling lay team to some nearby community or church to share their faith. For still others it means hand-to-hand grappling with the sin and suffering of the city.

How much else is happening? Perhaps we will never know,

and do not need to know. It is enough to know whether it is happening to us.

Questions for study and application:
1. How important is a vision for the future to any work done for God?
2. How wide and how deep should your own vision be for whatever ministry God has called you to?
3. At what point does the work of the Pittsburgh Experiment contribute most to your vision?

NUCLEAR WAR, NUCLEAR PEACE

NUCLEAR WAR, NUCLEAR PEACE

Leon Wieseltier

A New Republic Book

Holt, Rinehart and Winston/New York

This book is a slightly expanded version of an article that appeared in *The New Republic* magazine. Published by arrangement with *The New Republic*, 1220 19th Street, N.W., Washington, D.C. 20036.

Composed in Palatino by Chronicle Type & Design, Washington, D.C. 20036

Published by Holt, Rinehart and Winston, 383 Madison Avenue, New York, New York 10017.

Published simultaneously in Canada by Holt, Rinehart and Winston of Canada, Limited.

Grateful acknowledgment is made to the following for permission to reprint previously published material:

Random House, Inc.: For excerpts from *The Fate of the Earth* by Jonathan Schell (Alfred A. Knopf). Copyright ©1982 Jonathan Schell. For excerpts from *Beyond the Cold War* by E. P. Thompson (Pantheon). Copyright © 1982 E. P. Thompson.

International Security: For excerpts from "Nuclear Strategy: A Case for a Theory of Victory" by Colin S. Gray (Summer 1979). Copyright © 1979 by the President and Fellows of Harvard College.

Commentary: For excerpts from "How to Think About Nuclear War" by Edward N. Luttwak (August 1982). Copyright © 1982 by the American Jewish Committee.

Czeslaw Milosz: For lines from "A Song on the End of the World" in *Selected Poems* (New York, 1973).

Library of Congress Cataloging in Publication Data
Wieseltier, Leon.
Nuclear war, nuclear peace.
"A New Republic book."
Bibliography: p.
Includes index. 1. Atomic warfare. 2. Deterrence (Strategy). 3. Atomic weapons and disarmament. 4. United States—Military policy.
I. Title
U263.W53 1983 355'.0217 83-6125

ISBN Hardbound 0-03-064082-2
ISBN Paperback 0-03-064029-6
First Edition

Printed in the United States of America
10 9 8 7 6 5 4 3 2 1

for my parents

There will be no other end of the world,
There will be no other end of the world.

PUBLISHER'S NOTE

This book is an expanded and slightly altered version of an essay that was published in *The New Republic* magazine in a special combined issue dated January 10 and 17, 1983. The essay, which stands as the longest to have appeared in the magazine's pages since its founding in 1914, was immediately acclaimed as a crucial and durable contribution to the nuclear debate. It is published here in book form as a tribute to that durability, and in an attempt to bring it to the attention of the widest possible audience.

CONTENTS

PREFACE

The reader of this essay will not mistake its author for a military strategist, or a political expert, or a student of science of any sort. He is only a citizen who writes.

I embarked upon this essay because I found myself in deep dissatisfaction with the present nuclear debate. Almost nowhere did I find my own view of the problem precisely put. What was worse, my view of the problem, which is the view of others as well, was shouted down from both sides, from all of the right and almost all of the left. Its coherence was challenged. It was clamorously accused of "third campism," of a failure to follow certain political and philosophical conceptions to their "logical conclusion," of a refusal to "let the other shoe drop." I could not oppose the Soviet Union, some said, and still support a diminishment of our nuclear arsenal. I could not oppose the nuclear regime under which we live, said others, and still support the competition with the Soviet Union. I was told to choose, and I wrote this essay to expose the crudity of the choice. There is no contradiction between anti-Communism rightly considered and arms control rightly considered; what follows is an attempt at such right considerations. It is conceived, also, as an exercise in intellectual inconvenience. If I fall into a "third camp," it is the camp of concerned but careful analysis, which is always a third camp. Complexity is not the enemy of conviction. My other shoe does not drop because it belongs on my foot.

The more general subject of this essay is the relationship of national security policy to foreign policy, of the military strategy of the United States to its moral and political ends. It is not about the deadly devices themselves. I cannot really follow the physicists and the engineers. I have discovered, however, that for the purpose of understanding the nuclear dilemma you do not have to follow them very far. A rudimentary grasp of what missiles are, and what they do, and how many exist, is enough. The decisions that must be made—what weapons we shall have, what we shall do with them—are not scientific decisions. They are political decisions. A knowledge of history is needed, not merely a knowledge of hardware. Still, I accept the criticism, offered to me most constructively by Geoffrey Kemp, that my discussion of nuclear policy is perhaps too innocent of how this part of the world works. If a weapon can be built, Kemp objects, it will be built; and if it will be built, ideas about its use will not be far behind. Technology, in other words, is not the effect of strategic thinking, but its cause. I would like to believe that this is not always the case,

that the safety of this country is not hostage to research and development, that the intellectuals and
the politicians have as much impact upon public policy as the scientists and the industrialists, that we are
the masters of what we make and not the slaves. All
this, as I say, I would like to believe. Writing persua-
sively against "the alchemists of our times," Lord
Zuckerman has proposed that research and development be seriously controlled. It must be possible to
impose reason upon reality. In a matter of such urgency, and there is no more urgent matter than the
management of the nuclear danger, the attempt must
anyway be made.

I do not write in behalf of a new idea, but in
behalf of an old one. My review of the present nuclear
debate concludes with a dithyramb to deterrence.
This is not new ground. It is embattled ground. Arguing for deterrence, as I hope sadly to show, is no
longer like arguing for motherhood. But if nuclear
weapons are a curse, deterrence is a blessing. Feelings about the one must not be confused with feelings
about the other. Despite the moral and theoretical
infirmities of the idea of deterrence, which the Catholic bishops have recently brought to the attention of
millions, it must be defended without apology. Not
the least of its blandishments is the instruction it provides about methods of disarmament.

The reader will deduce that I am against the MX
but for the Trident II, against an "across-the-board"
freeze but for the cancellation of many nuclear contracts, against unilateral disarmament but for the
United States to take a modest but momentous lead in
lowering the danger. Such specific proposals, however, are not my main concern. They are much in the
media, where experts dispute experts before an exas-
perated public. The broader intellectual and political

dimensions of the problem are not. (The media are not made for these dimensions.) For this reason I have confined this essay largely to first principles.

This little book incurred a lot of debts. It was written during my final months at the Society of Fellows at Harvard University. I am grateful to Burton Dreben and the members of the Society for enabling me to turn my attention away from medieval Jewish history, and for encouraging me to turn it back. My erratic education in strategic studies took place in the quarters of the Center for Science and International Affairs at Harvard, where a simpleton's questions were cordially suffered. At *The New Republic*, which published an earlier version of this essay, I was lucky to have my work fall into the hands of Martin Peretz, Hendrik Hertzberg, and Dorothy Wickenden. A blessing on them, and on their pencils.

Marc Granetz of Holt, Rinehart and Winston insisted that this be a book, and made it into one. His editorial attention is exemplary. I thank him, and New Republic Books.

I have had sundry sorts of help, when I asked for it and when I did not, from Terry Castle, Peter Galison, Nathan Glazer, Judith Miller, Steven Miller, Allan Nadler, Jan Nolan, Max Palevsky, Martin Peretz, Ronald Radosh, Peter Spiro, Kathleen Tynan, Stephen Walt, Michael Walzer, Thea Wieseltier, and Sandra Merriman.

Without the criticism and the company of Mahnaz Ispahani this could not have been done. She knows why—I think.

My parents were in Poland when the Nazis came, and of their families only they survived. It is not just for love, then, that this book belongs to them.

Its subject is the frustration of the only fate that would be worse then theirs. Now they must contemplate that, too. I have made of Milosz's lines a prayer for my parents, who are the noblest people I know.

Washington, D.C.
February 6, 1983.

NUCLEAR WAR, NUCLEAR PEACE

INTRODUCTION

> How immensely simplified the world is when it
> is examined for its worthiness for destruction.
>
> WALTER BENJAMIN

A great debate is taking place in the West, where it
can take place. The subject is the prevention of nuclear war. That nuclear war is damnation, everybody
agrees. The horrors held out by nuclear weapons
have been harrowingly described. Thermal pulse,
blast wave, radiation fallout; air bursts and ground
bursts; the fast deaths and the slow; the destruction of
culture and the destruction of nature—the popular
imagination is now filled with the infernal images.
But the debate must not stop with the descriptions. It

must start with them. They do not, these chronicles of
carnage that are placed before the public, concentrate
the mind wonderfully, like the prospect of only a
hanging; they do not, in many cases, concentrate the
mind at all. They only fill it with fear, when it was
already afraid. Fear has been our fate since 1945. We
do not need to be called to the feeling. It animates the
policymakers as well as the protesters. Who is *for*
nuclear war?

The fear of nuclear war—the most intelligent feeling of our time—has once again taken the form of a
mass movement, with men, women, and children demanding not to be incinerated. The demand is moral,
but it is also quite general. The same may be said of
many of the demands of the movement's intellectuals. They linger long over the consequences of a nuclear exchange, and then leap to visions of a better
world. They write beautifully about the fate of the
species and the fate of the earth. But nuclear war will
not be prevented by poetry or philosophy; it will be
prevented by policy. Whatever else the bomb is, it is a
practical problem. It demands solutions, not merely
sentiments; and it demands solutions that are not
sure to be simple. There comes a point in the discussion of this very grave subject when eloquence is
egregious, when it must be replaced by a cool and
careful consideration of the danger in all its details. If
there is anything as foolish as not thinking about nuclear weapons, it is not thinking about them enough.

There are those, of course, who think about nuclear weapons all the time, whose profession it is to
think about them. These are the defense intellectuals,
and the nuclear debate must not be left to them, either. The scientists who produce the weapons and
the strategists who plan for their use have no particular competence in the matter of preserving living

things in life and human beings in history. All that
they can tell us is what the weapons are. They have
no special moral or political authority for having
made them. Indeed, they are too much with them,
too much at ease in the weapons' world. And they are
utterly in thrall to the imperatives of technology; they
invent first and ask questions later. What stands in
their way, however, is the political system in which
they live. They must seek approval in the society for
their designs and their devices. Physics is not policy;
nor is engineering; nor is strategy. In a democracy
even the matter of national security must come before
the public. Sooner or later research and development
must be justified. The stirring of popular opinion
against the arms race really represents democracy's
challenge to technocracy. The position of the United
States on nuclear weapons will be made in the town
hall and the think tank. There are those who believe
that this is a mixed blessing, that defense is too difficult a matter for democracies. It is a difficult matter;
and it is made no easier by the trouble that democracies have believing in the existence of their enemies.
Yet the alternative is an unmixed curse, a society in
which nobody can oppose the military and its mystifi-
cations because nobody can oppose anything. It may
irk the defense establishment that its conclusions are
not final, that it must carry its case before an untu-
tored citizenry; but it is precisely the participation of
all the people in all deliberations of public concern—
in sum, an open society—that the defense establishment was established to defend.

The nuclear debate, then, has been too frequently
diverted by the wrong kinds of discourse. It has consisted largely in fantasies that will profit us nothing

and facts that we cannot quite understand. The citizens of this nation, and of the nations of NATO, are trapped between visionaries and experts. They are given sermons or systems analysis.

Nor is that all. The nuclear debate has been infected by ideology. It had to happen; the ideologization of intellectual life in the United States is virtually complete. Almost the only views that are heard are world views. Political positions come in packages. Everything is said to be connected to everything else; or, as the theorists of the left used to put it, critical thinking is dominated on all sides by a concept of totality. According to *The Nation*, it follows from your opposition to the war in Vietnam that you oppose the free market, or the patriarchal family, or Camp David. According to *Commentary*, it follows from your opposition to the Soviet Union that you oppose environmentalism, or Jacobo Timerman, or homosexuality. Of course these things do not follow. (A man may hate Communism in the arms of another man.) To a certain extent the New Left was undone precisely by its extravagant ideological entailments; most Americans were unwilling to go the doctrinal distance. The New Right (the neoconservatives included) will be similarly undone. Many intellectuals, and even more politicians, will resist the regimentation.

Meanwhile the nuclear question is slapped into the service of the left and the right. The argument against an arms race has been placed under the sign of the sixties. The radical raptures of fifteen years ago, many of which were refuted by Soviet foreign policy and rejected by American public opinion, are said to have found an heir. Antinuclear activists speak as if the long dark night of the left is finally over. There is a peace movement again. And, like its predecessor, it is in the throes of a great ideological expansion. Nuclear weapons, it turns out, are not the real problem; they are only its most parlous expression. The real problem is America's ambitions. These ambitions are deemed to be the present danger to this country and to the world. Thus, many things come with the antinuclear position—neutralism, pacifism, and isolationism, to name a few. It is not only arms that must be controlled; so must American power.

The argument for an uncontrolled arms race, on the other hand, is an argument for uncontrolled American power. For the Reagan Administration, too, and for its intellectuals, nuclear weapons are not the real problem. The real problem is the Soviet Union's ambitions. These ambitions are deemed to be the present danger to this country and to the world. It is not far from this to a pronuclear position. The prevention of nuclear war, it is said, must take place in the context of the prevention of Soviet expansion. A nuclear strategy follows, as the night the day, from anti-Communism. Those who speak of disarmament, and even of peace, are "objectively" pro-Soviet. There is no way that the United States can limit or reduce the nuclear weapons in its possession, it is said, without playing into the hands of the Kremlin.

There is no gainsaying that the nuclear question cannot be addressed except in the thick of present political reality. Too many advocates of disarmament speak as if the issue is somehow too big for politics. They believe that the making of nuclear weapons was a revolution in human affairs; their unmaking, therefore, will also require a revolution ("the revolution in thought and in action if mankind is to go on living," in Jonathan Schell's discouraging words). This is a view of reality that is completely determined by tech-

nology. For these peace people, as for the military
planners they detest, history begins with the bomb,
even as it may end with it. All other considerations—
especially the contest between the values of democracy and the values of totalitarianism—are irrelevant.

The surprising thing about life since Hiroshima,
however, is the extent to which it has not changed.
There has been a great deal of moral and political
continuity. Nor can this be all attributed to denial.
The nuclear peril has never been really denied, as
Schell and others have claimed. (The notion of denial,
though, is a useful way to discredit psychologically
the views of those with whom you disagree.) It has
just never taken over. People went on living for the
old purposes, and politics remained as premised on
these purposes as it ever was. The values of democracy were still good, and the values of totalitarianism
were still evil. The struggle between democracy and
totalitarianism did not end in 1945, because it is a
struggle between different answers to some of the
most fundamental questions of human life. The nuclear danger has not robbed these questions of their
urgency.

Nuclear weapons may destroy the world and totalitarianism may ruin it. It is an abdication of responsibility and an admission of defeat to argue that both
cannot be beaten. We need not fight suicide at the risk
of slavery, as some "doves" would have us do, nor
slavery at the risk of suicide, as some "hawks" would
have us do. The antinuclear argument is too important to be conceded to the one, and the anti-Communist argument is too important to be conceded to the
other. The arguments belong together, not in the
world of ideology, but in the world of politics. The
anti-Communist argument reminds us that there are
forms of disarmament from which people may suf-

fer—the loss of their freedoms, certainly, and maybe also the loss of their lives. And the antinuclear argument reminds us that democracy may adopt certain means in its struggle against totalitarianism that will destroy it, too.

What is necessary is to proceed with the historically urgent task of nuclear disarmament in a manner that will not have an effect upon the historically urgent task of resisting the Russians. Of course this must not be merely stated, but shown. Yet first the nuclear controversy must be uncluttered, and some misconceptions on both sides removed. What is essential to the argument against nuclear weapons, and what is not? What are the real philosophical and political implications of the fear of nuclear war?

1

THE PARTY OF PEACE

The peace movement of the early 1980s began in Western Europe and spread to the United States. The immediate occasion for the antinuclear agitation in Western Europe was the 1979 NATO decision to install in Europe medium-range nuclear missiles, the Pershing II and the cruise, targeted on the Soviet Union; these would match, in range and in accuracy, the SS-20 missiles that the Soviet Union already had targeted on Western Europe. (112 cruise missiles are to be placed in Italy, 160 in Britain, 48 in Belgium, 48 in Holland, and 96 in West Germany. Germany is also to receive 108 Pershings.) This NATO decision had the appearance of lowering what is called the nuclear threshold; that is, it seemed to make the prospect of nuclear war more likely by basing the defense of

Western Europe upon nuclear weapons whose smaller size made them less inhibiting to use. When President Reagan spoke casually to reporters about a limited nuclear war in Europe, the fears of many Europeans were confirmed. Hundreds of thousands of
people took to the streets, and in some countries—
Germany especially—they became a formidable political force. They were not united, however, behind a
single antinuclear position. Many things were proposed: the repeal of the NATO decision, or the return
of the Pershings and the cruise after they are installed
(in 1983); the creation of nuclear-free zones in Europe—in Central Europe, or in the Baltic, or even
"from Poland to Portugal"; unilateral nuclear disarmament, to which Britain's Labour Party is now offi-
cially committed; and multilateral nuclear disarmament, probably through negotiations between the
United States and the Soviet Union.

In the United States the occasion for the peace movement was its new President's picture of the world. In
the name of a really metaphysical confidence in
America he appeared quite willing to wage a nuclear
war. (It must be said in fairness to Mr. Reagan that his
predecessor, who was known for his homilies about
nuclear horrors, was responsible for Presidential Directive 59, issued in July 1980—as ominous a document as any produced by the present Administration.) Mr. Reagan spoke of controlling nuclear war,
not of controlling arms. He seemed to think that nuclear wars can be won. The agency for arms control
was assigned to a man who had spent the past decade
peddling ideological justifications for the arms race.
More generally, the President stood for a vision of

America in which power had pride of place. This vision was perfectly expressed in his budget, which called for a radical expansion of the military and a radical contraction of everything else. Secretary of State Alexander Haig mumbled something to Congress about a nuclear demonstration shot, and Secretary of Defense Caspar Weinberger drafted plans, called the Defense Guidance, for a "protracted" nuclear war. Here, too, hundreds of thousands of people took to the streets, and here, too, the political climate was changed. It now appears that politicans will not be able to ignore the antinuclear anxiety of the people. The most popular antinuclear proposal is the Kennedy-Hatfield resolution, calling for "a mutual and verifiable freeze on the testing, production, and future deployment of nuclear warheads, missiles, and other delivery systems." In the elections of 1982, freeze referenda were approved in eight states out of nine, and in twenty-eight cities and counties. Many antinuclear activists, however, are not satisfied with the freeze, and speak of more dramatic forms of disarmament.

The peace movement is an eruption from below. It has about it an aspect of the popular will. Individuals with otherwise divergent political ideas and interests have realized that the existence of nuclear weapons transforms the citizenry of this country into a single community of fate. They share a presentiment about what is being prepared for them. The fear is absolutely faultless. But it is not only fear upon which the peace movement is founded. Its intellectuals argue from something more. They advance certain moral and historical judgments that do their cause no justice. It is these other propositions of the peace movement that must be examined. This concern about nuclear catastrophe must be rid of certain politi-

cal constructions that are placed upon it; they origi-
nate elsewhere.

Nuclear weapons are not like other weapons.
The difference was recognized as early as 1946 by
Bernard Brodie, who wrote with great wisdom that
"thus far the chief purpose of our military establishment has been to win wars. From now on its chief
purpose must be to avert them. It can have almost no
other useful purpose." This is the doctrine of deterrence, upon which defense policy in the nuclear age
has been based. The doctrine of deterrence is the exact opposite of the doctrine of use. The distinction
between deterrence and use, however, is not the only
thing that the intellectuals of the peace movement
have in mind when they insist upon the difference
between nuclear arms and conventional arms. They
have in mind, rather, a broader, and more momentous, distinction. The problem of nuclear weapons,
they maintain, calls for nothing less than a new analysis of history.

Jonathan Schell makes the call, though he does
not make the analysis. "Everything has changed," he
announces. Human history may be periodized according to the appearance in it of the bomb; and the
period after the appearance of the bomb, Schell explains, is characterized not merely by the fear of
death, but by the fear of "the death of death." The
change, in other words, is spiritual, and it is to the
realm of the spirit that Schell repairs. It is with "Gandhi's law of love" and little else that he leaves the
endangered human species. He writes of "a fundamental divorce between the prenuclear basis of our
whole approach to political life and the reality of our
nuclear world"; but about the manner of a postnu-
clear return of politics to reality we are told nothing,
except that the system of sovereign states must be

dissolved in favor of a world government. "The peril of extinction is the price that the world pays...for its insistence on continuing to divide itself up into sovereign nations...Our present system and the institutions that make it up are the debris of history. They have become inimical to life and must be swept away." This is an old idea; Einstein declared that "there is only *one* path to peace and security: the path of supranational organization." This is also something more than the idea of an international authority for atomic energy, which Neils Bohr proposed to Churchill in 1944, and which was embodied in the Baruch Plan, an American plan of moral merit. (The Soviets wouldn't hear of it.) Schell wants nothing less than "to reinvent politics, to reinvent the world." If that is what it will take to master the nuclear menace, however, we may all start living for the day, because we will surely die. Schell's book is a classic of irresponsible idealism.

A new analysis of history based upon the nuclear difference may be found, rather, in the writings of E. P. Thompson, the British social historian. Thompson may be considered the most influential intellectual in the peace movement. In 1980 he published his pamphlet *Protest and Survive*, which became the manifesto of the antinuclear movements in England and in Europe; last year he published a version of it as "A Letter to America" in *The Nation.* Thompson's arguments for disarmament—he is a practiced publicist— may all be found in his recent book, *Beyond the Cold War*.

The real distinction between conventional weapons and nuclear weapons, according to Thompson, is that nuclear weapons are not instruments of intention. They are, instead, makers of it. Conventional weapons are mere things, manipulated by men; the men must be understood, therefore, and not the things. In the world of conventional weapons, military facts must be broken down into political facts, into the ideas and interests that motivate the elite whom the military serves. Not so in the world of nuclear weapons. They are not things; they are systems. The production, deployment, and support of these weapons systems generates "a correspondent social system"—an organization of knowledge that leads to an organization of the economy that leads to an organization of society. What began with the splitting of the atom ended with the national security state. Nuclear weapons have a logic of their own, which eventually imposes itself upon every sector of society. The bomb defines the character of the society. And this character Thompson defines as "exterminism."

Exterminism, in Thompson's words, is an "order whose institutional base is the weapons-system, and the entire economic, scientific, political, and ideological support-system to that weapons-system—the social system which researches it, 'chooses' it, produces it, polices it, justifies it, and maintains it in being." There are, of course, only two such systems in existence—the United States and the Soviet Union. The two superpowers are distinguished by what Thompson calls an "isomorphism"; each is thrust by "its economy, its polity, and its ideology" in a direction "whose outcome must be the extermination of multitudes." "The U.S.A. and the U.S.S.R. do not *have* military-industrial complexes: they *are* such complexes"; for that reason, he concludes, "isomorphic replication is evident at every level: in cultural, political, but above all, in ideological life."

All these pseudo-scientific sonorities amount to this: that the United States and the Soviet Union are the devil and the deep blue sea. The nuclear power they share has eclipsed the differences between them. The choice that now confronts the world is not between capitalism and Communism, or between democracy and totalitarianism; it is the choice between extermination and survival. And so Thompson utters the silly remark that "the movement of Polish Solidarity is, in a critical sense, *of the same kind* as the movement in West Europe to resist nuclear rearmament." Schell, too, equally certain that the nuclear weapon is the essential characteristic of both the United States and the Soviet Union, compares Brezhnev's way of dealing with his critics to Nixon's; he speaks of an "alliance of the champions of peace in repression." Where there are nuclear weapons, in short, there are no rights.

"Isomorphism," in the sphere of politics, means neutralism. There is no need to take sides in the struggle between the United States and the Soviet Union if it makes no difference who wins. The resurgence that neutralism has enjoyed in Europe is owed in large measure to this association with the antinuclear argument. Neutralism—or, as Thompson prefers, "internationalism"—is presented as a logical requirement of disarmament. So, too, is "better Red than dead"; or, as one of Thompson's lieutenants in European Nuclear Disarmament said, "better Finnish than finished." So, too, is the idea of unilateral disarmament.

Unilateralism is a disgraceful notion, produced by people who think so little of themselves that they believe in nothing except life. Neutralism is an admission of philosophical exhaustion. Staying above the war of ideas is not a spiritual triumph; it is a spiritual collapse. It represents a loss of interest in the principles at stake in political systems. And "better Red than dead" is an insult to those who believe "better dead than Red." It is important to remember that there are such people. There were, after all, Hungarians, Czechs, Poles, and Afghanis, and indeed Russians, who died resisting Soviet power because they believed it was the rational thing to do. It will be objected that their resistance to the Russians carried no danger of nuclear catastrophe; but nuclear catastrophe, it cannot be sufficiently stressed, is not the only possible outcome of anti-Communism. "Better Red than dead," in any case, is a very big idea. It takes a lot down with it. It is not only a response to the threat of extinction; it is an attitude toward public life which affects the moral and psychological preparedness to resist totalitarianism at any time.

These ideas are easily enough refuted; and none of them, in any case, will in any way affect the targeting of Soviet missiles. The destruction of Western Europe's industrial capacity will remain an essential part of the Soviet Union's strategy in any war with the United States. But it is essential that those who are dedicated to peace be made to understand that none of these ideas are properly derived from the fear of nuclear war. They are derived only from the ideological and political preferences of their authors.

Consider the case of Thompson. He joined the Communist Party in 1940 and left it in 1956. He calls himself a "dissident Communist" and the totalitarian societies of the Soviet empire "pseudo-Communist." In an open letter to Leszek Kolakowski in 1973, an angry denunciation of Marxist disillusionment, Thompson wrote that "what we dissident Communists did in Britain—and for this achievement I still feel a stubborn pride—was to refuse to enter the well-worn paths of apostasy....We had, after all, our experiential political reasons for being opposed to capitalist society, independent of any evolution in Eastern Europe whatsoever." Later he made the same point more colorfully: "For no matter how hideous the alternative may seem, no word of mine will be willingly added to the comforts of that old bitch gone in the teeth, consumer capitalism." Communism, on the other hand, may be a bitch, but it is not yet gone in the teeth. "Fifty years is too short a time to judge a new social system." (This is exactly how Franz Mehring defended the Bolsheviks—"the long wind of history," he called it. He made his defense, however, in 1917.) The revolution in Russia, according to Thompson, was obstructed by "circumstances, contingencies, accidents, events," and "the logic of polarities within a divided world." The last phrase refers to the interference of the United States in the natural development of socialism. ("We must remember that the failure of '1956' was in part a failure imposed by 'the West.' ")

Thompson's ideological biography does not discredit his ideas; they discredit themselves. It does disclose, however, the intellectual predicament in which they were developed. This predicament must be understood if the antinuclear argument is to be shaken loose from them. Thompson is most emphatically anti-Soviet and he is most emphatically anti-American. He seeks "a third way." There is an equivalence of evil, he believes, between the superpowers. Thompson is pretty serene, in the passages quoted above, about the satanic statistics of Stalin's reign— fifty years may be too short a time to judge a new social system, but it was ample time to kill maybe a hundred million people—and such habits of historical judgment no doubt leave him with a certain theoretical predisposition to find unfreedom in America.

They leave him, too, with a willingness to give Soviet foreign policy the benefit of the doubt. "The basic postures of the Soviet Union seem to me, still, to be those of siege and aggressive defense; and even the brutal and botching intervention in Afghanistan appears to have followed upon sensitivity as to United States and Chinese strategies." On the other hand, "the United States seems to me to be more dangerous and provocative in its general military and diplomatic strategies, which press around the Soviet Union with menacing bases." This is the common left-wing theory according to which the Soviet Union is expanding because it is "encircled."

Still, even Thompson admits that the equivalence between the Soviet Union and the United States is rather rough. Speaking of Watergate, which he compares to Khrushchev's "demystificatory" speech at the Twentieth Party Congress, Thompson writes that "the rhetoric of constitutionalism and of personal liberty turned out to be somewhat tougher, more internalized, than one had come to suppose." It is grudging praise, but it is praise. Thus a problem for Thompson remained. The intellectual foundations for the third way were a little shaky. Capitalism may have been no better than Communism, but the United States looked a bit better than the Soviet Union. The discovery of the nuclear danger, however, solved the problem. The doctrine of "exterminism" makes the equivalence between the United States and the Soviet Union exact. Once these political systems are defined essentially by the bomb, they really are equals in evil. It is not the idea of disarmament, then, that requires the idea of neutralism; it is the idea of neutralism that requires the idea of disarmament.

Thompson's version of the antinuclear argument is not his alone. This constellation of ideas, which promotes the criticism of the arms race into a larger historical criticism, is shared by many on the left. (The Appeal for European Nuclear Disarmament, an influential document circulated in Western Europe in April 1980, warns that "the powers of the military and of internal security forces are enlarged, limitations are placed between free exchanges of ideas and between persons, and civil rights of independent-minded individuals are threatened, in the West as well as the East"; and it concludes that "we must commence to act as if a united, neutral, and pacific Europe already exists.") What are the merits of such an analysis? Beyond the call to arms control, they are not many. There is a false premise to Thompson's argument, which may be called nuclear reductionism. He is arguing, like Schell, backward from the apocalypse: because everything may be destroyed by the bomb, everything may be explained by it. But it is striking how much of social and political life since 1945 cannot be explained by the bomb. The frequency of war, most notably. Hiroshima was supposed to put an end to war; the stakes, it was commonly said, were now too high. But twenty-five million people have died in war since Hiroshima. The weak, moreover, have frequently defied the strong; the movements of national liberation were never deterred, and the existence of nuclear weapons did not keep smaller states that did not have them from waging war with larger states that did.

There are many political and economic features of the international situation upon which nuclear weapons have no bearing. The same is true about many politi-

cal and economic features of the states that possess
nuclear weapons. The security apparatus of the Soviet Union, for example, was in place long before it built
a bomb. The Lubyanka prison, and the philosophy of
control that it represents, was already in existence
when Soviet physicists went to work. The repression
by the Soviet regime of its own people was not generated by its technological ability to do so. Thompson's
thesis underestimates the place of such repression in
the Soviet scheme of things.

He overestimates its place in the American
scheme of things. It is hard to know how to reply to
the view that abuses of rights in the United States are
like abuses of rights in the Soviet Union. Plainly they
differ by many orders of magnitude. Nixon broke into
the office of his critic's psychiatrist; Brezhnev committed his critics to a psychiatric hospital. It is extremely
dubious, moreover, that abuses of rights in this country are related to its nuclear development. They, too,
took place before 1945. What has racism, for example,
to do with the Pentagon? It has been suggested, more
specifically, that the internal surveillance insanity that
overcame the Nixon government was a spillover from
the mentality of secrecy that attends all things nuclear. This is rather forced. The persecutions of COINTELPRO originated in a political style and a personality
disorder that cannot be laid at the Defense Department's door. COINTELPRO, moreover, was conducted
by the same Administration that conducted SALT.
And it was ended. A new Administration "leashed"
the F.B.I.—and unleashed the MX missile. The fight
for civil liberties, in short, scored its greatest successes in the nuclear age. The Bill of Rights was not
abrogated by the bomb.

The political culture of the United States cannot
be reduced to its military culture. Thompson thinks

too crudely about the relationship of internal security to external security. "Deterrence has repressed the violence towards the opposing bloc," he writes; "the repressed violence has backed up, and worked its way into the economy, the polity, the ideology, and the culture of the opposing blocs." But the state of weaponry is not directly reproduced in the state of society. Can the author of *The Making of the British Working Class* really believe that the social process is so simple? Or the foreign policy process? The state of society is not directly reproduced in the state of foreign policy, either; free nations may sin against freedom, as Thompson is often the first to proclaim. The introduction of nuclear power raised the stakes of foreign policy—statesmen are now responsible for more than they have ever been—but it did not reduce foreign policy to military strategy.

The present Administration also seems not to know this. Its national security policy is ultimately underwritten by the demented doctrine of nuclear use. Thompson's consternation, therefore, is not without foundation. But he cannot be followed his whole way. His argument against nuclear weapons is an argument against too much. Thompson is like the bewildered girl in Randall Jarrell's novel, who looked under her bed and discovered a horse. He looked under his bed and discovered a missile.

The antinuclear agitation has included another attitude that must be challenged. This is the new disreputability of defense. There has grown up in the midst of those who oppose the arms race a great distaste for all things military. Because they hate war, they hate armies. They think that armies are the cause of wars; or, as C. Wright Mills put it, "the immediate cause of World War III is the preparation of it." The scientific establishment that is appended to the military has also come in for a fair share of the popular contempt, despite the fact that it was from among its ranks that the alarm about nuclear arms was first sounded. This antimilitary attitude takes a number of forms. Foremost among them is the opposition to defense spending, both in the United States and in Europe. What began as a campaign against bombs has become a campaign against tanks. The defense budget has been attacked not merely for its details, but also for its principles. Many of its details, to be sure, are dubious, particularly its provisions for some of the extravagant electronics that are so beloved by American military planners. And it includes among its principles the preparedness to fight and win a protracted nuclear war—a promise of death for millions. There is an absence of conscience in the nuclear budget of this government. But the absence of conscience stops there.

The economic argument against defense spending is of two kinds. The first is made from a vision of American security; it has been advanced most sensibly by James Fallows, an important figure in the liberal reawakening to problems of defense. He has shown that money is being wasted on weapons that are not required, or that will not work. The basis of his criticism is a constructive concern that the United States be efficiently defended; the criterion for military spending, it is agreed, must be military need. The second kind of economic argument is made from a vision of American society. According to this argument the criterion of military spending must be social need. Money spent on weapons, after all, is money not spent on something else; and staggering sums are spent on weapons. Dollars given to the Pentagon are dollars taken away from the poor. There is a more ideological inflection to this argument—the citizens of this country are told to choose between the welfare state and the warfare state. It is also argued, in a similar vein, that the criterion of military spending must be economic need, that capital must be transferred from the military industries to the civilian industries if the decline in American economic power is to be reversed. John Kenneth Galbraith finds a direct correlation between the lower percentage of the gross national product that Germany and Japan devoted to their military in the 1970s and the economic eminence they achieved in those years. (This is a curious explanation of the strength of the Japanese, and no explanation at all of the new German weakness.) Spending for defense distorts the economy, then, or it distorts the society.

It is true that the economic consequences of the military buildup proposed by the Reagan Administration will be dire; but these may be remedied by a change not in the military policy, but in the economic policy. A change in the military policy can be justified only on military grounds. (Lester Thurow has made this point.) It is precisely on such grounds, for example, that the MX missile is not justified. In a time of hardship, it is especially galling that some of these stupendous sums may be kept from Aid to Families with Dependent Children. In such a time, if it is not necessary that a weapon be built, it is necessary that it not be built. But if the MX, or any other equally expensive weapon, can be shown to be essential to the country's security, the money should go to it. The government can tax; and only because it refuses to tax does it seem as if we must choose between Social Security and national security. What's more, the economic argument against defense spending turns against its makers in the case of NATO; a conventional defense of Europe would be much more expensive than a nuclear defense. It was for the sake of frugality ("more bang for the buck") that the Eisenhower Administration first adopted the notorious notion of "massive retaliation" as the basis of American military strategy.

The social argument against defense spending is, in one respect, quite easily disposed of; families with dependent children must be alive if they are to be aided. But the argument raises serious questions about the dispositions of democracies in matters of defense. The philosophical foundations of the welfare state, it is sometimes said, dissuade its population from the military dimensions of foreign policy. As one scholar has written, "the modern emphasis on the education, health, and welfare of the common man is in fundamental conflict with foreign policies based on regarding man elsewhere as a legitimate object of aggression and oppression." Of this, certainly, we may be proud; and this philosophical condition accounts in part for the difficulty faced by recent administrations in winning popular support for double standards in their positions on human rights. But emphasis on "education, health, and welfare" may also lead to an introversion of political interests, to a decreasing preoccupation with foreign affairs. Which would be no danger at all, if political interests in the Soviet Union were an impediment to the men who govern it. The military budget of the Soviet Union, however, requires nobody's approval. Andropov has no need of Boll Weevils.

The authors of the Constitution did not have militarism in mind when they put providing for the common defense before promoting the general welfare, and it is not militarism that I wish to defend. I wish only to defend defense. The opposition to spending for conventional weapons has opportunistically borrowed its moral prestige from the opposition to spending for nuclear weapons. The antiwar movement: there is moral prestige already in the name. But the antiwar movement of the 1960s fought a real war. The antiwar movement of the 1980s fights a possible war. It is invariably a good fight, if it is against a possible nuclear war. But many possible wars are not nuclear. The purpose of an antiwar movement in the absence of a real war, then, may be problematic. The problem is not pacifism, which does not exist as a serious political force in the United States. (It does, to a more significant degree, in Europe, where there may be found a phenomenon that might be called the pacifist in the Palestinian headdress, or Sandinistas for SALT—people who prefer the loss of innocent lives in revolution to the loss of innocent lives in war.) The problem is, rather, a much more serious proposition, which is that the use of force is not a legitimate instrument of national policy in the nuclear age.

Jonathan Schell writes that "the ruin of war by nuclear weapons has brought about a divorce between violence and politics." We live "in the prenuclear world," he maintains, when we believe that "sovereign nations could still employ the instruments of violence as instruments of policy." A similar conclusion appears in the Report of the Independent Commission on Disarmament and Security Issues, which was chaired by Olaf Palme of Sweden. The report, entitled *Common Security*, lists among its conditions for such security that "military force is not a legitimate instrument for resolving disputes among nations." It explains: "Historically, the use of force as an instrument of national policy has only rarely been effective in the long run.[!] In the nuclear age, it raises risks which are disproportionate to any conceivable gain." The injunction, please note, includes all forms of force, not merely nuclear war. The report goes on to say that "prevailing definitions of self-defense must be tightened and narrowed," so as to rob war of its most acceptable justification. On this last point, however, the Palme Commission is admirably ambivalent. "Nevertheless, all states must retain the right to use force in their own defense and, in accord with the conditions and procedures specified in the Charter of the United Nations, in collective defense of victims of aggression." Which brings war's justification back.

The delegitimation of war in the nuclear age is not completely without reason. The reason is the fear of escalation. The threshold between conventional war and nuclear war is more easily crossed than the threshold between war and peace; and so the surest way to avoid nuclear conflict is to avoid all conflict. Unfortunately not all the peace movement's objections to war are so responsible. There lurks within it the conviction, formulated most vocally by the churches, that after the invention of nuclear weapons there can no longer be a just war. The truth is that the notion of the just war was discredited for many of the marchers not so much by Hiroshima as by Vietnam, particularly by the filthy way the war was fought. And so the argument is heard, as it was in Europe even as Hitler's troops were barreling across the borders, that to defeat the enemy you must become like the enemy. The enemy, therefore, is not Russia, or Germany—the enemy is war. There is a sense, of course, in which this is true. There are no clean wars; and the consequences of only a conventional war would be ruinous enough. There are, however, just wars.

Writing of the motives for the arms race, Galbraith observes that the most influential motive of all is "the belief, strong in the United States, much cited in oratory, that we are defending an economic, social and political system." Galbraith's irony is ill-judged. We *are* defending such a system. We may be defending it poorly, and there may be those who are battening unfairly upon its defense. But there will be a high price to pay in the moral condition of the country if the attack upon the military and industrial particulars of the United States becomes an attack upon its purposes. There is a moral basis to the idea of security. It is in this matter of the relation of moral principle to military power that the influence of Vietnam has been most baleful; and it is in this matter, too, that the peace movement of the 1980s is most sadly the heir of the peace movement of the 1960s. Those for whom Vietnam was the primal political scene have difficulty in discerning the relation of power to principle. Those for whom World War II was the primal political scene do not. They know that there may come a time when there is no higher expression of the values by which we live than the fight for them. The hatred of all things military is finally a sign that you do not believe in what you are, that you do not believe that you have something to lose. This may be the state of a growing number of young Europeans, to judge by recent public opinion polls; a poll taken in Germany last year, for example, showed 56 percent of the 16- to 20-year-olds

surveyed preferring Soviet domination to war, and
only 25 percent agreeing that democracy is worth de
fending.

Of course, there can never be a nuclear war that
is just. There is no moral standard that can sanction it.
The remnants of the civilization that caused such a
catastrophe would have no right to the values it had
created; these values for which whole populations
lived would die when whole populations died. Michael Walzer has precisely analyzed the moral illegit-
imacy of nuclear war. "It would violate both of the
proportionality limits fixed by the theory of war: the
number of people killed in the war as a whole would
not be warranted by the goals of the war—particularly
since the dead would include many if not most of the
people for whose defense the war was being fought;
and the number of killed in individual actions would
be disproportionate...to the value of the targets directly attacked." All this comes, however, at the end
of a scrupulous defense of the notion of the just war.
There have been wars that had to be fought.

To be antinuclear, then, is not to be antimilitary. Nor
is it to be anti-American. Nuclear weapons have introduced a new circumspection into the conduct of international affairs, but the circumspection must not go
so far as to deny our assistance to those whose freedoms have been confiscated by Communism (or, for
that matter, by Fascism). Unfortunately the fear of
nuclear weapons is having just that effect. It has become the new argument for neutralism—the argument that silences all criticism. It has also become the
new argument for isolationism. The nuclear danger is
invoked to inhibit not only military interventions, but
political and economic interventions as well. The re-

sponse of some liberal intellectuals to the recent repression in Poland offers a good example. A prominent liberal commentator who is no admirer of the Soviet Union argued that the United States must blunt its reaction to the smashing of Solidarity because "a sudden collapse" of Russia's empire in Eastern Europe "could be dangerous if it triggers a violent Soviet reaction. We do, after all, live in an age of nuclear weapons." It is extremely unlikely, however, that the Soviets would have responded to a default on the Polish debt by firing an SS-20. A few German banks would probably have collapsed, that is all; and the Soviets would have been properly punished by political means only. This liberal's analysis is a perfect illustration of the way in which the fear of nuclear war becomes an excuse for any projection of Soviet power.

But then there is the White House, and the Department of Defense, and the Arms Control and Disarmament Agency, where the fear of the Soviet Union is an excuse for any projection of nuclear power.

2

THE PARTY OF WAR

Like the antinuclearists in the peace movement, nuclearists in power defend their position with a view of the world and a view of the weapons. The official nuclear strategy of the United States, which has been slowly evolving in a sinister direction since the Schlesinger stewardship of the Pentagon, is based upon two sets of conclusions, both of them highly contestable. The first concerns the nuclear strategy, and more generally the political intentions, of the Soviet Union, which, according to Richard Pipes, "thinks it can fight and win a nuclear war"; the second concerns the nuclear arsenal's reason for being, which, according to the present Pentagon, is to be used. It now looks as if the United States thinks it can fight and win a nuclear war, too.

It is not true, as some "hawks" have maintained, that the concept of deterrence does not appear in Soviet military thinking; it does, most prominently in the basic treatise of Soviet military doctrine edited by Marshal V. D. Sokolovsky, where it is stated that "the greater the buildup of means of mass destruction, the greater the conviction in the impossibility of their use." The text speaks also of "balance" and "parity" and "stalemate," as do other Soviet sources. Still, there does exist a great divergence in nuclear doctrine between the United States and the Soviet Union. That is indisputable. To judge by many of the texts of its military planners that have reached the West, often against the wishes of the Kremlin, the Soviet Union thinks about nuclear war less gingerly than does the United States. Deterrence does not seem to have been the controlling concept of Soviet strategic thinking. The point of departure for Soviet military writers on nuclear war is not Brodie's dictum on deterrence, cited above; they depart, rather, from the dictum of Clausewitz, enthusiastically endorsed by Lenin, that war is a continuation of politics by other means. In the words of one Soviet general,

> this does not mean that nuclear war...has ceased to be an instrument of politics, as is claimed by the overwhelming majority of representatives of pacifist, anti-war movements in the bourgeois world. This is a subjective judgement. It merely expresses protest against nuclear war.

And he continues:

> There is profound error and harm in the disorienting claims that there will be no victor in a thermonuclear world war. The peoples of the

world will put an end to imperialism, which is
causing mankind incalculable suffering.

There are many more such passages in the or-
gans of the Soviet military establishment. They seem
strange, and they are. The strangeness of the Soviet
military mentality, however, is no reason for it not to
be taken seriously. Liberals have a hard time taking
strangeness seriously; and there has existed in the
liberal community the belief that the Soviet Union will
catch up to the United States in strategy as in science,
that there will be a convergence in the nuclear dog-
mas of the superpowers as the Russians come to share
the American faith in the rationality of deterrence.
This has not happened. The Soviet Union has its own
ideas and idioms in nuclear matters. Its approach to
nuclear war has not quite broken with the traditional
approach to war.

Many reasons for this have been given. It is said,
for example, that the difference between its approach
and ours is the difference between the military mind
and the civilian mind. There does not exist in the
Soviet Union the phenomenon of civilians making
military policy. Membership in the military, however,
has not prevented many American generals from
adopting the doctrine of deterrence, and the Soviet
defense minister happens to be a civilian. Historical
and cultural reasons have also been adduced, from
the role of the army in the development of Russia
(Professor Pipes feels that the Russian subjugation of
Kazan and Astrakhan in the sixteenth century has
some bearing upon the Kremlin's plans for its ICBMs)
to the infatuation of Marx and Lenin with Clausewitz
and Darwin. It has even been suggested that the loss
of twenty million people in the Second World War
makes it much less difficult for the Soviet leadership

to contemplate suffering such losses in the Third. Whatever the reason, when it comes to considering the consequences of nuclear war, the Soviets seem less spooked.

The principal tenets of Soviet nuclear doctrine, as they have been established by scholars, are these: that a nuclear-war-fighting capacity must be maintained, because the security of the Soviet Union must be based not upon the good sense of the enemy not to attack, but upon the ability of Soviet forces to withstand an attack; that victory is possible in a nuclear war; that the advantage in a nuclear war will accrue to whichever side strikes first; that "the creation and constant maintenance of qualitative and quantitative superiority over the enemy in this means of armed conflict" is essential; and that there are effective forms of civil defense against nuclear weapons, and practical programs for survival. "Soviet strategic doctrine," in the words of Benjamin Lambeth, the author of a RAND study of the subject, "is manifestly a combat-oriented operational philosophy that treats the possibility of nuclear war as a threat that cannot simply be wished away."

There are elements of official Soviet thinking about nuclear war that are fantastic. These may be found in connection with its objective of "total victory." After a strategic nuclear exchange, the Soviets have plans for the burning cities of America. "Combat operations will continue for the purpose of the final defeat of the enemy on his own territory" because "that side which manages during the first days of the war to penetrate more deeply into enemy territory naturally acquires the capability for more effectively using the results of its nuclear attacks and disrupting the mobilization of the enemy." The territory will be occupied; its population will be politically controlled and ideologically converted. "As for ideological struggle, in conditions of nuclear war...it will be conducted through all possible channels and in the most active forms. The war itself is a competition of the spirit, ideas, world outlook, ideologies, and moral stability of the personnel of the armed forces and the population of the country." Marxism, in short, will rule the ruins.

Soviet doctrine is reproduced in Soviet development. The Brezhnev era began with a historic rapprochement between the Party and the military. The immediate cause of the happy new relationship was Khrushchev's humiliation in Cuba, which would not have happened, it was said, if the Soviet Union had been better armed. But there was a deeper cause, which is that the government and the army came to have common purposes. The government relied more upon the army for its authority; militarism is inevitable in a political system without legitimacy. The Soviet Union, as Cornelius Castoriadis has brilliantly described it, has been slowly militarized. This means not only that generals are now prominent in the making of foreign and domestic policy, but also that the economy and the society of the Soviet Union have been sedulously reorganized according to the needs of its military forces and industries. It is now commonly acknowledged that Brezhnev presided over the most dramatic military buildup in Soviet history. The Soviet Union is more or less equal to the United States in its nuclear capacity, and superior to the United States (if not to the West as a whole) in its conventional capacity. The militarization of the Soviet Union is certainly the most disturbing development in many decades. It has transformed a state founded upon a dream of world domination into a military power of monstrous proportions. And so the "hawks" cry havoc.

There is a danger, obviously. The "hawks" have been more correct about the Russians than the "doves." But they have not been completely correct, particularly in their conclusions concerning Soviet nuclear policy. Consider, for example, the Soviet belief in "striking first," which they have amply documented. This is simply not the same as a belief in "a first strike." The Soviet doctrine of "preemption," as it is called, means only that the Soviet Union would fire its missiles first if a crisis with the United States reached the point at which a nuclear exchange seemed inevitable. But this is tactics, not strategy. "Preemptive" war is not "preventive" war. It is, quite the contrary, similar to what is known in the West as "launch on warning"; and it is identical to a consideration put forward by a member of the Carter Administration when he wrote that "resorting to intercontinental nuclear attack would likely be the result of a conviction that a nuclear exchange had become inevitable, and that some advantage would obtain from going first." This is a provision for the brink of war, not for the breaking of the peace. There is no evidence at all that the Soviets believe in "first strike," or that they have plans to start a nuclear war, or that their nuclear strategy is, as Pipes put it, "not retaliation but offensive action." (Many of the Soviet scenarios for fighting a nuclear war include the saving subordinate clause "if it is unleashed by the imperialists.") If the Soviets believe in "first strike," why have they not struck? After all, the United States, according to the "hawks," has never been weaker. The Soviets know as well as Pipes what their strength is. Perhaps they know better than he what our strength is.

Soviet doctrine, moreover, is not all that determines Soviet behavior. Despite the chilling certitudes of Soviet planning for nuclear war, it is impossible—

for us as well as for them—to be sure that the plans
describe how the planners would conduct themselves
in a crisis. No one knows exactly how a nuclear war
will be fought; this uncertainty unnerves all who ever
perfunctorily study the problem, and it must be reckoned alongside the Soviet swagger. The state of Soviet forces, too, must be reckoned. They are formidable,
to be sure; but they are not maintained in a state of
preparedness that implies an intention to act. The
deployment of Soviet nuclear forces in peacetime is
not in keeping with Soviet nuclear doctrine. Soviet
bombers are on the ground more than American
bombers, and Soviet submarines are in port more
than American submarines; and Soviet nuclear forces
are less frequently "on alert" than their American
counterparts. There is evidence, furthermore, that
nuclear weapons in the forward area of the Warsaw
Pact are not collocated to their delivery systems, and
that responsibility for these weapons in peacetime
falls not to the military command but to the K.G.B.

Some of the Soviet Union's nuclear notions are
evil, yes; but they are also absurd. What does it matter
if they are making plans for after the apocalypse? The
fantasies of seizing smoldering radio stations are fearful, but they are of no consequence. Nor is the fantasy
of civilian defense. Shelters will not work wherever
they are. They will save no one from a direct hit, or
from the fallout of a direct hit, in Moscow or in Manhattan.

The most seductive of the Soviet Union's nuclear fic-
tions is probably the notion of nuclear superiority. It
is a notion to which the American government seems
to subscribe—for example, in the report of the Secretary of Defense to Congress for the fiscal year 1983

where it states that although our "modernization program is not designed to achieve nuclear 'superiority' for the United States, by the same token, we will make every necessary effort to prevent the Soviet Union from acquiring such superiority and to insure the margin of safety necessary for our security." There is an unsettling confusion here, perfectly expressed by those quotation marks—we do not want " 'superiority,' " but we will not let them have "superiority." Here it is meaningless and there it is meaningful. Whatever the Administration's view of the notion of nuclear superiority, it clearly subscribes to the notion of nuclear inferiority. The President warns that the land-based Minuteman missiles of the United States, all 1,052 of them, are "a window of vulnerability" in the American deterrent. He is right. Why have the Soviets not taken them out, however, if they can do so with such ease? The answer, of course, is that they cannot take them out with any ease at all. They would have to destroy most of our missiles to avoid the retaliatory power of those that remained. The United States, moreover, will hardly wait to see if a Soviet strike is a success. Missiles fired from American submarines would find their targets behind the Urals before missiles fired from Soviet bases would find their targets behind the Rockies. Our nuclear force at sea is impossible to detect, and impossible to defend against. (It is worth noting that opponents of the arms race such as Hans Bethe support the improvement of the American marine deterrent, particularly of the Trident II missiles—which a freeze would not allow.) To be sure, the vulnerability of our land-based missiles is a real problem, but it may have no solution. Such missiles may be in a state of strategic senescence. This should worry the Soviets more, however; three-quarters of their nuclear force consists of

ICBMs. We think that we are vulnerable through a window, but they know that they are vulnerable through the front door.

Still, we are not in a position of superiority, because there is no such thing. Our submarines ensure only that our adversary, too, will not survive. The notion of nuclear superiority is without meaning, because the losses on either side will be too much to bear if only a single missile gets through, and more than a single missile will. There is a sense in which "Soviet" strategy is like "Soviet" genetics. The United States would be as foolish to believe that the numbers any longer matter, or that a nuclear war can be won, as it would be to believe that winter wheat will grow in the spring. The strategy is determined by the weapon. The missiles have only to exist, and deterrence is the law of their existence. For this reason the Soviet union acts in accordance with the doctrine of deterrence even if it does not think in accordance with it. Deterrence may go with the American grain or against the Russian grain; it may suit the philosophical and cultural bias of a nation that knows little about war and wants to dwell apart, or it may suit the philosophical and cultural bias of a nation that knows a great deal about war and wants the world; but it suits the weapons. That is why many of the doctrinal differences between the United States and the Soviet Union do not matter. *Any* strategy that respects the lethality and the invulnerability of these arms will deter a war between the powers that possess them. As Brodie wrote, "their being there is quite enough."

The nuclearists in and out of government cannot justify their position, then, with reference to Soviet strategy, even if Soviet strategy is in many ways deeply disturbing. But these people are not exactly disturbed by it. The "hawks" do not attack Soviet strategy; they admire it. That is their dirty little secret. They accept a great deal of the Soviet approach to nuclear weapons. There is indeed a convergence in doctrine taking place between the United States and the Soviet Union. But they are not coming around to our way of thinking; we are coming around to theirs. Something terrible is happening in the defense community of the United States, and it is the Sovietization of American strategy. A balance of terror is now threatened by a balance of error. When both sides believe these things, there may be trouble.

The Sovietization of American strategy began well before Reagan came to office. It was conceived, without irony, for the sake of deterrence. The Deputy Undersecretary of Defense for Policy Planning in the Carter Administration, for example, expressed this lucidly: "Our policies must take account of what we know of Soviet perspectives on these issues. For by definition, deterrence requires shaping Soviet assessments about the risks of war, assessments that will be made using their models, even if we think those models less accurate than our own." There is some sense in this; deterrence is, after all, a communication of intent, and the communication must be made in a language that will be understood. But it did not stop there. The Carter Administration came to bless and stayed to curse. In 1977 and 1978 it requested large allocations from Congress for the purpose of civil defense; the debate about that dubious idea was immediately renewed, and Congress awarded the President less than he asked. Secretary of Defense James Schlesinger had converted American strategy to "counterforce," to the targeting of military sites instead of civilian sites, for the purpose of providing the

United States with more options in the waging of a
nuclear war. His successor, Harold Brown, perpetrat-
ed Presidential Directive 59; this, in the words of one
commentator, "aimed to improve deterrence by im-
proving the capacity for a prolonged but limited nuclear war." The muddle in such thinking is macabre.
The Administration that began with ideas of minimal
nuclear deterrence ended with ideas of limited nuclear war. It is always in the name of deterrence that
deterrence is undone. It must be made "flexible," it
was said, as it was said in the 1950s and again in the
1960s—flexible enough, that is, to include a fight.
Such refinements in American strategy have led
Theodore Draper to observe dourly that deterrence
"may yet equal liberty for the number of crimes committed in its name."

Draper made his observation about the Reagan
Administration, and quite rightly. What Carter started Reagan finished. The Sovietization of American
strategy has been perfected in the Weinberger Pentagon. "The assessments that truly matter," an adviser
to the Administration has written, "are those made in
Moscow." On May 30, 1982 Richard Halloran of *The
New York Times* published the outlines of a classified
document described as "the first complete defense
guidance of this administration." The document defines a five-year plan for defense that might indeed
have been made in Moscow. It is a strategy for fighting a nuclear war "over a protracted period." American nuclear forces in such a conflict, it declares, "must
prevail and be able to force the Soviet Union to seek
earliest termination on terms favorable to the United
States." How is this to be accomplished? "Decapitation," that is how; the objective of the United States in
a nuclear war is "to render ineffective the total Soviet
(and Soviet-allied) military and political structure,"

which includes the destruction of communications lines within the Soviet Union. (This repeats Carter's hope of finding Soviet leaders in their bunkers, of depriving the enemy of "its own ability to maintain control after a war starts.")

Nor is this all. The Defense Guidance provides for the development of ballistic missile defense systems; and it makes bold to suggest that the United States might revise the A.B.M. treaty—one of the very few achievements of arms control negotiations, and a monument to the doctrine of deterrence—if a new generation of ICBMs requires such a revision. Defense against nuclear weapons appears to rank high in the present Administration's priorities. The Deputy Undersecretary of Defense for Strategic and Nuclear Forces told a reporter last January that a proper civil defense program would enable the United States to recover fully from an all-out nuclear war with the Soviet Union in only two to four years; and according to the Federal Emergency Management Agency, which would carry out the plans for civil defense, "the United States could survive a nuclear attack and then go on to recovery within a relatively few years."

"Protracted," "prevail," "survive"—this is the semantics of suicide. It is important to make clear what these words mean in the real world. "Protracted" means that hostilities will not end with the end of Washington and Moscow, or New York and Leningrad. Many missiles will fly many times. The fight for the rubble over there will continue from the rubble over here. After all, if all goes according to plan, we will not have been "decapitated"; they will have been. But how do you end a war with an enemy whose head you have cut off? What is the sense in destroying the people with whom we may negotiate? Negotiations, however, are not the object of the war; the object of the war, rather, is to "prevail."

The idea of "prevailing" in a nuclear war looks a lot like the idea of winning a nuclear war. Secretary Weinberger insists that this is not so. He declares his belief that nuclear wars cannot be won, but then he goes on to say that "we certainly are planning not to be defeated." A senior White House adviser, in a speech on national security approved by President Reagan, announced that "prevailing with pride is the principal new ingredient of American security policy." Never mind that after a nuclear war all we will have left to be proud of is the performance of our missiles. If we are to prevail, let us at least prevail with shame. We will, anyway, prevail posthumously. But what exactly does "prevailing" mean? Presumably it has something to do with the "termination of hostilities on terms favorable to the United States." But what can such terms be? What remnant of the Soviet Union will the United States make its demands of? And what remnant of the United States will be making the demands? Perhaps we will want to occupy their territory. Then we can put out their fires. Perhaps we will want to control their population. Then we can dig their graves.

There is another assumption in all this tough talk about "prevailing" in a "protracted" nuclear war, which is that the people upon whom the missiles have fallen will still see some reason for the war. The Defense Guidance is under the impression that individuals who are not incinerated will continue to carry the flag. This is asking a lot. The principles for which the war was started will not command very much allegiance a few strategic exchanges later, nor should they. The survivors of the kind of war contemplated by the patriots at the Pentagon probably will hate everything this country ever stood for. Will their leaders, when they surface from their safe holes in the ground, remind them that Russia was worse? Patriotism will also die by radiation. Brodie made the point well. "Whether the survivors be many or few," he wrote in 1957, "in the midst of a land scarred and ruined beyond all present comprehension, they should not be expected to show much concern for the further pursuit of political-military objectives." That the Communists lost the war will be no consolation. The survivors will look around and see that they did, too.

Of all the Administration's circumlocutions, however, "survival" is the most contemptible, because it means exactly its opposite. These official critics of the peace movement angrily deny that a nuclear war will mean the end of humanity; this, they say, is hysteria. They are right. Somebody will almost certainly have the bad luck to live on. Senator Claiborne Pell of Rhode Island asked Eugene Rostow the critical question at his confirmation hearings: "In the event of nuclear exchange between the Soviet Union and the United States, do you envision either country surviving?" Rostow, who was confirmed as director of the Arms Control and Disarmament Agency, replied: "The human race is very resilient, Senator Pell." The man takes the long view. He regards ground zero under the aspect of eternity. Rostow went on to explain that there would be "10 million dead on one side and 100 million on the other, but that is not the whole population." The 10 million dead are American, presumably, and the 100 million are Russian—we win again. This actuarial attitude toward suffering on such a scale is astonishing. Rostow's figures, more-

over, are false. The demographic distributions of the
United States and the Soviet Union make it likely that
millions more would die here and millions less would
die there. But it is not only the figures that are so
frightening. It is the sentiment. It brings to mind another thinker about the future, Edward Teller, who is
advising the Administration; he has assured his countrymen just as philosophically that "the biggest nuclear conflict would be a catastrophe beyond imagination. But it will not be the end." Teller, of course,
believes that we can save humanity from the worst if
only we build shelters, but there is no evidence that
Rostow believes in shelters. He believes in acceptable
losses. Just as the Soviets do, in fact. "Survival,"
then, is just another version of the long wind of history. It is a euphemism for extermination.

This is what they have done to deterrence. They have
not abandoned it, to be sure, but they have diluted it.
The idea of mutual assured destruction, upon which
deterrence is based, competes in our defense planning with the idea of counterforce, upon which nuclear use is based; and it is losing the competition. There
is a confusion of concepts in current American strategy. This confusion appeared nakedly in a speech giv-
en by Secretary of State Alexander Haig last year.
"Deterrence depends," he said, "upon our capability,
even after suffering a massive nuclear blow, to prevent an aggressor from securing a military advantage
and prevailing in a conflict. Only if we maintain such
a capability can we deter such a blow." Now this is
precisely what deterrence is not. After receiving "a
massive nuclear blow," that is, a first strike, all that
remains is to return "a massive nuclear blow," that is,
a second strike; it is the certainty of the second strike

that keeps the peace by promising the side that strikes first the same fate as the side that was first struck. Two strikes, in any case, and both sides will be out. This is the structure of deterrence. It is not the structure of what Haig was proposing. The war he imagined will not end with the devastation of the dreaded first and second strikes. He imagined, quite the contrary, an extended series of devastations—the two nations on their knees, punching wildly, redundantly sending missiles into faraway seas of fire. And yet the Secretary thought that he was describing deterrence.

In fairness to the Reagan Administration, it must be said that its dilution of deterrence is not new. And in fairness to the Carter Administration, it must be said that Secretary of Defense Brown was right when he insisted that Presidential Directive 59 was not "a radical departure" from doctrines developed by his recent predecessors. It has been shown, in fact, that American plans for fighting a nuclear war already existed in the mid-1950s. But they were evil then and they are evil now. Consider, for example, the sequence of strikes contemplated by our current strategy; study the targets, not just the weapons. They begin by "rendering ineffective" the Soviet "military and political power structure"; they move from this hardest of "hard" targets to "nuclear and conventional military forces and industry critical to military power"; and from these still pretty "hard" targets to Soviet industry. Nowhere in the Defense Guidance is there any mention of "soft" targets—that is, of strikes against civilians. The strategy seems clean—all counterforce and no countervalue. The authors of the Defense Guidance may even be congratulating themselves on the morality of a strategy that does not target cities. But where is Soviet industry, and Soviet communications, and Soviet centers of political and military control, if not in Soviet cities? You cannot destroy the Kremlin without destroying the life around it. There are no surgical strikes in a nuclear war.

At least not yet. The Pentagon is now pushing a new kind of nuclear weapon whose objective is precisely a surgical strike. Known as "the third generation," such a weapon would destroy its target without any side effects. The elimination of the side effects known as "collateral damage" from military calculations would make nuclear weapons finally usable. "The third generation" is really a nuclear bullet. There has never been a weapon more precise and less damaging to anything but its target than a bullet. The intercontinental nuclear bullet would seem to transform the present situation by removing the danger. It would seem to return nuclear warfare to a sort of technologically magnificent conventional warfare, and make strategic weapons behave tactically. But it is not as it seems. The "dirty" weapons are not about to be retired. In fact, nothing will make the use of the "dirty" ones more likely than the use of the "clean" ones. The more precise and less damaging strikes will be made first, which means that a war will have started which feels like a conventional war but is a nuclear war. The less precise and more damaging strikes will probably follow. The technology the Pentagon is developing is deceptively undangerous, because it will only lull us into an illusion of security. In a nuclear world the only thing more dangerous than nonusable weapons are usable weapons. There is no return to innocence. "The third generation" promises the final perfection of counterforce, but counterforce offers no protection against catastrophe.

As things now stand, none of our weapons are "clean." Counterforce was conceived as a consequence of improvement in the accuracy of intercontinental ballistic missiles, which made it possible to hit small targets very far away, but the accuracy of missiles does not yet limit the damage they cause. A more direct hit is still as costly as a less direct hit. In this sense the counterforce strategy of the present Pentagon is what counterforce strategy has always been—sheer sophistry. The concern of counterforce for innocent lives is purely cosmetic. Innocent lives will surely be lost; and the lie that they will not, which flourishes in the strategic formulas of the Soviet Union and the United States, only makes the loss of these lives more likely.

The Sovietization of American strategy that is reflected in the Defense Guidance is of a piece with the recent revival of a certain school of thought among defense intellectuals. The man whose work most perfidiously represents this school of thought is Colin Gray, an analyst at the National Institute for Public Policy in Fairfax, Virginia. "For the U.S. government to endorse a full-fledged war-fighting doctrine in the strategic realm," Gray writes, "would constitute a doctrinal revolution." This is the revolution that Gray is helping to bring about. "It is unlikely that the United States will be able to overcome its fundamental skepticism over the wisdom of approaching a central nuclear war as one should approach...non-nuclear war." Presidential Directive 59, he complained, was "flawed but useful." The conceptions of counterforce elaborated since Schlesinger do not satisfy Gray; they are only small steps in the right direction. They provide "a richer menu of attack options," but they do provide the full strategic feast in which these options make sense—"a theory of victory in war (or satisfactory war termination)." Gray's contribution to strategic studies consists in the elaboration of such a theory. "The Marines raising the flag on Mt. Suribachi is the way in which the President should think of wars being terminated," he writes rousingly. In the same vein, he observes that "the same Department of Defense policy-making hierarchy that could not (or would not) design a theory of victory for Vietnam, similarly abandoned such an apparently extravagant notion in the realm of strategic nuclear policy." It is not enough that the Soviet Union be deterred, Gray maintains; it must be defeated. For "first and foremost the Soviet leadership fears *defeat*, not the suffering of damage—and *defeat*…has to entail the forcible demise of the Soviet state."

This last observation holds the key to the kind of thinking that was eventually embodied in the Pentagon's present plans. The victory that Gray seeks is not military, but political. What would such a victory be? Most generally, "the destruction of Soviet political authority and the emergence of a post-war world order compatible with Western values." Specifically, the strategy calls for a situation in which "the brain of the Soviet system [is] destroyed or degraded."

> Striking the U.S.S.R. should entail targeting the relocation bunkers of the top political and bureaucratic leadership, including those of the K.G.B.; key communications centers of the Communist party, the military, and the government; and many of the economic, political, and military records….The U.S.S.R., with its gross overcentralization of authority, epitomized by its vast bureaucracy in Moscow, should be highly vulnerable…to such an attack.

> The Soviet Union might cease to function if its
> security agency, the K.G.B., were severely crip-
> pled. If the Moscow bureaucracy could be
> eliminated, damaged, or isolated, the U.S.S.R.
> might disintegrate into anarchy...

These are the intellectual origins of the doctrine of
decapitation. Decapitation, however, is not all. Once
the file cabinets in Red Square have been taken out by
an intercontinental ballistic missile, "disaffected Warsaw Pact allies and ethnic groups inside the Soviet
Union...can assert their own values in very active political ways." In sum, the Soviet system will be "encouraged to dissolve itself."

This is anti-Communism at its craziest. It is also not at
all counterforce. Counterforce would be required for a
military victory. The political victory about which
Gray hallucinates, however, requires something
more—countervalue, the targeting not of silos but of
cities. This is exactly what he provides. His "counter-
political" objective calls for countervalue of an especially cynical kind. Gray denounces the doctrine of
mutual assured destruction for being "immoral," because it directs American missiles at Soviet civilians.
Mutual assured destruction, he argues in anger,
promises only to punish; "a mass murder theory," he
calls it. But where does he direct the missiles? And
what does he promise? It makes no difference if Moscow is destroyed as punishment for a first strike that
destroyed Washington, as deterrence has it; or if it is
destroyed in the name of life, liberty, and the pursuit
of happiness, as Gray has it. One thing is certain: the
war he contemplates will kill the people it is designed
to free. Gray is dishonest, therefore, when he pre-

tends that he wishes only "to wage war against the Soviet state as opposed to Soviet society"; the distinction does not exist, because there is no nuclear way to crush the Soviet state without crushing Soviet society. The center of control that Gray lists are civilian centers. For this reason, too, the distinction between "defeating" the Soviets and "damaging" the Soviets is nonsense. The damage that the Soviets would suffer would be the same as defeat. It would be genocide.

The notion of victory is not the only nuclear fiction that Gray has in common with the Russians. He believes also that "the concept of strategic superiority should be revived," as should "a serious civil defense program." This last item is part of Gray's brave new view of nuclear defenses in general. Last year he argued that "there is a strong case for reassessing every aspect of Ballistic Missile Defense." Noting that there exist technologies for such defense that did not exist when the treaty forbidding it was written, Gray calls for "a new debate." He distinguishes between the defense of military forces ("hard-point defense") and the defense of society ("urban-industrial defense"), and comes out for both. His preferred form of military defense is the Army system known as LOADS (Low Altitude Defense System), which consists of a small, hardened radar and guided interceptor missiles. This will effectively protect the Minuteman missiles, he suggests, though it is "ideally suited" to the MX. (It is implied, of course, that this makes the MX attractive; but it must be first established that missile defense is attractive.) LOADS, in any event, will protect little else. The low altitude of its engagement with incoming missiles makes it too dangerous to use for the sake of air bases, for example, or any military force that is

deployed in or near a city. This is not really a sticking
point for Gray, however, who writes even about the
defense of society that "it is not true that an imperfect
city defense is valueless." " 'Leakage' " [now there
is nuclear language at its best] "can be controlled by
deploying more interceptor missiles." But Gray is no
fool. He is not in favor of "urban-industrial defense"
because he knows that it will work. Quite the contrary. "No matter how proficient the ballistic missile
defenses may be," he writes quite candidly, "there
can be no guarantee that a few warheads could not
penetrate. No defense system should be expected to
'work' with absolute and total success." The catastrophe, in other words, will come to pass. What, then?
Gray has an answer—civil defense, or what he calls "a
measure of 'hardening' for urban-industrial America." And if this does not work "with absolute and
total success"? He has another answer—"an acceptable failure rate."

What is America's "acceptable failure rate"? Gray
names a number: "An intelligent U.S. offensive strategy wedded to homeland defenses" he concludes,
"could reduce U.S. casualties to approximately 20
million." Which makes Gray exactly twice as realistic
as Rostow, but that is damning with very faint praise.
Like the 10-million man, the 20-million man won the
attention of this Administration. Recently the Defense Department asked Gray's advice concerning the
basing of the MX. He is a member of the General
Advisory Committee, a group of experts regularly
consulted by the Pentagon. (A dense pack that
works.) And according to members of the Senate
staff, Gray had a hand in the drafting of the Defense
Guidance. The influence of his ideas upon that document are obvious. The policymakers at the Pentagon
swear their devotion to the doctrine of deterrence, but

they seek the counsel of deterrence's critics, and they heed it.

The criticism of deterrence that has been rehabilitated in official circles is based upon a rather simple consideration—that deterrence, strictly speaking, is not a strategy. This is correct. Deterrence teaches nothing about the manner in which nuclear weapons may be employed. It is, rather, a device to make their employment unnecessary. In this sense it is the very opposite of strategy. It provides only for before the war. What happens, however, when deterrence fails?

It has been remarked that the principal difference in doctrine between the United States and the Soviet Union is that we focus on the prevention of war and they focus on the manner in which the war that was not prevented will be fought; we plan mainly for pre-war deterrence, and they for post-deterrence war. Obviously both must be planned for. There was never a weapon that was not used. It would be morally and politically reckless not to entertain the eventuality that deterrence might fail, that the United States might have to use its nuclear weapons. As Gray puts it, "a central nuclear war really could occur"; for this reason, he concludes, "there is a role for strategy."

Operational thinking about nuclear weapons is not in itself odious, as the peace movement often claims; but there are kinds of operational thinking about nuclear weapons that are odious. For example, the kind that orders a nuclear war to be fought until it is won. A need for strategy is not the same as a need for victory. It is a question of war aims. Gray and his ilk simply assume that the traditional aims of war are still good, and pledge allegiance. But there must be a different aim in a nuclear war. The aim in a nuclear war must be to end it, and end it fast. Brodie—the intellectual hero of the nuclear age—observed that "the main war goal upon the beginning of a strategic exchange should surely be to terminate it as quickly as possible and with the least amount of damage possible—on both sides." This is the only sane solution to a mad war. Such sanity, however, has met with scorn by the "hawks" hovering over Washington. Gray, for example, dismissed Brodie's remark by saying that "the best prospect of all for minimizing (prompt) damage lies in surrendering preemptively," which is demagoguery. Pipes attacked "the philosophical premises underlying the mutual-deterrence doctrine" on the grounds that they "ran contrary to all the tenets of traditional military theory, which had always... viewed the objective of war to be victory." Pipes prefers the old-fashioned way, like the Russians.

Such views are simply not relevant to reality. They do not face up to the firepower of these weapons. If they did, they could never conceive of them as rational instruments of American interests. There does not exist a doctrine of damage-limitation that our present weapons will not disobey. Deterrence, moreover, was never as dumb as its critics contend. It has always meant more than keeping our fingers crossed. There has been a finger on the trigger, too. American planning has hoped for the best; but, as the distinguished career of counterforce in our military thinking shows, it has also considered the worst. It has not, however, made the worst the norm. That is the intellectual style of the nuclear-war fighters. They do not merely provide for pessimism; they turn it into policy. These worst-casers may fulfill their own fears. Under cover of post-deterrence planning they are creating the military and psychological conditions for the greatest tragedy in history.

The objection to relying upon the good will of the enemy is well taken. Such a degree of dependence is a shaky basis for security. Sooner or later deterrence may fail; our luck cannot last forever. Measures must be taken, therefore, to cut our losses, and theirs. But these measures must not consist in proposals to prosecute a nuclear war more prettily. They must consist, rather, in the preparation of protocols for the termination of hostilities. Brodie's observation has tremendous implications for nuclear diplomacy. Post-deterrence planning should involve the manufacture of mutually agreed-upon mechanisms for bringing a wicked war quickly to an end. The superpowers must agree on rules for the immediate renunciation of any further use of nuclear weapons after the war has begun. They must throw their prodigious technical prowess into the creation of lines of communication that will survive strategic nuclear exchanges. They must develop diplomatic drills for such a purpose. For once the missiles have started to fly, everything will depend on the mental reflexes of the men who give the orders. They must be able to rely upon habits of mind that dissuade them from pressing on.

But these are not the habits of mind in which they are being trained. They are imbued with ideas and inclinations that say, be soldiers. There will be no soldiers, however, in a strategic nuclear exchange with the Soviet Union. There will be only the projectiles and the people. And it will profit nothing to counsel courage, as the "prevailers with pride" do. You cannot be brave against a missile. The best you can do is not fire another one. But this is not how our defenders think. They want to win the war they want to deter. They may have a lot to answer for; if deterrence collapses, it may be in part because it was corrupted.

3

THE CASE OF EUROPE

The degradation of Western strategy by the doctrine of use, and the degradation of Western values by the doctrine of unilateralism, mar the debate about Europe, too. The deployment by NATO of theater nuclear forces—the Pershing II and cruise missiles—may be justified in two ways. The first is that NATO needs these weapons in order to fight a limited nuclear war in Europe. The second is that NATO needs these weapons in order not to fight a limited nuclear war in Europe.

The first view has been championed forthrightly by Edward Luttwak. He considers the conundrum that NATO will face in the event of a Soviet attack. Its conventional defenses may fail, he observes correctly, and it may be forced to resort to the use of battlefield nuclear weapons. The Soviets, presumably, will respond in kind, but they can also raise the stakes by threatening the cities of Europe with theater nuclear weapons, the intermediate range SS-20s, that are already abundantly in place. How could NATO meet such a threat? "A better response to such a Soviet threat," he writes,

> would be possible if by then NATO had acquired its own theater nuclear forces which, like the Soviet forces that already exist in considerable numbers, would be suitable to threaten not merely cities indiscriminately, but rather such specific targets as political and military command centers, airfields, nuclear storage sites, and even large concentrations of ground forces—that threat being all the more credible for being less catastrophic.

Once again, the counterforce chimera. It is even more of a chimera in the European setting, where the population is all around; there is no Nevada desert to make at least a counter-military strike look clean. A counter-political strike is dirty everywhere. The military action contemplated by Luttwak will accomplish not the defeat of an army but the demise of a society. It is hard to understand the sense in which such an action will be "less catastrophic." Less than what? And for whom? "U.S. scenarios for limited war in the European theater do not amuse us," E. P. Thompson has complained. "This is where we happen to live." That they do. Arguments like Luttwak's only win sympathy for arguments like Thompson's.

But let us stay with Luttwak's strategy. The Russians have attacked, and the Pershings are there. They are used. And suddenly, according to Luttwak, it is an age of reason. "By far the most likely outcome

is that a war would end very soon if any nuclear
weapons, however small, were actually to be detonat-
ed by any side on any target." No theory of victory
here, at least. Still, no man has been given this much
to know. In the matter of the outcome of a nuclear
war there are no experts. Luttwak is only speculating.
He believes that a nuclear war will limit itself, and
that this is "likely." But it is just as "likely" that it will
not. The threshold, after all, will have been crossed.
The unthinkable will not only have been thought; it
will have been done. Surely, then, it may be done
once more. It is impossible to predict the actions of
statesmen and soldiers at such a terrible time, but this
much seems evident: that each missile that will be
launched will make it easier to launch another. If the
difference between conventional weapons and nuclear weapons is not respected, there is no reason to
believe that the difference between one type of nuclear weapon and another will be. The greater escalation
makes the lesser escalation more likely, not less likely. Luttwak, however, argues the other way around.
The use of nuclear weapons will end the use of nuclear weapons, he maintains. Such reasoning is not reas-
suring.

What makes Luttwak so certain that the war will
stay limited? "The shock effect upon leaders on both
sides—but especially on the Soviet leaders who had
started the war." This is a surprising endorsement of
the good sense of the Soviets. That the Soviets would
stay cool in a nuclear situation is to be wished. But it
is, once again, a belief in reason when the hour is late.
The Soviets, in any case, have made it known that
they would interpret an attack by NATO as an attack by
the United States. It is the official policy of the Russians to turn a theater nuclear war with Europe into a
strategic nuclear war with the United States. If

Luttwak does not believe that this is their intention, he must show why not. If he does believe that this is their intention, however, he must admit that after the Atlantic alliance has fired its Pershings, the limitation of the war to Europe is out of its hands.

Luttwak offers another reason for his sanguine scenario for nuclear war in Europe.

> The devastating psychological impact [of the use of nuclear weapons] upon the forces in the field would most likely arrest the conflict there and then. It is fully to be expected that military units whose men would see the flash, hear the detonation, feel the blast, or merely hear of such things, would swiftly disintegrate, except perhaps for a handful of units particularly elite.... The entire 'software' of discipline, or morale, of unit cohesion and *esprit de corps*...are simply not built to withstand such terror as nuclear weapons would cause—even if at the end of the day it were to be discovered that the dead on all sides are surprisingly few.

This last remark refers, presumably, to the casualties caused by tactical nuclear weapons; theater nuclear weapons would leave no such surprise for the day's end. Unfortunately it is not the case that battlefield nuclear weapons would bring a halt to the hostilities. In an admirable essay on "The Human Face of Deterrence," John Keegan has shown that troops may continue to fight even in the aftermath of such an attack. Keegan cites the remarkable resilience of German infantry at Cassino and at Normandy, where they were subjected to bombings so intense that they approached the level of a tactical nuclear burst. To the astonishment of the Allies, the enemy troops continued to fire their guns. Keegan attributes this perseverance to the durability of "instinctive habits of obedience" acquired as a result of countless drills in training. Keegan's skepticism may be carried further. The efficacy of tactical nuclear weapons depends upon their early use. If they do not stop the advancing Warsaw Pact army at once, they will quickly become too costly to use, because as the adversary army continued its advance it would come closer to NATO forces, and to the civilian population that these forces are present to protect. Tactical nuclear weapons used at that point in the fighting would turn upon their users.

There is no guarantee that battlefield nuclear weapons will limit the war. They cannot be counted upon to stop all the soldiers. Thus, it is said, NATO must have theater nuclear weapons waiting in the wings. But these weapons do not discriminate between soldiers and civilians, particularly not in the counter-political manner that Luttwak proposes they be used. They will destroy not the *esprit* but the *corps*. The "theater" will become a charnel-house. In short, such a war cannot, in good conscience, be called "limited." The United States, it is true, will be outside its "limits," though probably not for long. But for the people of Europe who are within its "limits," limited nuclear war is total nuclear war.

Like the conception of counterforce at the strategic level, the conception of counterforce at the theater level claims the cachet of deterrence. Luttwak concludes his argument for a war-fighting strategy for Europe with a short disquisition on deterrence. "Deterrence does not rest on the theoretical ultimate of all-out population destruction," he observes. "Whether nuclear or not, the workings of deterrence depend on threats of punishment that others will find believable. This requires that the act of retaliation be

in itself purposeful, and less catastrophic than more."
Luttwak's remark about "all-out population destruction" sounds a little like Rostow's remark about the
resilience of the human race. It is true that deterrence
does not work because everybody will die. Everybody
will not. But the certainty that somebody will survive
is hardly a warrant for fighting a nuclear war.
Luttwak is arguing against a straw man. Nobody ever
said that deterrence rests on the possibility of "all-out
population destruction." What it rests on, rather, is
the possibility of vast undifferentiated devastation.
Yet the devastation imagined by a war-fighting strategy is highly differentiated. Military targets are differentiated from political targets, and both these targets
are differentiated from civilian targets. Tactical nuclear weapons are differentiated from theater nuclear
weapons, and both these weapons are differentiated
from strategic nuclear weapons. The aim of all these
differentiations is to weaken the compunctions of
military commanders, to make a war that is without
limit and without purpose seem "limited" and "purposeful." Deterrence, then, may be less than "all-out
population destruction," but it is more than "purposeful" nuclear use.

The possibility of undifferentiated devastation,
moreover, is perfectly "believable," in Luttwak's
term; it is made believable by the power of an intermediate-range missile to destroy its target by destroying the entire place where its target is to be found.
The requirement that deterrence be "believable" is
frequently used as an excuse for counterforce planning. In fact, deterrence does not require your enemy
to believe that you will strike back; it requires only
that he not believe that you will not. Deterrence does
not, in other words, require certainty. Doubt is quite
enough.

Deterrence is the real reason for the installation of the intermediate-range missiles by NATO—deterrence, to be precise, at all levels. Deterrence at all levels does not now exist, and it is this that makes the use of theater nuclear weapons in Europe more likely. The peace movement, in other words, has it backward. It is in order *not* to fight a nuclear war limited to Europe that the missiles will be delivered to NATO. The last thing that the United States should do, if it intends to limit a nuclear war to Europe, is to put missiles in Europe that can reach the Soviet Union.

The decision to deploy the Pershing and the cruise was based upon a sound understanding of the political dangers posed by the present military balance in Europe. The Soviet superiority in theater nuclear weapons threatens Western Europe with political domination or physical destruction, because it discourages the United States from coming to Western Europe's defense. In the event of a confrontation between NATO and the Warsaw Pact, the Warsaw Pact can inflict upon NATO a nuclear blow for which NATO cannot retaliate in kind. NATO must rely, therefore, upon the nuclear capacity of the United States. The United States would have to choose, however, between a strategic nuclear exchange with the Soviet Union and the surrender of Europe. As long as the intermediate-range missiles of the Russians are met only by the long-range missiles of the Americans, as long as the decision to move to the direst nuclear attack must be made by the United States, the security of Europe rests on the readiness of the United States for suicide. And that, obviously, is no security at all. The Pershing and the cruise were developed as a solution to this problem. In the words of Michael Howard, they are designed to "assuage the fears of Western Europeans that, confronted by a threat that did not extend to their own continent, the Americans would be effectively deterred from intervening." These missiles lower the cost of retaliation for the United States and raise the cost of attack for the Soviet Union. They will be there not to be used, but to prevent their Soviet counterparts from being used. There is, after all, one way that nuclear war may be limited, and that is by the firing of the SS-20s at states that have no Pershings or cruise. Such a war will indeed be limited—to Western Europe.

These missiles make possible retaliation without escalation. In a word, they deter. They restore the mutual hostage relationship in which deterrence is said to consist; the present predicament may be characterized as a single-hostage relationship, with Western Europe as the hostage. Still, the problem of the alliance is not solved. The new weapons with which NATO will be furnished make it less probable that the United States will be laid waste for the sake of Europe, but only less probable. They do not make it impossible. It is easy to defend the NATO missile decision against the illusions of the peace movement, but it is hard to defend it without bitterness. For the Pershings and the cruise, as the governments of Western Europe freely admit, are still a way of tying America to Europe's fate; and this is necessary, as they do not freely admit, because Europe is not prepared to take responsibility for its fate on its own.

If the United States ever fights a nuclear war with the Soviet Union, it will almost certainly not be because the Soviet Union attacked the United States. It will be because the Soviet Union attacked an ally of the United States. The war will not begin with a strategic nuclear exchange, but it will probably escalate to it. The defense policy of the Atlantic alliance is based upon the inexorability of escalation. The official metaphors for escalation are "chain of deterrence," "web of deterrence," "continuum of deterrence"; the new missiles will be installed to complete this chain, this web, this continuum. Deterrence must hold at all levels if the worst nuclear fear of the age is not to come to pass. Thus, conventional warfare must be abjured, lest tactical theater nuclear weapons must be used; tactical nuclear weapons must be abjured, lest strategic nuclear weapons be used; and strategic nuclear weapons must be abjured. The promise of escalation is what stays everybody's hand. When there is peace, it is a promise of good. But when there is war, it is a promise of evil. The metaphors of deterrence are, after all, metaphors of entanglement. When deterrence fails, it may fail at all its levels. That is its dark side. The United States has remorselessly declared its intention, in its famous policy of "first use," to rescue Europe's armies by the use of nuclear weapons, that is, to promote a conventional war into a nuclear war. And the Soviet Union has declared its intention to interpret any nuclear attack by NATO as an attack by the United States—that is, to promote a theater nuclear war into a strategic nuclear war.

But it is not only doctrine that will make escalation inexorable. It is the real situation on the ground. The single most decisive fact about that situation is the inadequacy of our Allies' conventional defenses. NATO and the Warsaw Pact are roughly equal in manpower, but the Warsaw Pact has particularly large advantages in tanks (2.64 to 1), artillery pieces (2.07 to 1), land-based bombers (4.83 to 1), fighters (5.07 to 1) and interceptors (7.14 to 1); and its supply lines are less of a problem than NATO's. (These figures are drawn from *The Military Balance 1982-83* of the International Institute for Strategic Studies, which concludes that "the numerical balance over the last 20 years has moved slowly but steadily in favor of the East," while "the West has largely lost the technological edge which allowed NATO to believe that quality could substitute for numbers.") If a war goes badly, for this reason, there is escalation. A "first use" is really a last resort. In order to make a nuclear defense more credible (not least to the citizens of the democracies to be defended), the destructive consequences of first use were concealed for a time behind the doctrine of "flexible response," according to which the most horrible nuclear strikes would be averted, or in any case saved for last. The deficiencies in the doctrine of flexible response, however, have been amply illustrated. The less horrible strikes are pretty horrible. And the nuclear strikes would have to begin at once, as we have observed. But "political leaders would never sanction such early use of nuclear weapons," according to Lawrence Freedman (the author of *The Evolution of Nuclear Strategy*, the best single book about strategic studies that I have read). Freedman concludes, instead, that "Western European leaders have long considered the real virtue of theater nuclear forces, e.g., the Pershing and the cruise, to be the link the weapons provide to the U.S. strategic arsenal."

The defense of Europe, then, requires a readiness for nuclear war. Rostow, in a speech at Yale, made the point plainly. "There is no way to build an impermeable wall between the use of nuclear and conventional weapons," he said. "The President of the United States must never be put in a position where he would have to choose between abandoning a vital American interest and launching a nuclear war." Of course this has been precisely the position of every President since 1945; nuclear war in Europe has been avoided not because we were unwilling to launch it, but because political means for the resolution of crises have not yet failed. The weakness of NATO determines not merely its policy on defense, furthermore, but its policy on arms control as well. Rostow made the connection clear. "In order to prevent the unthinkable horror of nuclear war, we must enforce the rules of public order against all forms of aggression, conventional and nuclear." Or, more simply, "in order to eliminate nuclear war, you must eliminate war itself."

Now, one of the interesting things about Rostow's view is that it is shared by Schell. "In the present global political system," writes Schell,

> a leader of a nuclear power who comes to believe that his nation's vital interests are being threatened by another nuclear power faces a pair of alternatives that never confronted any statesman of pre-nuclear times: he can acquiesce in the aggression...or he can threaten to unleash a holocaust in which the life of mankind might be lost.

And there are implications for arms control, also much like Rostow's, only given more grandiloquently:

> For the world, in freeing itself of one burden, the peril of extinction, must inevitably shoulder another: it must assume full responsibility for settling human differences peacefully.... Nuclear disarmament cannot occur if conventional arms are left in place.... If we are serious about nuclear disarmament—the minimum technical requirement for real safety from extinction—then we must accept conventional disarmament as well.

Of course these men reason differently. Since we must fight wars, we must fight nuclear wars, reasons

Rostow. Since we must not fight nuclear wars, we must not fight wars, reasons Schell. But there is, in the dystopia of Rostow and the utopia of Schell, a common assumption, which is that we no longer can fight conventional wars.

Can we? According to the four distinguished architects of deterrence who proposed that the United States adopt a policy of "no first use," we can.

No first use makes no sense in the context of the current conventional balance, as Bundy, Kennan, McNamara, and Smith almost acknowledged; no sooner had they pitched their idea than they were arguing "on behalf of strengthened conventional forces." They acknowledged, too, that "no one on either side could guarantee beyond all possible doubt that if conventional warfare broke out on a large scale there would in fact be no use of nuclear weapons." The Soviet Union, always on the alert for propaganda opportunities, made a declaration of no first use at the United Nations in June, shortly after the article in *Foreign Affairs* appeared. The United States, quite correctly, did not at all modify its policy as a result of the Soviet declaration. "We could not make that assumption about the Soviet leaders," the "Gang of Four" wrote in a premonitory passage; "and we must recognize," they continued, at great cost to their argument, "that the Soviet leaders could not make it about us. As long as the weapons themselves exist, the possibility of their use will remain."

And yet the notion of no first use was greeted with great enthusiasm in the United States, despite the rather obvious fact that it struck at the foundation of European defense at a time of real conventional weakness. The reason for this enthusiasm is not far to seek. The notion of no first use spoke for a hope that the United States has hidden for the entire history of the alliance—the hope to which Secretary of State Haig referred when he retorted that no first use would "make Europe safe for conventional warfare." Europe, of course, like the rest of the world, has always been "safe" for conventional warfare. No first use dares to suggest that it still is. It denies the most dangerous discontinuity of the nuclear age. There is a thrilling thesis about history in no first use, which is that there remains before us not the choice between peace and extinction, which is the conventional wisdom about the nuclear age, but the choice between peace and war. No first use, in other words, is a proposal for the normalization of the nuclear world. For the nuclear world will be normal when wars may be waged between states that have nuclear weapons without their being used. In such a world, escalation is no longer inexorable. The defense of Europe no longer asks the sacrifice of America. No first use is addressed to America's nerves, which have been sorely exposed by NATO.

No first use owes its popularity to what may be called the fantasy of the firebreak. The firebreak is the technical term for the difference between conventional war and nuclear war; it is the opposite of escalation. The firebreak is a worthy objective. It is not hard, in the nuclear age, to praise conventional war. The smaller scale of the catastrophe, of course, is what most recommends a conventional war. But there are other such recommendations. Nuclear weapons do not deter anything except nuclear weapons; the years since 1945 have been riddled with confrontations and conflicts. Moreover, nuclear weapons are a military deterrent, but not a political deterrent. Perhaps the best proof of this is the postwar period in Europe. The Soviet Union created its empire in Eastern Europe in the very years that the United States enjoyed not merely nuclear superiority, but nuclear monopoly. Insofar as it warns against too great a reliance upon a nuclear defense, then, no first use is a constructive suggestion.

Except for the Europeans. They hate no first use. "How will we fight back?" asks a senior editor of *Die Zeit*. "Given a renunciation of first use," four fearful West German defense specialists remind us, "conventional war in Europe would once again become possible." It is true that as you decrease the possibility of nuclear war, you increase the possibility of conventional war; but this would seem worth the gamble, especially for Germany, which would probably be annihilated by the nuclear conflagration in question. The Germans, however, prefer the possibility of annihilation to the preparedness for something less. This has been the case since the 1950s, when a nuclear bias was introduced into the force structure and the defense doctrines of NATO. Since then it has been fatalistically assumed that NATO will never be able to match the Warsaw Pact in conventional strength. Unfortunately, this fatalism is related to finance. The recovery of conventional parity by Western Europe, it is commonly believed, demands an increase in defense spending so great that it might place the economies of these countries on a different footing. This is an exaggeration; according to General Bernard Rogers, the Supreme Allied Commander of NATO, the Soviet advantage can be offset by an increase of 4 percent in what the member states now spend on defense. The general is probably too sanguine. Still, for the Europeans that is 4 percent too many. They are reluctant to meet even their existing commitments, the 3 percent of GNP they have already pledged, and Rogers was talking of less. In short, they prefer the nuclear peril to higher taxes. That is what is so galling about the defense policy of the Atlantic alliance. It is not only themselves that our allies place in jeopardy. Their economic objection to a conventional defense has consequences for the United States as well. Their pleas for the American nuclear guarantee mean that they would sacrifice us for the sake of their standard of living.

If the firebreak is a fantasy, it is not America's fault. Nor is it America's fault if doubts about the alliance are heard on this side of the Atlantic. (Intellectuals as different as Ronald Steel and Irving Kristol have voiced such doubts.) It must be understood, in the matter of NATO, who is dragging whom to their doom. E. P. Thompson cries that he is "not ready to accept the obliteration of the material resources and inheritance of this island, and of some half of its inhabitants, in order to further the strategies of NATO." This is sheer effrontery. The world is the other way around. It is the material resources and the inhabitants of the United States that will be obliterated in defense of NATO, not the material resources and inhabitants of NATO that will be obliterated in defense of the United States. The installation of the Pershings and the cruise—which Thompson opposes, of course—will correct the apportionment of risk within the alliance, but only slightly. If these missiles are ever launched against the Soviet Union, deterrence will have failed not only for Europe, but for the United States, too. Against E. P. Thompson, who portrays NATO as a collection of small nations cowed by the United States into serving its interests, NATO must be defended as a community of principle. But along come the West German defense specialists and they do not speak of a community of principle. They speak only of "a community of risk." This, too, is sheer effrontery. They are asking the United States to do for them what they will not do for themselves. (The conservative government of Helmut Kohl proposed to spend less on defense than the liberal government of Helmut Schmidt.) And they are asking the civilization of Europe to countenance its own end so that they may compete in the world's markets.

NATO is a security arrangement based upon a common morality. For moral ends the United States has made an extraordinary commitment to Europe. It has "extended" deterrence. No first use would undermine that commitment. It would take deterrence back; it would, therefore, weaken NATO as a security arrangement. Still, no first use is a noble idea, refuted by an ignoble reality. It intends to put nuclear weapons out of play. But nuclear weapons can be put out of play in only two ways—deterrence and disarmament. No first use cripples deterrence but offers nothing in the way of disarmament. And it encourages the delusion that words will do away with the nuclear danger, when only deeds will. For deterrence to work, weapons must have been made. For disarmament to work, weapons must have been unmade. The announcement that the weapons are there but there is no need to worry means nothing.

4

AND SO, DETERRENCE

The great nuclear debate, then, has consisted mainly in the trashing of deterrence. It is trashed on the right and trashed on the left. There is arresting agreement on this matter. In 1973, for example, the present Undersecretary for Policy in the Department of Defense, Fred C. Iklé, published an article called, "Can Nuclear Deterrence Last Out the Century?" which helped inaugurate the right-wing revisionism that has come to rule; and in 1981 E. P. Thompson published "Deterrence and Addiction," a lecture given before the British Association for the Advancement of Science. These texts must be read together if our full fall from our senses is to be understood. The planner and the professor concur that it is the dogma of deterrence that stands in our way. They think it is immoral. Ac-

cording to Iklé, it is really "mutually assured genocide," and "Tomas de Torquemada, who burned ten
thousand heretics at the stake, could claim principles
more humane tnan our nuclear strategy"; and according to Thompson, it is "inducing nuclear war," and is
"carrying us towards the Final Solution." And they
think it is irrational. According to Iklé, "there exists no
rational basis" for deterrence, because "those calculat-
ed decisions which our deterrent seeks to prevent are
not the sole processes that could lead to nuclear
war....We are making survival depend on the rationality of all future leaders in all major wars"; and according to Thompson, deterrence "proceeds by attributing a rationality to states which can rarely be found
in History ...untroubled by those non-rational surges
(of panic or of national self-assertion) which mark the
historical record....What if the Russians are playing a
different game from the Americans, and each ignores
or misunderstands the other's rules?" Then the planner and the professor part company. The one takes to
the Pentagon, to find ways to win with nuclear weapons. The other takes to the streets, to find ways to
abolish them. Many follow both. And the only idea
that has so far come between us and these weapons,
and equilibrated this evil world, is left almost friend-
less.

There is a sense in which deterrence is certainly
immoral. It is a promise of murder. We prevent them
from using their weapons by threatening to kill millions of people, and by making them believe that we
mean it; and they do the same. If the deed cannot be
called moral, the threat cannot be called moral. This is
the objection that is made in the pastoral letter on
nuclear weapons drafted for the National Conference
of Catholic Bishops. Drawing upon the congressional
testimony of Cardinal Krol of Philadelphia against

SALT II, a pronouncement that marked an important
moment in the politicization of the Catholic clergy,
the pastoral letter states that "not only the *use* of strategic nuclear weapons, but also the *declared intent* to
use them involved in our deterrence policy, are both
wrong." The bishops continue that "the nature of the
deterrent in the nuclear age has raised the most severe moral questions for Catholic teaching on warfare," and proceed to detail what they call "the negative dimensions of deterrence." They conclude that
"under no circumstances may nuclear weapons or
other instruments of mass slaughter be used for the
purpose of destroying population centers....Our condemnation applies especially to the retaliatory use of
weapons striking enemy cities after our own have
already been struck." What their condemnation applies to especially, in other words, is the second
strike. While the second strike certainly poses a shattering moral difficulty, it (or the plausible threat of it)
is the essence of deterrence. The bishops have done
much, then, to bring deterrence into disrepute,
though they conclude rather correctly by accepting it
as "the lesser of the two evils." It must be said to the
credit of the bishops that their reservations about the
Administration's strategic agenda are not crazy, that
they have correctly decoded the Pentagon's present
counter-political plans, which is the slaughter of inno-
cents by another name; and it must be said to the
discredit of the Pentagon that its plans for the fighting
of a nuclear war have been so deceitfully disguised as
deterrence that doubts about the one have led to
doubts about the other. Still, the disparagement of
deterrence in the present intellectual and political climate is more than a little irresponsible.

There is a sense, too, in which deterrence is irrational. It is irrational to think highly of human nature.

Our intelligence has placed intercontinental ballistic missiles at the disposal of our instincts. Nothing in the past can have been so attractive to the aggressive drives of men, so seductive to their desire for self-destruction, as nuclear weapons. "Men have gained cont ol over the forces of nature to such an extent that with their help they would have no difficulty in exterminating one another to the last man": Freud made this observation a full fifteen years before the explosion at Almagordo. No policy on nuclear weapons, except for the immediate unscrewing of every one of them, can guarantee against an accidental war, but there is something even worse to consider. Who can say with any certainty that there will never be somebody with a finger on the button who will not want to push it? The world may one day pay dearly for somebody's experience of his or her parents. This is the happiest time in history for sick minds.

Deterrence, moreover, is not peace. It is a condition of crisis. Indeed, deterrence is another word for danger, a brief expression for the first stage of nuclear confrontation, for the fact that what we fear most may have already begun. Deterrence is often said to have "worked," and if anything has "worked," it has; but we cannot be sure. Even if it "worked" in the past, we cannot be confident that it will "work" in the future. (Deterrence must be the only public arrangement that is a total failure if it is successful only 99.9 percent of the time.) Thompson is correct that deterrence is "a counter-factual proposition that does not admit of proof." To be a little more precise, deterrence is a proposition that may be known to be false, but not to be true. When it fails, we will know that it was false, or a few of us will. Until then we will persist in believing that it is true, and not entirely without reason. Deterrence is probably more than a necessary fiction and probably less than a law of history.

The criticism of deterrence, then, is not quite groundless. But many of the conclusions drawn from this criticism are. The alternatives to deterrence that have been proposed are no more moral or rational, they are in fact less so. The razing of Moscow known as "decapitation" is ethically no more satisfactory than the razing of Moscow known as "mutual assured destruction." Nor is it particularly moral to place our populations in still greater peril simply by taking back the threat, or taking back the weapons. The only thing more menacing to our security than nuclear strength is nuclear weakness. Any scheme for dealing with the nuclear danger that would disarm only one side, or upset the balance between the two sides, would leave us more exposed, not less. It is just as irrational to invite a war with ICBMs as it is to fight a war with ICBMs.

The proper conclusion to be drawn from the shortcomings of deterrence is, rather, that deterrence is not enough. It must not be rejected. It must be completed. And it is completed by disarmament, in the form of arms control. Deterrence and disarmament are complementary concepts. The proper policy for the nuclear powers may be put this way: no deterrence without disarmament, no disarmament without deterrence. But this is a slogan, whose meaning must be spelled out.

The need of deterrence for disarmament is pretty plain. The existence of such weapons means that we already exist in a state of emergency. They simply cannot be left to the pacific tendencies of people in power. They must be controlled, limited, reduced, and abolished—that is, they must be more than deterred. It follows from the nature of the emergency, furthermore, that all this must happen bilaterally.

Anybody who is sincerely concerned about the nuclear danger will agree that the world will be no safer if cuts are made in only one arsenal. Nuclear superiority does not lessen the possibility of nuclear use; the United States dropped the bomb on Hiroshima when it had a nuclear monopoly. (It is worth noting, too, that if Japan had had the bomb, Hiroshima would not have been hit, because the United States would have been deterred.) The only real disarmament, then, is mutual disarmament. It is the only form of disarmament that will not advance the national interests of one side at the expense of the other's, and the only form of disarmament that will advance the higher interests of both.

The need of disarmament for deterrence is perhaps less plain. Put simply, deterrence serves as the proper regulating principle for arms control. It determines how many weapons, and of what kind, may be limited or reduced without upsetting the balance—without tempting either side to think that there would be a greater advantage in using force than in controlling it. There follows from deterrence the ideal for disarmament, which is the ideal of stockpiles shrinking more or less symmetrically. They continue to deter each other as they are diminished; and if they did not deter, they would not be diminished. This is not very rousing—unlike, say, Schell's summons to "rise up to cleanse the earth of nuclear weapons"—but it is very responsible.

Some say that the reliance upon negotiations to rid us of the risk is a counsel of despair. As anybody knows who has read Gerard Smith's comfortless account of the SALT I talks, there is some truth to this. Arms control talks have almost always smothered their purpose with the political ends of the parties. In such critical areas as strategic nuclear weapons they have not been able to agree even upon the definition of the reality that they have been mandated to modify; different measures of nuclear strength are proposed in order to disguise advantages that nobody is prepared to give away. The effort at the table has often been not to renounce, but to retain, as many weapons as possible. To be sure, SALT I and SALT II were not exactly futile; there are fifty thousand nuclear weapons alive in the world, and every cut counts. The symbolic significance of nuclear negotiations, furthermore, should not be sacrificed. But arms control is not the solution to the nuclear problem, at least not for a long time to come. Ronald Reagan has called for the reduction by a third of the nuclear warheads in the land-based and sea-based missiles of both superpowers, to be followed by an "equal ceiling" on the number of land-based warheads. George Kennan has called for "an across-the-board reduction by 50 percent of the nuclear arsenals now being maintained." Both are fine proposals, and both would leave intact the power to destroy the world. That is the most pressing reason for preserving the doctrine of deterrence—these missiles and warheads are not going away. If you do not believe that we should unilaterally disarm, and you do not believe that we should fight a war, and you do not believe that the arms race should forever be run, then you must believe in deterrence.

This last point should be clarified. The relationship of deterrence to the arms race is a matter of dispute. It is true that there has been no military buildup in the atomic age that has not been made in the name of deterrence, and in many cases (the "bomber gap" and the "missile gap") its name was taken in vain. Deterrence has become an idea behind which a major sector of the American economy frequently hides. This is the version of deterrence that does not include a principle of limits. It is, in this version, a purely relative idea—we must have whatever they have. And if they have more, then so must we. Such a doctrine of keeping up is a perfect rationale for an arms race. Strategic stability is a worthy goal, but strategic stability applies also to the most swollen arsenals, which is exactly the present predicament. The other side is allowed to raise the ante, and to dictate the size and style of our forces. It is not on the basis of this version of deterrence, then, that the arms race may be restrained.

There is another version of deterrence, however, which flies in the face of the arms race. This version originates not in the idea of strategic stability, but in the idea of mutual assured destruction, which it takes very seriously. The strategic criterion for the research, development, and production of nuclear weapons is taken to be simply the capacity to inflict an unacceptable degree of damage upon any aggressor. During the McNamara administration at the Pentagon, when the idea of mutual assured destruction was adopted as American policy, such unacceptable damage was deemed to be 20 to 33 percent of the Soviet population and 50 to 75 percent of Soviet industry. Obviously a lower level of damage would be equally unacceptable. The point is that whatever the definition of unacceptable damage, the capacity to inflict it already exists. It existed twenty years ago. For this version of deterrence the numbers are not relative but absolute. The manufacture of nuclear weaponry beyond the requirements of assured destruction is redundant, and so is its research and development; and according to this version of deterrence, the arms race is exactly that—an exercise in redundancy.

There is a kind of redundancy, of course, that deterrence requires. The United States must ready itself with the ability to strike at the Soviet Union after it has itself been struck, and so its forces are structured in a "triad" of land, sea, and air forces, each of which can do the deadly work of the other. But the arms race is a redundancy not of structure, which is necessary for security, but of numbers, which is necessary for business. "And the result," as Kennan remarked, "is that today we have achieved, we and the Russians together, in the creation of these devices and their means of delivery, levels of redundancy of such grotesque dimensions as to defy rational understanding." Kennan then scoffs at "something called deterrence," again from the perfectibilian point of view, but it is precisely the technological and military situation to which he points that is deterrence's reason for being. Unless a weapon must be made it must not be made. This is what is known as "minimal deterrence." In the early Nixon years it was known as "sufficiency." It would lead to a kind of selective freeze, with some projects of research and development properly frozen.

Deterrence, finally, is more than a military dispensation. It is a political dispensation, too. It permits nations that have the power to kill each other to prosecute their interests without killing each other. This is part of its offense to many in the peace movement, who want everything called off until the nuclear problem is solved. The most prominent spokesman for the suspension of politics due to the nuclear peril is George Kennan. In a recent speech in Frankfurt, Kennan succinctly delivered his well-known views on the way in which American policy toward the Soviet Union must adapt to the nuclear condition. "We must immediately stop every type of economic warfare...these are means for preparing a new war, not the means for preventing one." And "we have to put an end to the often systematic condemnation of another great people and its government—a condemnation which if not stopped will really make war inevitable by making it seem inevitable." And we must "exercise restraint in the tragic question of human rights and national independence," bearing in mind always "that a new war would not help those who are considered victims of Communist arbitrariness." The argument is simple. Because of the possibility of nuclear war, the United States may do nothing, in words or in deeds, to express its profound philosophical differences with the Soviet Union. It may challenge Soviet influence, and the Soviet ideal of life, only in ways that will not matter.

To "put an end to the systematic condemnation" of the Soviet Union, however, is to put an end to the telling of the truth. (Kennan disagrees. In 1976 he told an interviewer that "I can see very little merit in organizing ourselves to defend from the Russians the porno shops in central Washington. In fact, the Russians are much better in holding pornography at bay than we are." They certainly are.) Furthermore, to "exercise restraint in the tragic question of human rights" is to deprive the victims of "Communist arbitrariness" of their only hope. The course that Kennan counsels is the compromise of America's deepest convictions. It is also political paralysis. A "tragic question" is a question you can do nothing about. Kennan is a man unnerved by a nightmare. He would unnerve his countrymen, too. He would have them be-

lieve that the tightening of credit to the Russians, or
the public support of Soviet dissidents, or the linkage
of favorable trade agreements to the free emigration
of Jews and others from the Soviet Union, will lead to
war. This is especially odd in a man who denies that
the Soviets are "aggressively disposed."

There is a part of politics, to be sure, that must
never be linked to the rivalry between the superpowers, and that is nuclear politics. Arms control must
not be a pawn in the game. It must be recognized as a
different dimension, and dissociated from the ordinary political world. But ordinary politics must go on.
Just as the bomb must not become a tool of political
principle, political principle must not become a tool of
the bomb. It is the divorce of the two that deterrence
accomplishes. Deterrence does not depart from the
consideration of the Soviet Union as an enemy—as an
enemy of which the United States may be proud.
Deterrence and arms control are quite compatible
with the cold war. Their objective is simply to keep
the cold war cold.

That is not to say that deterrence is incompatible
with détente. Obviously it is not. But if détente is to
be defended, it must be on its own grounds. The military relationship of the United States with the Soviet
Union must not be confused with its political relationship. (Détente, in its first try, did not change the pace
of Soviet weapons production, as it was hoped it
would.) The management of the military relationship
has a single objective, the avoidance of war. For this a
stalemate will suffice. The management of the political relationship is considerably more complicated. It
must not be conducted, therefore, in Geneva. Unfortunately arms control has been laden with too heavy a
political burden. Many of its advocates look to it not
merely for the terms of our national security policy,

but for the terms of our foreign policy, too. This is a mistake. It will make agreements on arms more difficult to achieve; and the full panoply of differences between the superpowers cannot be adequately addressed within the narrow framework of such negotiations, which must be narrow if they are to succeed. Arms control may lead to a lessening of tension, and it may not. If it does not, it must still stay on course, tension and all. Before it is anything else, then, arms control is "a managerial concept," in Freedman's words. That may not seem like much, but if you are serious about reducing the nuclear danger, you will not mind.

There is no contradiction between anti-Communism and arms control. But it works both ways. If anti-Communists must not be daunted by arms controllers, arms controllers must not be daunted by anti-Communists. For the ultimate reason for the absence of a contradiction between anti-Communism and arms control is the grotesque size of the nuclear arsenal itself. The United States has 1,052 intercontinental ballistic missiles, on which there are 2,152 warheads; and 520 submarine-launched ballistic missiles, on which there are 4,768 warheads; and 316 long-range bombers. In this decade, furthermore, the United States will deploy air-launched cruise missiles and sea-launched cruise missiles, making its strategic triad into a strategic pentad. The requirements of deterrence, then, are well satisfied. This means that a good deal of arms controlling may take place before this country, and the campaign against totalitarianism, is put in jeopardy. Because the numbers are so great we have room in which to move. Let us, to show that we are serious about arms control, volunteer to take apart some of what we have, because the gesture may make a change in the hearts of Americans and in the hearts of Russians; and let us default on the Polish debt. These actions will cost us nothing in security. They will profit us much in morality.

This, then, is the situation. There is the party of peace, and the party of war, and the party of deterrence. The party of deterrence is too little esteemed by the public. This is not surprising; no masses ever marched in the name of realism. But the public must be made to see that freedom's immediate future lies with this party, and that there is much work to be done. "It is not for you to finish the work," said a rabbi of the second century, "but neither are you free to desist from it." The rabbi was martyred by the Romans, but he spoke like a man who knew he would be survived.

NOTES

Dedication

Page

    v   *There will be no other end* . . . . : Czeslaw Milosz, "A Song on the End of the World," *Selected Poems* (New York, 1973), p. 57. The poem was written in Warsaw in 1944.

Preface

Page

    xi   "the alchemists of our time" : Solly Zuckerman, *Nuclear Illusion and Reality* (New York, 1982), p. 106. This chapter on "The Advice of Scientists" is perhaps the wisest part of a very wise book.

Introduction

Page

1 How immensely simplified . . . : Walter Benjamin, "The Destructive Character," *One-Way Street and Other Writings,* tr. Edmund Jephcott and Kingsley Shorter (London, 1979), p. 157. I have slightly altered the translation.

5 "the revolution in thought . . ." : Jonathan Schell *The Fate of the Earth* (New York, 1982), p. 160.

6 The notion of denial: Schell, pp. 148-150. See also Robert Jay Lifton and Richard Falk, *Indefensible Weapons: The Political and Psychological Case Against Nuclearism* (New York, 1982), pp. 100-110, where denial is called "numbing," and is alleged to have distorted almost every precinct of American life.

The Party of Peace

Page

10 "the repeal of the NATO decision . . . the creation of nuclear free zones . . ." : E. P. Thompson and Dan Smith, eds. *Protest and Survive* (Middlesex, England, 1980), pp. 223-256. See the critical discussion of nuclear free zones in Lawrence Freedman, *Arms Control in Europe*, Chatham House Papers (London, 1981), pp. 37-40, where it is stated, " . . . a nuclear-free zone is not equivalent to a nuclear-safe zone . . . The range and mobility of modern weapons tend to make a nonsense of all geographical constraints."

10 Presidential Directive 59: *Report of Secretary of Defense Harold Brown to the Congress on the FY 1982 Budget, FY 1983 Authorization Request, and FY 1982-86 Defense Programs* (Washington, D.C., 1981), pp. 38-45. For the intellectual and political context of the document, see Lawrence Freedman, *The Evolution of Nuclear Strategy* (New York, 1981), pp. 372-394.

11 Haig mumbled something : Bernard Gwertzman, "Allied Contingency Plan Envisions a Warning Atom Blast, Haig Says," *The New York Times*, November 5, 1981.

11 the Defense Guidance: Richard Halloran, "Pentagon Draws Up First Strategy for Fighting a Long Nuclear War," *The New York Times*, May 30, 1982.

12 "thus far the chief purpose . . ." : Bernard Brodie, ed., *The Absolute Weapon* (New York, 1946), p. 76.

12 "Everything has changed" : Schell, p. 185.

12 "the death of death" : Schell, p. 119.

12 "Gandhi's law of love" : Schell, p. 224. This was an early blow struck on behalf of Gandhi's new relevance to all our troubles.

12 "a fundamental divorce . . ." : Schell, p. 196.

13 "The peril of extinction . . ." : Schell, p.219.

13 "there is only *one* path. . ." : Albert Einstein, *On Peace* (New York, 1960), p. 416.

13 the Baruch Plan: See Michael Mandelbaum, *The Nuclear Question: The United States and Nuclear Weapons, 1946-1976* (Cambridge, 1979), pp. 23-33; and also Stephen E. Ambrose, *Rise to Globalism: American Foreign Policy, 1938-1980* (New York, 1980), pp. 118-120. Some historians believe that the Baruch Plan was purely propaganda. Recently the controversy erupted again (*Washington Post*, January 3, 29, February 7, 1983), perhaps because the Reagan Administration's "zero option" for nuclear missiles in Europe raises similar questions about the relationship of the morally ideal to the political real in the control of nuclear weapons.

13 "to reinvent politics. . .": Schell, p. 226.

14 "a correspondent social system": E.P. Thompson, *Beyond the Cold War: A New Approach to the Arms Race and Nuclear Annihilation* (New York, 1982), p. 45.

14 "order whose institutional base. . .": Thompson, *Beyond the Cold War*, p. 65.

14 "isomorphism": Thompson, *Beyond the Cold War*, p. 66.

14 "its economy. . .whose outcome. . .": Thompson, *Beyond the Cold War*, p. 64.

14 "The U.S.A . .": Thompson, *Beyond the Cold War*, p. 66.

14 "isomorphic replication. . .": Thompson, *Beyond the Cold War*, p. 67.

15 "the movement of Polish Solidarity. . .": E. P. Thompson, "A Letter to America," in *Protest and Survive*, ed. E. P. Thompson and Dan Smith (New York, 1981), p. 50. This is the American edition of a popular collection of essays produced by the peace movement in Britain. It is rather memorably introduced by Daniel Ellsberg's "Call to Mutiny," in which his countrymen are counselled that "these European marchers are saying with their presence on the road what the mothers and fathers at Jonestown waited too long to say. . ."

15 "alliance of the champions. . .": Schell, p. 135.

15 "better Finnish than finished": Jolyan Howarth of the Campaign for Nuclear Disarmament at the Center for European Studies at Harvard University, in a conversation with the author.

16 "dissident Communist...pseudo-Communist": E. P. Thompson, "An Open Letter to Leszek Kolakowski," *The Poverty of Theory and Other Essays* (New York, 1978), p. 306, 381.

16 "what we dissident Communists did. . .": Thompson, *Poverty*, p. 305.

17 "For no matter how hideous. .": Thompson, *Poverty*, p. 392.

17 "Fifty years is too short a time.   .": Thompson, *Poverty*, p. 372.

17 "the long wind of history": See Peter Nettl, *Rosa Luxemburg* (London, 1969), p. 428.

17 "circumstances. . .within a divided world": Thompson, *Poverty*, p. 372.

17 "We must remember. . .": Thompson, *Poverty*, p. 378.

17 'a third way": Thompson, *Beyond the Cold War*, p. 67. This is the controlling concept of the entire book.

1, maybe a hundred million people: This almost unbelievable figure is drawn from Anton Antonov-Ovseyenko, *The Time of Stalin, Portrait of a Tyranny* (New York, 1982), pp. 210-213. Antonov-Ovseyenko is a professional historian whose unbearable book is based in part upon extensive excerpts from the official inquiry of the Khrushchev years into Stalin's crimes. The diabolical arithmetic is this: in the civil war and famine of 1921-22, 16 million died; in the collectivization of agriculture and its concomitant executions of 1931-32, 22 million died; in the purges of the 1930s, 19 million died; in the Second World War, 32 million died; in the postwar purges, 9 million died. Concerning these figures Harrison Salisbury observed (*The New York Times Book Review*, January 17, 1982): "Many previous historians have attempted to estimate the number of lives lost in the years of the Stalin regime, and some other estimates are close to these appalling figures. But no exact count is possible."

18 "The basic postures of the Soviet Union. . .menacing bases": E. P. Thompson, "Protest and Survive," *Protest and Survive* (Middlesex, England, 1980), p. 49.

18 "the rhetoric of constitutionalism. . .": Thompson, *Poverty*, p. 378.

19 "the powers of the military   .pacific Europe already exists": "Appeal for European Nuclear Disarmament,

April 28, 1980," *Protest and Survive* (Middlesex, England, 1980), pp. 224-225.

21 "Deterrence has repressed. . .": Thompson, "Protest and Survive," *Protest and Survive* (Middlesex, England, 1980), p. 54.

21 "the immediate cause of World War III. . .": C. Wright Mills, *The Causes of World War III* (New York, 1958), p. 47.

22 James Fallows, *National Defense* (New York, 1981).

23 Galbraith finds a direct correlation: John Kenneth Galbraith, "Economics of the Arms Race," *Boston Review* (August, 1982), p. 4.

23 Lester Thurow has made this point: "The Reagan military policies lead to some very adverse economic consequences, but most of these are avoidable consequences if a different set of economic policies accompanied the military build-up. Personally I oppose the Reagan policies because I do not agree with his interpretation of the threat or his military strategy for countering the threat, but I do not think you can base your opposition on economic foundations." Lester Thurow in "News of the Week in Review," *The New York Times*, November 15, 1981.

24 "the modern emphasis on the education, health, and welfare. . .": Klaus Knorr, *On the Uses of Military Power in the Nuclear Age* (Princeton, 1980) p. 49.

25 "the ruin of war by nuclear weapons. . .": Schell, p. 220.

25 "in the pre-nuclear world. . .instruments of policy": Schell, p. 188.

25 "military force is not a legitimate instrument. . .victims of aggression": *Common Security, A Blueprint for Survival*, The Independent Commission on Disarmament and Security Issues (New York, 1982), pp.8-9.

27 "the belief, strong in the United States. . .": Galbraith, p. 3.

27 a poll taken in Germany last year: John Vinocur, "The German Malaise," *The New York Times Magazine* (November 15, 1981), p. 116.

28 "It would violate both of the proportionality limits. . .": Michael Walzer, *Just and Unjust Wars: A Moral Argument with Historical Illustrations* (New York, 1977), pp. 276-277.

29 "a sudden collapse": Ronald Steel, *The New Republic* (February 17, 1982), p. 2.

The Party of War

Page

30 "thinks it can fight. . .": Richard Pipes, "Why the Soviet Union Thinks It Could Fight and Win a Nuclear War," *Commentary* (July 1977).

31 "the greater the buildup. . .": See Raymond L. Garthoff, "Mutual Deterrence and Strategic Arms Limitation in Soviet Policy," *International Security* (Summer 1978), p. 123. This article is the most comprehensive collection of evidence for the view that Soviet nuclear thinking includes among its principles the ideas of deterrence and arms control.

31 "this does not mean that nuclear war. . .": Maj. Gen. A.S. Milovidov, in Joseph D. Douglass, Jr. and Amoretta M. Hoeber, *Soviet Strategy for Nuclear War* (Stanford, 1979), p. 7. This publication of the Hoover Institution is a primary sourcebook on its subject for many national security hardliners. The authors' analysis is rather meager, but they reproduce Soviet military materials that must not be scanted.

31 "There is profound error. . .": Douglass and Hoeber, p. 10, 91, and *passim*.

32 Professor Pipes feels: Richard Pipes, "Militarism and the Soviet State," *Daedalus* (Fall 1980), p. 2.

33 "the creation and constant maintenance. . .": Douglass and Hoeber, p. 57, 91, and *passim*.

33 "Soviet strategic doctrine. . .be wished away": Benjamin Lambeth, "How to Think About Soviet Military Doctrine," (RAND paper P-5939, Feb. 1978) in *Soviet Strategy*, ed. John Baylis and Gerald Segal (London, 1981), p. 121. The introduction to this volume is an excellent review of the state of scholarly opinion on the subject. See also Lambeth, "The Political Potential of Soviet Equivalence," *International Security* (Fall 1979) and, with a slightly different emphasis, "Uncertainties for the Soviet War Planner," *International Security* (Winter 1982/1983).

33 "Combat operations will continue. . .of the enemy": Douglass and Hoeber, pp. 22-23.

34 "As for ideological struggle. . .": Douglass and Hoeber, pp. 42-43.

34 as Cornelius Castoriadis has brilliantly described it: Cornelius Castoriadis, *Devant la guerre* (Paris, 1981). This book is a model of tough-minded, unideologized anti-Soviet analysis. It should be translated into English.

35 The Soviet doctrine of "preemption": Douglass and Hoeber, pp. 9, 36, 98.

35 "resorting to intercontinental nuclear attack. . .": Walter Slocombe, "The United States and Nuclear War," *Rethinking the U.S. Strategic Posture*, ed. Barry M. Blechman (Cambridge, 1982), p. 37.

35 "not retaliation but offensive action": Pipes, p. 31.

37 "modernization program is not designed. . .": *Report of Secretary of Defense Caspar W. Weinberger to the Congress on the FY 1983 Budget, FY 1984 Authorization Request, and FY 1983-87 Defense Programs* (Washington, D.C., 1982), pp. 1-17.

37 Hans Bethe: From an interview with Robert Scheer, *Los Angeles Times*, April 11, 1982. It is not clear how Bethe reconciles this view with his sonorous support for a nuclear freeze.

38 "their being there. . .": Bernard Brodie, *War and Politics* (New York, 1973), p. 404.

39 there may be trouble: Robert Jervis has explained why very well: "Even if the Russians were to say that they believed a [counterforce] war of attrition was possible, the United States would not have to adopt such a view. While it takes the agreement of both sides to fight a counterforce war, this is not true for [Mutual Assured Destruction]. If one side denies that counterforce wars can be kept limited and convinces the other side that it believes this, the other cannot safely act on its doctrine." From "Why Nuclear Superiority Doesn't Matter," *Political Science Quarterly* (Winter 1979-80), pp. 630-631.

39 "Our policies must take account. . .": Walter Slocombe, "The Countervailing Strategy," *International Security* (Spring 1979), pp. 19-20.

40 "aimed to improve deterrence. . .": Freedman, *The Evolution of Nuclear Strategy*, p. 393.

40 "may yet equal liberty. . .": Theodore Draper, "How Not To Think About Nuclear War," *The New York Review of Books* (July 15, 1982), p. 42.

40 "The assessments that truly matter. . .": Colin Gray, in Keith B. Payne, *Nuclear Deterrence in U.S.-Soviet Relations* (Boulder, 1982), p. xiii. Payne's book, which appeared late in the writing of this essay, is a perfect synopsis of some of the ideas now in the air at the Pentagon.

40 "Decapitation. . .to render ineffective. . .": Richard Halloran, "Pentagon Draws Up First Strategy for Fighting a Long Nuclear War," *The New York Times*, May 30, 1982, p. 12.

11 "its own ability.   ": Freedman, *Evolution*, p. 393.

41 The Deputy Undersecretary of Defense. . .and according to the Federal Emergency Management Agency: Robert Scheer, "U.S. Could Survive War in Administration's View," *Los Angeles Times*, January 16, 1982.

42 "we certainly are planning. . .": Richard Halloran, "Weinberger Defends His Plan to Fight Long Nuclear War," *The New York Times*, August 10, 1982.

42 "prevailing with pride. . .": "Revised U.S. Policy Said to Focus on 'Prevailing' Over the Russians," *The New York Times*, June 17, 1982.

43 'Whether the survivors may be many or few": Bernard Brodie, "Implications of Nuclear Weapons on Total War," RAND Memorandum, p. 1118, July 1957, cited in Michael Howard, "On Fighting a Nuclear War," *International Security* (Spring 1981), p. 14.

43 "In the event of nuclear exchange. . .Senator Pell": Robert Scheer, "Rostow Sees Potential for Soviet First Strike," *Los Angeles Times*, September 29, 1981.

44 "the biggest nuclear conflict. . .": *Arms and Foreign Policy in the Nuclear Age*, ed. Milton L. Rakove (New York, 1972), p. 478.

44 "Deterrence depends. . .": "Haig's Speech on American Nuclear Strategy," *The New York Times*, April 7, 1982. This is the text of an important statement made at the Center for Strategic and International Studies at Georgetown University.

45 It has been shown: David Alan Rosenberg," 'A Smoking Radiating Ruin at the End of Two Hours': Documents on American Plans for Nuclear War with the Soviet Union," *International Security* (Winter 1981-1982). See also Desmond Ball, "U.S. Strategic Forces: How Would They Be Used?" *International Security* (Winter 1982/1983), pp. 31-38, 51-60. This article contains a great deal of precise (and troubling) information about American targeting policies.

46 "the third generation": Judith Miller, "New Generation of Nuclear Weapons With Controlled Effects
Foreseen," *The New York Times*, October 27, 1982.

47 The concern of counterforce for innocent lives: The
distribution of Soviet forces makes counterforce
meaningless even from a strictly countermilitary
point of view. Desmond Ball observes ("U.S. Strategic
Forces," p. 40) that 22 of the 32 major Soviet air bases,
3/4 of their intermediate range ballistic missile and
medium range ballistic missile sites, and more than
half of their 26 intercontinental ballistic missile fields,
are all west of the Urals, "many of them in some of the
most densely populated areas of the USSR." No Nevada deserts, then, or lonely dense packs, to ease the
American conscience about the costs of counterforce.

47 "For the U.S. government to endorse. . .": Colin S.
Gray, "Nuclear Strategy: A Case for a Theory of Victory," *International Security* (Summer 1979), p. 78.

47 "It is unlikely that the United States. . .": Gray, "Nuclear Strategy," p. 78.

47 "flawed but useful": Colin S. Gray, "Presidential Directive 59: Flawed But Useful," *Parameters: Journal of
the U.S. Army War College* (March 1981).

47 "a richer menu. . .": Gray, "Nuclear Strategy," p. 63.

48 "a theory of victory. . .": Gray, "Nuclear Strategy,"
p. 62.

48 "The Marines raising the flag. . .": Gray, "Nuclear
Strategy," p. 71.

48 "the same Department of Defense. . .": Gray, "Nuclear Strategy, p. 71.

48 "first and foremost the Soviet leadership. . .": Gray,
"Nuclear Strategy," p. 61.

48 "the destruction of Soviet political authority. . .":
Colin S. Gray and Keith Payne, "Victory is Possible,"
Foreign Policy (Summer 1980), p. 21.

48 "the brain of the Soviet system.   ": Gray, "Nuclear
Strategy," p. 68.

49 "Striking the USSR. . ": Gray and Payne, "Victory is
Possible," pp. 21,24.

49 "disaffected Warsaw Pact allies. . .": Gray, "Nuclear
Strategy," p. 80.

49 "encouraged to dissolve itself": Gray, "Nuclear Strategy," p. 69.

49 "immoral": Gray and Payne, "Victory is Possible,"
p. 17.

49 "a mass murder theory": Gray, "Nuclear Strategy,"
p. 65.

50 "to wage war. . .": Gray, "Nuclear Strategy," p. 68.

50 "the concept of strategic superiority. . .": Gray,
"Nuclear Strategy," p. 85.

50 "a serious civil defense program": Gray, "Nuclear
Strategy," p. 84.

50 ". . .a strong case. . .": Colin Gray, "A New Debate
on Ballistic Missile Defense," *Survival* (March-April
1981), p. 60.

51 "it is not true. .interceptor missiles": Gray, "A
New Debate," p. 62.

51 "No matter how proficient. . .": Gray, "A New Debate," p. 62.

51 "a measure of 'hardening'.   ": Gray, "A New Debate," p. 62.

51 "an acceptable failure rate": Gray, "A New Debate,"
p. 69.

51 "An intelligent U.S offensive strategy. . .": Gray and Payne, "Victory is Possible," p. 25.

52 "a central nuclear war. . .": Gray, "Nuclear Strategy," p. 57.

53 "the main war goal. . .": Bernard Brodie, "The Development of Nuclear Strategy," *International Security* (Spring 1978), p. 79. This essay is an essential commentary on the nuclear-war-fighting school of thought.

53 "the best prospect of all. . .": Gray, "Nuclear Strategy," p. 75.

53 "the philosophical premises. . .": Pipes, p. 24.

54 diplomatic drills for such a purpose: See the bleak assessment of our present provisions for "war termination" in Desmond Ball, "U.S. Strategic Forces," pp. 44-47.

The Case of Europe

Page

57 "A better response. . .": Edward N. Luttwak, "How to Think About Nuclear War," *Commentary* (August 1982), p. 25.

57 "U.S. scenarios for limited war. . .": E. P. Thompson, "Protest and Survive," *Protest and Survive* (Middlesex, England, 1980), p. 51.

57 "By far the most likely outcome. . .": Luttwak, "How to Think," p. 25.

58 "The shock effect upon leaders. . .": Luttwak, "How to Think," p. 25.

59 "The devastating psychological impact. . .": Luttwak, "How to Think," p. 25.

59 "The Human Face of Deterrence": John Keegan, "The Human Face of Deterrence," *International Security* (Summer 1981).

60 "Deterrence does not rest. . .": Luttwak, "How to Think," p. 28.

61 Doubt is quite enough: It is doubt, too, that obviates the rather difficult question about the credibility of the second strike, which would, after all, be the second most immoral and irrational act in history. As Kenneth Waltz has written, "To ask why a country should carry out its deterrent threat once deterrence has failed is to ask the wrong question. The question suggests that an aggressor may attack believing that the attacked country may not retaliate. This invokes the conventional logic that analysts find so hard to forsake. In a conventional world, a country can sensibly attack if it believes that success is probable. In a nuclear world, a country cannot sensibly attack unless it believes that success is assured. An attacker is deterred even if he believes only that the attacked *may* retaliate. Uncertainty of response, not certainty, is required for deterrence because, if retaliation occurs, one risks losing all. In a nuclear world, we should look less at the retaliator's conceivable inhibitions and more at the challenger's obvious risks." From *The Spread of Nuclear Weapons: More May Be Better*, Adelphi Papers (London, 1981), p. 18.

62 "assuage the fears of Western Europeans. . .": Michael Howard, "Surviving A Protest: A Reply to E. P. Thompson's Polemic," *Encounter* (November 1980), p. 19.

64 "the numerical balance over the last 20 years.   .": *The Military Balance 1982-1983*, The International Institute for Strategic Studies (London, 1982), p. 131.

65 If a war goes badly: A less dolorous estimate of our conventional defenses in Europe is given in John J. Mearsheimer, "Why the Soviets Can't Win Quickly in Central Europe," *International Security* (Summer 1982).

65 "political leaders would never sanction. . .": Lawrence Freedman, "NATO Myths," *Foreign Policy* (Winter 1981-82), p. 53.

65 "Western European leaders. . .": Freedman, "NATO Myths," p. 53.

65 "There is no way to build. . .all forms of war, conventional and nuclear,": Eugene V. Rostow, "The Great Nuclear Debate," a speech delivered at Yale Law School, April 23, 1982.

66 "in order to eliminate nuclear war. . .": Ronald Brownstein and Nina Easton, "Why Are These Men Negotiating for Us?" *The Village Voice*, June 15, 1982, p. 8.

66 "In the present global system. . .": Schell, p. 213.

66 "For the world. . .": Schell, pp. 225-226.

67 "on behalf of strengthened conventional forces": McGeorge Bundy, George F. Kennan, Robert S. McNamara, Gerard Smith, "Nuclear Weapons and the Atlantic Alliance," *Foreign Affairs* (Spring 1982), p. 763. A more thorough and candid consideration of no first use has been produced by the Union of Concerned Scientists (*No First Use*, Cambridge, 1983). While endorsing the idea, and arguing clearly for it, this report is not deluded that it can be implemented in the current military and political situation. It calls instead for a process of conventional reinforcement and strategic rethinking that would create the conditions in which a declaration of no first use would lessen the nuclear danger without increasing the nonnuclear danger.

67 "no one on either side. . .": Bundy, et al, p. 766.

67 "We could not make that assumption. . .": Bundy, et al, p. 766.

68 "make Europe safe. . .": Bernard Gwertzman, "U.S. Refuses to Bar Possible First Use of Nuclear Weapons," *The New York Times*, April 7, 1982.

69 "How will we fight back?": Josef Joffe, "Retain First Use," *The New York Times*, June 16, 1982.

69 "Given a renunciation of first use. . .": Karl Kaiser, Georg Lieber, Alois Mertes, Franz-Josef Schultze, "Nuclear Weapons and the Preservation of Peace," *Foreign Affairs* (Summer 1982), p. 1163.

69 too sanguine: The Union of Concerned Scientists is even more sanguine. It estimates that NATO's conventional strength may be enhanced to the degree to which a declaration of no first use would be meaningful without requiring even General Rogers' recommended increase—indeed, that the conventional balance may be restored within the financial commitments that NATO's members have already undertaken. (*No First Use*, p. 46.)

70 Ronald Steel: Ronald Steel, "Ending the American Protectorate of Europe," *Harper's* (July 1982).

70 Irving Kristol: Irving Kristol, "Reconstructing NATO: A New Role for Europe," *The Wall Street Journal*, August 12, 1982. See also his comments in *The Transatlantic Crisis, A Conference of the Committee for the Free World* (New York, 1982) pp. 18-20, which include an endorsement of no first use.

70 "not ready to accept the obliteration. . .": E.P. Thompson, "Protest and Survive," *Protest and Survive* (Middlesex, England, 1980) p. 40.

70 "a community of risk": Kaiser, et al, p. 1162.

And So, Deterrence

Page

73 "mutually assured genocide. . .more humane than our nuclear strategy": Fred Charles Iklé, "Can Nuclear Deterrence Last Out the Century?" *Foreign Affairs* (January 1973), p. 281.

73 "inducing nuclear war": Thompson, *Beyond the Cold War*, p. 15.

73 "carrying us towards. . .the Final Solution": Thompson, *Beyond the Cold War*, p. 7.

73 "there exists no rational basis": Iklé, p. 269.

73 "proceeds by attributing a rationality. . .": Thompson, *Beyond the Cold War*, p. 12.

74 "not only the *use*. . .": *The Challenge of Peace: God's Promise and Our Response, Pastoral Letter of the National Conference of Catholic Bishops on War and Peace* (Washington, D.C., 1982), p. 54.

74 "the nature of the deterrent. . .": *The Challenge of Peace*, p. 49.

74 "the negative dimensions of deterrence": *The Challenge of Peace*, p. 49.

74 "under no circumstances. . .": *The Challenge of Peace*, pp. 41-43.

74 "the lesser of two evils": *The Challenge of Peace*, p. 54. The phrase is Cardinal Krol's.

75 "Men have gained control. . .": Sigmund Freud, *Civilization and Its Discontents*, tr. and ed. James Strachey (New York, 1962), p. 92.

75 "a counter-factual proposition. . .": Thompson, *Beyond the Cold War*, p. 13.

76 no deterrence without disarmament: The Catholic Bishops arrive at a similar conclusion. "As clearly unsatisfactory as the deterrent posture of the United States is from a moral point of view, use of nuclear weapons by any of the nuclear powers would be an even greater evil." (*The Challenge of Peace*, p. 57). Thus deterrence, which cannot be defended "as an end in itself," as Pope John Paul II put it, can be defended "conditionally," if it is allied to arms control. (*The Challenge of Peace*, pp. 56-57). The defense of deter-

rence is a tricky thing. An undue emphasis upon its negative dimensions and an undue emphasis upon its positive dimensions may be equally disastrous. For an example of the latter, see Kenneth Waltz, "The Spread of Nuclear Weapons: More May Be Better." I know no more precise description of the many political and military benefits of deterrence than this essay, no more ringing defense of deterrence "as an end in itself"; and yet, as its title indicates, it becomes perverse. "A happy nuclear past," writes Waltz, means a happy nuclear future (p. 7). And "Concentrating attention on the destructive power of nuclear weapons has obscured the important benefits they promise to states trying to coexist in a self-help world" (p. 7). And "I have found many reasons for believing that with more nuclear states the world will have a promising future" (p. 30). And then this sentence, which is a perfect example of the casuistry of which political science is capable: "Nuclear weapons make it possible to approach the deterrent ideal" (p. 30). This is backwards. Nuclear weapons are not there to create deterrence. Deterrence is there to cope with nuclear weapons. In short, just as your abhorrence of nuclear weapons must not lead you to abhor deterrence, your admiration of deterrence must not lead you to admire nuclear weapons.

77 "rise up to cleanse the earth. . .": Schell, p. 231.

78 "an across-the-board reduction. . .": George Kennan, *The Nuclear Delusion, Soviet-American Relations in the Atomic Age* (New York, 1982), p. 180.

80 an exercise in redundancy: Secretary of Defense Harold Brown made this point in his Annual Report for 1980: "It is tempting to believe, I realize, that the threat to destroy some number of cities—along with their population and industry—will serve as an all-purpose deterrent. The forces required to implement such a threat can be relatively modest, and their size can perhaps be made substantially, though not completely, insensitive to changes in the posture of an opponent. In that way, at least our side of the arms

race could be ended, since an opponent could never be certain that the threat of city-destruction would not be executed." (*Report of the Secretary of Defense Harold Brown to the Congress on the FY 1980 Budget, FY 1981 Authorization Request, and FY 1980-1984 Defense Programs* (Washington, D.C., 1979), p. 75.) Brown goes on to observe, however, that "unfortunately. . .a strategy based on assured destruction alone is no longer wholly credible"; he considers "counterforce and damage-limiting campaigns," but without any enthusiasm; and ends up with his famous "countervailing strategy." These pages of this official report reveal the intellectual pathos of Carter's Pentagon, which tried to find a strategy of use that would go beyond mutual assured destruction without becoming a doctrine of nuclear-war fighting. There is little such pathos in Reagan's Pentagon.

80 "And the result. . . .": Kennan, *Nuclear Delusion*, p. 177.

81 "We must immediately stop. . .victims of Communist arbitrariness": "George Kennan Calls on the West to End Sanctions Against Soviet," *The New York Times*, October 11, 1982.

81 "I can see very little merit. . .": Kennan, *Nuclear Delusion*, p. 74.

83 "A managerial concept": Lawrence Freedman, "Arms Control: No Hiding Place," *SAIS Review* (Winter-Spring 1983), p. 4.

84 "It is not for you. . . .": Rabbi Tarfon, *Pirke Avot* (Wisdom of the Fathers), II, 21.

SUGGESTED READINGS

A look at the length of the nuclear bookshelf makes it hard to believe that the subject is young. The literature is vast. It is also intimidating—it includes physics, engineering, history, strategy, politics, and ethics—until you immerse yourself in it. Soon it becomes apparent that in this field there have been more new words than new ideas; there are only a few things that can be done with only a few kinds of nuclear weapons. The intellectual effort required of the citizen who wishes to hold an intelligent opinion on this subject is not substantially greater than the intellectual effort required of the citizen who wishes to hold an intelligent opinion on any public subject (the economy, for example). Such a citizen must read. The media, as usual, will not do.

An excellent beginning is Michael Mandelbaum's *The Nuclear Question, The United States and Nuclear Weapons, 1946-1976* (Cambridge, 1979), which has withstood the temptation to turgidity that so many other works in the field have not. A more complete history of the subject is Lawrence Freedman's *The Evolution of Nuclear Strategy* (New York, 1981), a work of scholarship that is also a public service. The most instructive study of the strategy and politics of nuclear weapons is Bernard Brodie's *Strategy in the Missile Age* (Princeton, 1965). The reader of these books may participate in the present debate with confidence.

It will be obvious from my notes that I have found much profit in *International Security*. I can think of no better way to get acquainted with the present debate than the reading of this journal; it publishes articles of different political persuasions but of the same intellectual quality.

Much of the present debate does not take place in books, and in my notes I have referred to those articles most representative of their positions. Still, some books have recently appeared that will together furnish the student with a mental map. The antinuclear argument may best be found in *The Nuclear Delusion* by George Kennan (New York, 1982) and *Protest and Survive*, edited by E. P. Thompson and Dan Smith (New York, 1982). The nuclear-war-fighting argument may best be found in *Nuclear Deterrence in U.S.-Soviet Relations* by Keith B. Payne (Boulder, 1982). The argument of what I have called "the party of deterrence" may best be found in *Nuclear Illusion and Reality* by Solly Zuckerman (New York, 1982), *Rethinking the U.S. Strategic Posture* edited by Barry Blechman (Cambridge, 1982), and *Present History* by Theodore Draper (New York, 1983).

INDEX

The Author

Leon Wieseltier was born in Brooklyn in 1952. He was educated at Columbia, Oxford, and Harvard, where he was a member of the Society of Fellows. His writings have appeared in *The New Republic*, *The New York Review of Books*, *Dissent*, *Harper's*, and other publications. He is presently a senior editor of *The New Republic*, and a contributing editor to *Partisan Review*.